METHODS OF THOUGHT

Current Issues in Thinking and Reasoning
Series editor: Kenneth J. Gilhooly

Current Issues in Thinking and Reasoning is a series of edited books that will reflect the state-of-the-art in areas of current and emerging interest in the psychological study of thinking processes. Each volume is tightly focused on a particular topic and consists of seven to ten chapters contributed by international experts. The editors of individual volumes are leading figures in their areas and provide an introductory overview. Example topics include, thinking and working memory, visual imagery in problem solving, evolutionary approaches to thinking, cognitive processes in planning, creative thinking, decision making processes, pathologies of thinking, individual differences, neuropsychological approaches and applications of thinking research.

Also available in this series:

Imagery, Language, and Visuo-spatial Thinking
Edited by Michel Denis, Robert H. Logie, Cesare Cornoldi, Manolo De Vega and Johannes Engelkamp

Working Memory and Thinking
Edited by Robert H. Logie and Kenneth Gilhooly

Evolution and the Psychology of Thinking
Edited by David E. Over

The Cognitive Psychology of Planning
Edited by Robin Morris and Geoff Ward

Methods of Thought

Individual Differences in Reasoning Strategies

edited by
Maxwell J. Roberts
University of Essex, UK

and

Elizabeth J. Newton
University College London, UK

Psychology Press
Taylor & Francis Group

HOVE AND NEW YORK

First published 2005
by Psychology Press
27 Church Road, Hove, East Sussex BN3 2FA

Simultaneously published in the USA and Canada
by Psychology Press
270 Madison Avenue, New York NY 10016

Psychology Press is part of the Taylor & Francis Group

Typeset in Times by RefineCatch Limited, Bungay, Suffolk
Printed and bound in Great Britain by
TJ International Ltd, Padstow, Cornwall
Cover design by Jim Wilkie

British Library Cataloguing in Publication Data
A catalogue record for this book is available from the British Library

Library of Congress Cataloging-in-Publication Data
Roberts, Maxwell J.
  Methods of thought : individual differences in reasoning strategies /
Maxwell Roberts and Elizabeth Newton.
      p.   cm. – (Current issues in thinking & reasoning)
  Includes bibliographical references and index.
  ISBN 1-84169-395-2
  1. Reasoning (Psychology)   2. Methodology.   I. Newton, Elizabeth,
1962–. II. Title.   III. Series.

  BF442.R63 2004
  153.4′3–dc22   2004009265

ISBN 1-84169-395-2

MJR
I dedicate this book to all of the students who have listened to me, and some of the ones who haven't

EJN
for Tim and Oliver

Contents

List of contributors

Alison M. Bacon, Centre for Thinking and Language, Department of Psychology, University of Plymouth, Drake Circus, Plymouth PL4 8AA, UK

Vicky Dierckx, Department of Experimental Psychology, Ghent University, Henri Dunantlaan 2, B-9000 Gent, Belgium

Ludovic Fabre, LPC-CNRS & Université de Provence, Case 66, 3 Place Victor Hugo, 13331 Marseille, France

K. J. Gilhooly, School of Psychology, University of Hertfordshire, Hatfield AL10 9AB, UK

Simon J. Handley, Centre for Thinking and Language, Department of Psychology, University of Plymouth, Drake Circus, Plymouth PL4 8AA, UK

Patrick Lemaire, LPC-CNRS & Université de Provence, Case 66, 3 Place Victor Hugo, 13331 Marseille, France

Bradley J. Morris, Department of Psychology, Grand Valley State University, 2129 AuSable Hall, One Campus Drive, Allendale, MI 49401, USA

Stephen E. Newstead, Centre for Thinking and Language, Department of Psychology, University of Plymouth, Drake Circus, Plymouth PL4 8AA, UK

Elizabeth J. Newton, Department of Human Communication Science, University College London, Chandler House, 2 Wakefield St, London WC1N 1PF

Maxwell J. Roberts, Department of Psychology, University of Essex, Wivenhoe Park, Colchester, Essex CO4 3SQ, UK

Christian D. Schunn, Learning Research and Development Center, University of Pittsburgh, 3939 O'Hara St., Pittsburgh, PA 15260, USA

André Vandierendonck, Department of Experimental Psychology, Ghent University, Henri Dunantlaan 2, B-9000 Gent, Belgium

Introduction: Individual differences in reasoning strategies

Maxwell J. Roberts
Department of Psychology, University of Essex, UK

Elizabeth J. Newton
Department of Human Communication Science, University College London, UK

How do people make inferences? For several decades, researchers have been attempting to answer this question, but have often conceptualised the possible answers as being mutually exclusive. For example, in the past we have been presented with the option of choosing between two different types of general-purpose reasoning theory. On the one hand, it has been asserted that all people reason by the use of *mental models* every time they attempt to make an inference. For this type of process, information is represented in the form of spatial arrays, akin to mental diagrams, from which further information can be inferred (e.g., Johnson-Laird & Byrne, 1991). On the other hand, it has been asserted that deduction rules are the exclusive tools of thought. Here, abstract rules are applied to verbal/propositional representations (e.g., Rips, 1994). We therefore supposedly need to be able to decide upon the nature of a hypothesised *fundamental reasoning mechanism*: a device, or module, whose operation underpins all reasoning (Roberts, 1993, 1997, 2000a).

If there really were a fundamental reasoning mechanism, what might we expect to see in our data? If it were always utilised, then the procedures used by an individual (whatever these might be) would always match the claimed fundamental procedures. Mutually exclusive theories would be easy to compare, and data would unequivocally match the predictions of one rather than another. Deviant responses would easily be explained as experimental error. Can we really dismiss such patterns of data in this way? If they imply the use of bizarre or inexplicable processes, then yes. Unfortunately, all too often these patterns are somewhat more coherent, and in fact may even directly

1

match those expected were people using a different reasoning mechanism (e.g., Roberts, 2000b). Such a situation would be compatible with the existence of a fundamental reasoning mechanism whose action is not always detectable. In other words, fundamental processes may be obscured in certain circumstances by a sort of 'strategic smog'. The problem is, how can we know which processes are fundamental and which are smog? Not only is this question impossible to resolve empirically (Roberts, 1993, 2000a), but from the point of view of observing the behaviour of an individual, this scenario is indistinguishable from one in which there is no fundamental reasoning mechanism, and instead people utilise a collection of tools and techniques acquired from experience, or borrowed from other cognitive domains. The exact use of tools therefore depends upon the person and the task, and no type of process can be asserted to enjoy the privilege of being fundamental.

If the question *is there a fundamental reasoning mechanism?* cannot be answered, and the question *how do people reason?* does not have a simple answer, then what is left for researchers to investigate? In fact, although the issues become more complex, they remain tractable. We need to know what reasoning strategies people apply, how these are acquired, how they are chosen between, and how acquisition and selection are influenced by individual and task properties. The chapters in this volume address all of these issues, with particular reference to deductive reasoning tasks.

Before continuing, we need to be clear as to what is meant by 'strategy', as there are at least two types of definition in the literature (Roberts & Newton, 2003). *Broad definitions* minimally specify a strategy as a self-contained set of processes that need not be applied for solving a task. For example, Siegler and Jenkins (1989) suggest that a strategy is 'any procedure that is non-obligatory and goal directed' (p. 11). There is an important distinction between an individual process, or component (e.g., Sternberg, 1985), or tactic (e.g., Johnson-Laird, Savary, & Bucciarelli, 2000) and the *sequence* of linked processes needed to complete a task. The entire series forms a strategy, but there is no guarantee that any individual will apply it. In contrast, *narrow definitions* have additional requirements. For instance, there must be a conscious decision to apply a strategy and/or conscious awareness of its operation. Fundamental, or hard-wired processes do not count (even where their action can be overridden, or ignored) so that a strategy must be applied in addition to what would normally happen, and this should require more effort than not applying it, at least to begin with. For example, Evans (2000) defines a strategy as 'thought processes that are elaborated in time, systematic, goal-directed, and under explicit conscious control' (p. 2).

The problem with narrow definitions, as Roberts and Newton (2003) argue, is that they presuppose that we can say for sure whether a set of procedures possess or fail to possess these properties. At the moment we cannot, and hence narrow definitions implicitly deflect research from the key issue, which has to be: *How do people differ in their approaches to reasoning, and why?* Instead, they run the risk of triggering less important debates, such as what name should be given to a particular set of processes, i.e., can they really be said to constitute a strategy? All contributors to this volume use a broad definition for 'strategy'.

Another line of thinking adopted by all contributors to this book is that people have *interstrategic* differences in reasoning which are worthy of investigation. In other words, people differ qualitatively in the strategies that they apply, applying different *types* of representation and process in order to make inferences. Hence, some people may reason by using mental models, others by deduction rules, others by using strategies that do not fit into either category (see Roberts, 2000a; Roberts & Newton, 2003). This should be contrasted with studies of *intrastrategic* differences. Here, the interest is in how people differ in precise details when implementing one particular category of strategy (e.g., mental models). Examples of the latter include Bucciarelli and Johnson-Laird, 1999; Roberts (in press) and Van der Henst, Yang, and Johnson-Laird (2002), but this type of difference is not the focus of the current book.

A deductive reasoning task is one in which all information necessary for a solution is given. Assuming that the information is true, the solution is therefore guaranteed to be correct. Traditionally, such tasks take the forms of conditional, categorical, and linear syllogisms, thus (respectively):

> If Tom is in London, then Linda is in Paris
> Tom is not in London
> Therefore, Linda is not in Paris, TRUE or FALSE

> All of the chefs are chess players
> All of the teachers are chess players
> Therefore, some of the chefs are chess players, TRUE or FALSE

> Ian is taller than Bob
> Bob is shorter than Tim
> Therefore, Tim is shorter than Ian, TRUE or FALSE

Throughout this book, the reader will see that numerous variants of the basic problems have been investigated over the years, and many other types of task can be categorised as 'deductive'. Although some researchers have recently queried whether deduction genuinely forms a coherent 'natural kind' for the purposes of reasoning research (e.g., Evans, 2002), from the point of view of individual differences in strategy usage, these types of task have a number of properties that make them interesting:

(1) Adults generally find them challenging, and there are considerable individual differences in levels of performance.
(2) Even within a type of task, there are considerable differences in item difficulty. Some are trivially easy to solve, others very difficult.
(3) Many different solution methods are available. General procedures, such as those based upon mental models or deduction rules, appear to be widely applicable if inefficient at times, and the use of both can be identified in different people (e.g., Bacon, Handley, & Newstead, chapter 4).
(4) People's procedures seem to change with time: Usually they become more refined, although sometimes pathological strategies may develop (e.g., Roberts & Newton, chapter 6; Newton & Roberts, chapter 7).

In fact, there has been a long tradition of researchers who have investigated individual differences in strategy usage for deductive reasoning tasks. Initially, these focused on linear reasoning (e.g., Potts & Scholz, 1975; Quinton & Fellows, 1975; Shaver, Pierson, & Lang, 1985; Sternberg & Weil, 1980; Wood, 1969) and one key issue was how strategy usage changes with practice. Sentence–picture verification later captured people's interest (e.g., Coney, 1988; Macleod, Hunt, & Mathews, 1978; Marquer & Pereira; 1990; Roberts, Wood, & Gilmore, 1994) and later still, categorical reasoning (e.g., Ford, 1995; Gilhooly, Logie, Wetherick, & Wynne, 1993). A recurring issue of interest for researchers investigating the latter two tasks has been whether different individuals prefer to represent information spatially versus verbally.

The chapters in this book represent ongoing research that recognises and builds upon past findings, reflecting a recent upsurge in interest in reasoning strategies (e.g., Schaeken, De Vooght, Vandierendonck, & d'Ydewalle, 2000). As such, these chapters are relevant not only to people who investigate deductive reasoning, but also to people who research into strategy usage in general, whether in the domains of arithmetic (e.g., Siegler & Lemaire, 1997), problem solving (e.g., Schunn & Reder, 2001), spelling (e.g., Rittle-Johnson & Siegler, 1999), or scientific reasoning (e.g., Kuhn & Pearsall, 1998). Deduction tasks enable theories of strategy selection and discovery to be tested in novel domains, on adults or children, and have also supplied new findings that general theories of individual differences in strategy usage will need to account for.

At least three different components can be identified when researching into individual differences in strategy usage, and all of these are discussed by the chapters in this book. First, it is necessary to identify the strategies that are used, or might potentially be used, for a task or a category of tasks: Researchers need to know what they might be looking for. This process is described as identifying the *strategy repertoire* (Lemaire & Fabre, chapter 1) and should be both empirically and theoretically driven. This may be informed by the possession of a suitable taxonomy of strategies, and the beginnings of an ambitious attempt at this are also discussed (Morris & Schunn, chapter 2). In fact, identifying the strategies used by individuals is not necessarily a straightforward process, and issues surrounding this are discussed both in general (Lemaire & Fabre, chapter 1) and, in particular, as applied to reasoning with linear and categorical syllogisms (Bacon, Handley, & Newstead, chapter 4) and for a compass point directions task that requires deductive reasoning (Roberts & Newton, chapter 6). One particular technique for identifying users of different strategies is to interfere with the various components of working memory, and see whether these differentially affect users of different strategies (Gilhooly, chapter 3; Bacon, Handley, & Newstead, chapter 4).

Once the strategies that people use have been identified, we then have to understand why individuals differ. One aspect of this that can be investigated is how people select between different strategies. This is likely to be driven by the degree of fit between (1) the type of task, its content, and the way in which it is presented, and (2) the strategies that are available for use and the abilities/resources available to the reasoner (Morris and Schunn, chapter 2). Different people may have tendencies to approach tasks in different ways, for example, some preferring spatial, concrete solution processes, others preferring more verbal, abstract methods, although so far this has proved difficult to explain (Bacon, Handley, & Newstead, chapter 4). There is evidence that interfering with working memory resources can change the types of strategy that people select (Gilhooly, chapter 3). Overall, strategy selections are generally effective in the sense that people tend to choose the most appropriate available strategy for solving a particular task, although there appear to be individual differences in the extent to which they are able to do this, as well as situational differences in the extent to which it is advantageous for people to attempt to do so (Dierckx & Vandierendonck, chapter 5). One possible influence on how likely people are to choose the most effective strategy is just how much more efficient it is in comparison with its competitors (Roberts & Newton, chapter 6).

The strategy selection process is unlikely to be confined to the first trial of a task. It *is* possible to identify situations in which the majority of people select a strategy, and then apply it throughout a task, but many researchers assert that high trial-by-trial variability is more characteristic of human higher cognition (e.g., Siegler, 1999). Hence, we need to understand differences in strategy usage *within* as well as between individuals (Lemaire & Fabre, chapter 1). Often, this variability reflects the fact that even within a single type of task, different strategies are optimal for different items. This therefore leads to questions concerning whether all people are equally adept at varying strategies in line with task demands, and whether such a level of vigilance is always justified (Dierckx & Vandierendonck, chapter 5).

Of course, another reason why people use different strategies is that they know different ones. Indeed, this is one of the recurring findings of studies comparing expert versus novice problem solving (e.g., Ericsson & Lehmann, 1996). If the best strategy is not available to an individual, then it cannot be used unless it is identified while solving the task. Hence, what do people learn about a task while they are performing it? How do they identify and capitalise on redundancies and regularities to develop more efficient methods, and avoid the discovery of pathological strategies? Strategy discovery is particularly difficult to investigate, but several recent findings suggest a success-based model: The people who perform best at a task are those who are most likely to discover new, improved methods, evaluate them as valid, and select them (Roberts & Newton, chapter 6). Unfortunately, strategy discovery appears to be far easier to inhibit than promote, and this has led to a *window of opportunity* model, in which strategy discovery is most likely to occur when tasks are easy enough to enable strategy discovery and, simultaneously, difficult enough to encourage strategy discovery (Newton & Roberts, chapter 7)

In this book, readers will find all of the major types of deductive reasoning task represented, particularly categorical (Morris & Schunn, chapter 2; Gilhooly, chapter 3; Bacon, Handley, & Newstead, chapter 4) and linear (Bacon, Handley, & Newstead, chapter 4; Dierckx & Vandierendonck, chapter 5) as well as other non-standard tasks (Roberts & Newton, chapter 6; Newton and Roberts; chapter 7). The purpose of their use is twofold. On the one hand, they form excellent tools for the investigation of how and why people differ in their strategy use, and on the other, they are core tasks in the deductive reasoning literature. By understanding individual differences in strategy selection for these, we hope that we will understand reasoning in general. However, deduction researchers will note that there are far fewer mentions of conditional/propositional reasoning compared with the rest (but see Lemaire & Fabre, chapter 1; Morris & Schunn, chapter 2; Gilhooly, chapter 3; Roberts & Newton, chapter 6). Surely people differ in their strategy usage for these tasks too? They almost certainly do, and given that research has developed sequentially as regards deduction tasks – first linear reasoning, then sentence–picture verification, then categorical reasoning – we might expect individual differences in conditional reasoning strategies to be the next domain to interest researchers.

The lack of current interest in interstrategic differences in conditional reasoning might appear strange when we consider the total number of experiments conducted, especially as this figure should include the Wason selection task. However, this is not so odd when we consider that a typical selection task will only involve the presentation of a few trials. In order to see how people differ, and how they change with time, we need to present many people with many trials. Not only this, but research into the selection task has focused on content and context effects (e.g., Holyoak & Cheng, 1995) and attentional processes (e.g., Roberts & Newton, 2001). Assuming that people have similar relevant knowledge and experience, and that attentional processes are low level and fundamental to all, then it is unlikely that such research would yield interesting individual differences in reasoning strategies (but see Stanovich & West, 1998). In addition, research into conditional reasoning has focused on attempting to identify whether people achieve this by the use of deduction rules, or by mental models. In retrospect these theories are rather similar in their predictions in this domain (e.g., Evans, Ellis, & Newstead, 1996), and both can be easily modified to account for the available data (e.g., Schroyens, Schaeken, & d'Ydewalle, 2001). Hence, it is hard even to identify whether either of the possibilities predominate for a group of people. In order to understand strategy usage, we need to identify this at the level of the individual, which will always be harder than identifying the dominant reasoning strategy of a group (Roberts, 2000a). Hence, identifying individual differences in this particular domain will have to wait until mental model and deduction rule theories develop such that they make distinctly different predictions in terms of patterns of errors, or until improved methodologies go beyond measuring simple error rates.

Strategy development is a fundamental component of learning. Children who discover, or who are more receptive to the teaching of new strategies, and are more likely to select the best in any given situation – both within and between tasks – will inevitably do better than their peers, whether this is at arithmetic, spelling, or solving intelligence test items. Strategy development does not end when school does. Adults differ too, with similar potential for differences in performance. Making inferences is an important element of everyday cognition, and given that different strategies are associated with different levels of effectiveness, we therefore hope to understand why some people are better at making inferences than others from the point of view of the strategies that they discover and select. In doing so, we will be better placed to assist people's learning and performance in any domain where appropriate strategy selection is important.

REFERENCES

Bucciarelli, M., & Johnson-Laird, P. N. (1999). Strategies in syllogistic reasoning. *Cognitive Science, 23*, 247–303.

Coney, J. (1988). Individual differences and task format in sentence verification. *Current Psychological Research and Reviews, 7*, 122–135.

Ericsson, K. A., & Lehmann, A. C. (1996). Expert and exceptional performance: Evidence of maximal adaptation to task constraints *Annual Review of Psychology, 47*, 273–305.

Evans, J. St. B. T. (2000). What could and could not be a strategy in reasoning? In W. Schaeken, G. De Vooght, A. Vandierendonck, & G. d'Ydewalle (Eds.), *Deductive reasoning and strategies* (pp. 1–22). Mahwah, NJ: Lawrence Erlbaum Associates, Inc.

Evans, J. St. B. T. (2002). Logic and human reasoning: An assessment of the deduction paradigm. *Psychological Bulletin*, *128*, 978–996.

Evans, J. St. B. T., Ellis, C. F., & Newstead, S. E. (1996). On the mental representation of conditional sentences. *Quarterly Journal of Experimental Psychology*, *49A*, 1086–1114.

Ford. M. (1995). Two models of mental representation and problem solving in syllogistic reasoning. *Cognition*, *54*, 1–71.

Gilhooly, K. J., Logie, R. H., Wetherick, N. E., & Wynn, V. (1993). Working memory and strategies in syllogistic-reasoning tasks. *Memory and Cognition*, *21*, 115–124.

Holyoak, K. J., & Cheng, P. W. (1995). Pragmatic reasoning with a point of view. *Thinking and Reasoning*, *1*, 289–400.

Johnson-Laird, P. N., & Byrne, R. M. J. (1991). *Deduction*. Hove, UK: Psychology Press.

Johnson-Laird, P. N., Savary, F., & Bucciarelli, M. (1999). Strategies and tactics in reasoning. In W. Schaeken, G. De Vooght, A. Vandierendonck, & G. d'Ydewalle (Eds.), *Deductive reasoning and strategies* (pp. 209–240). Mahwah, NJ: Lawrence Erlbaum Associates, Inc.

Kuhn, D., & Pearsall, S. (1998). Relations between metastrategic knowledge and strategic performance. *Cognitive Development*, *13*, 227–247.

MacLeod, C. M., Hunt, E. B., & Mathews, N. N. (1978). Individual differences in the verification of sentence–picture relationships. *Journal of Verbal Learning and Verbal Behavior*, *17*, 493–507.

Marquer, J. M., & Pereira, M. (1990). Reaction times in the study of strategies in sentence–picture verification: A reconsideration. *Quarterly Journal of Experimental Psychology*, *42A*, 147–168.

Potts, G. R., & Scholz, K. W. (1975). The internal representation of a three-term series problem. *Journal of Verbal Learning and Verbal Behavior*, *14*, 439–452.

Quinton, G., & Fellows, B. J. (1975). 'Perceptual' strategies in the solving of three-term series problems. *British Journal of Psychology*, *66*, 69–78.

Rittle-Johnson, B., & Siegler, R. S. (1999). Learning to spell: Variability, choice, and change in children's strategy use. *Child Development*, *70*, 332–348.

Rips, L. J. (1994). *The psychology of proof*. Cambridge, MA: MIT Press.

Roberts, M. J. (1993). Human reasoning: Deduction rules or mental models, or both? *Quarterly Journal of Experimental Psychology*, *46A*, 569–589.

Roberts, M. J. (1997). On dichotomies and deductive reasoning research. *Cahiers de Psychologie Cognitive/Current Psychology of Cognition*, *16*, 196–204.

Roberts, M. J. (2000a). Individual differences in reasoning strategies: A problem to solve or an opportunity to seize? In W. Schaeken, G. De Vooght, A. Vandierendonck, & G. d'Ydewalle (Eds.), *Deductive reasoning and strategies* (pp. 23–48). Mahwah, NJ: Lawrence Erlbaum Associates, Inc.

Roberts, M. J. (2000b). Strategies in relational inference. *Thinking and Reasoning*, *6*, 1–26.

Roberts, M. J. (in press). Falsification and mental models: It depends on the task. In W. Schaeken, A. Vandierendonck, W. Schroyens, & G. d'Ydewalle (Eds.), *The mental models theory of reasoning: Refinements and extensions*. Mahwah, NJ: Lawrence Erlbaum Associates, Inc.

Roberts, M. J., & Newton, E. J. (2001). Inspection times, the change task, and the rapid-response selection task. *Quarterly Journal of Experimental Psychology*, *54A*, 1031–1048.

Roberts, M. J., & Newton, E. J. (2003). Individual differences in the development of reasoning strategies. In D. Hardman & L. Macci (Eds.), *The international handbook of reasoning and decision making* (pp. 23–43). Chichester: Wiley.

Roberts, M. J., Wood, D. J., & Gilmore, D. J. (1994). The sentence–picture verification task: Methodological and theoretical difficulties. *British Journal of Psychology*, *85*, 413–432.

Schaeken, W., De Vooght, G., Vandierendonck, A., & d'Ydewalle, G. (2000). *Deductive reasoning and strategies*. Mahwah, NJ: Lawrence Erlbaum Associates, Inc.

Schroyens, W., Schaeken, W., & d'Ydewalle, G. (2001). The processing of negations in conditional reasoning: A meta-analytic case study in mental model and/or mental logic theory. *Thinking and Reasoning*, *7*, 121–172.

Schunn, C. D., & Reder, L. M. (2001). Another source of individual differences: Strategy adaptivity to changing rates of success. *Journal of Experimental Psychology: General*, *130*, 59–76.

Shaver, P., Pierson, L., & Lang, S. (1985). Converging evidence for the functional significance of imagery in problem solving. *Cognition*, *3*, 359–375.

Siegler, R. S. (1999). Strategic development. *Trends in Cognitive Sciences*, *3*, 430–435.

Siegler, R. S., & Jenkins, E. A. (1989). *How children discover new strategies*. Hillsdale, NJ: Lawrence Erlbaum Associates, Inc.

Siegler, R. S., & Lemaire, P. (1997). Older and younger adults' strategy choices in multiplication: Testing predictions of ASCM using the choice/no-choice method. *Journal of Experimental Psychology: General*, *126*, 71–92.

Stanovich, K. E., & West, R. F. (1998). Cognitive ability and variation in selection task performance. *Thinking and Reasoning*, *4*, 193–231.

Sternberg, R. J. (1985). *Beyond IQ*. Cambridge: Cambridge University Press.

Sternberg, R. J., & Weil, E. M. (1980). An aptitude × strategy interaction in linear syllogistic reasoning. *Journal of Educational Psychology*, *72*, 226–239.

Van der Henst J. B., Yang Y. R., & Johnson-Laird P. N. (2002). Strategies in sentential reasoning. *Cognitive Science*, *26*, 425–468.

Wood, D. J. (1969). *The nature and development of problem solving strategies*. Unpublished doctoral thesis, University of Nottingham, UK.

CHAPTER ONE

Strategic aspects of human cognition: Implications for understanding human reasoning

Patrick Lemaire
CNRS, Université de Provence, and Institut Universitaire de France,
Marseille, France

Ludovic Fabre
CNRS & Université de Provence, Marseille, France

One of the most fascinating aspects of human reasoning is the recent discovery that people use many different strategies when making inferences. This
changes the research agenda, and has numerous implications for issues that
will need to be addressed in order to better understand this domain. In this
chapter, we will discuss some of the most important conceptual and methodological issues that have been identified when accounting for the fact that
people may accomplish a cognitive task by using different strategies. To do
this, we will first give an overview of general issues, such as what is a strategy,
how to distinguish between strategies, and which aspects of strategy usage
need to be investigated, and we will discuss the various methods used to
investigate these. General principles will be illustrated using examples from
the domain of arithmetic problem solving. Here, strategy usage has been
investigated for more than two decades, and there is clear-cut evidence for the
use of different strategies, and for how this affects people's performance. In
the second section, we will show that the general lessons that have been learnt
from studies of problem solving have clear repercussions for understanding
human reasoning.

GENERAL ISSUES IN COGNITIVE STRATEGIES

Since Newell and Simon's (1972) *Human Problem Solving*, in which the
investigation of strategic aspects of human cognition was advocated as a
fruitful line of research in order to further understand performance, several

definitions of 'strategy' have been proposed. These all view a strategy as a 'method used for solving a problem' (Schunn & Reder, 2001, p. 59) or as 'a procedure or set of procedures for achieving a higher level goal or task' (Lemaire & Reder, 1999, p. 365). In other words, a strategy is the series of processes an individual uses to accomplish a cognitive task.

Many psychologists view the study of strategic aspects of cognition as crucial to understanding behaviour. Thus, differences in (1) the performance between two individuals, and (2) the performance of a single individual under two different experimental conditions, may be accounted for by differences in their underlying cognitive processes, i.e., their strategies. By looking at strategic aspects of human performance, cognitive psychologists aim to account for cognition in mechanistic terms. In this respect, they are like chemists trying to understand chemical reactions via elementary steps, and in particular, trying to understand how the same start products can be converted to the same end products, but via different reaction pathways.

As an example, suppose you participate in a study on arithmetic problem solving in which you are asked to verify a series of equations (e.g., $8 + 4 = 12$: TRUE or FALSE). $8 + 4 = 13$? is an example of a false equation that is also a *small-split problem* because its proposed answer is close to the correct one. $8 + 4 = 19$? is also false, but is a *large-split problem* because its given answer is distant from the correct one. For the false equations, researchers have established that people use two different strategies to verify them, involving different processes (e.g., Ashcraft & Battaglia, 1978; De Rammelaere, Stuyven, & Vandierendonck, 2001; Duverne & Lemaire, 2004; El yagoubi, Lemaire, & Besson, 2003; Zbrodoff & Logan, 1990). An *exhaustive-verification strategy* is used to solve small-split problems. For this, people encode the problems, search for the correct answer in memory, compare the proposed and correct answers, and make a true/false decision. This strategy is also applied to true problems. Large-split problems do not require searching for correct solutions, as the proposed answers are too far away from the correct answers to be plausible. Instead, a *self-terminated verification strategy* is used in which people encode the problem, make a fast implausibility judgement, and then make a false decision.

When we view strategies as sets of procedures that people use to accomplish cognitive tasks, this raises the fundamental issue of generality versus specificity. Certain strategies are general in the sense that they may be used for a variety of tasks, or in different domains. Other strategies may be specific to a particular domain (e.g., strategies for mental rotation are different from those for arithmetic problem solving; reasoning strategies differ from decision-making strategies) or to a particular task within a domain (e.g., strategies to *verify* conclusions presented with pairs of premises may be different from those used to *derive* conclusions from them; inductive reasoning strategies may be different from scientific reasoning strategies). Specific strategies may require knowledge of a particular domain in order for them to be applied. People may use either general or specific strategies, depending upon the task and whether knowledge is required or available. When specific strategies are not available, general problem-solving strategies (e.g., means–end analysis, subgoal analysis, forward/backward moves) are used instead.

As an example, arithmetic problem solving involves the use of strategies that are useless for solving anagrams, and hence are very specific. At a finer level of analysis, strategies used to verify arithmetic problems (e.g., $8 \times 7 = 54$: TRUE or FALSE) may differ from those used for production tasks (e.g., $8 \times 7 = ??$). For the latter, proposed and correct answers need not be compared, but there are fewer cues to assist in the search for a correct answer. Sometimes people will be able to retrieve the solution directly from long-term memory (LTM), otherwise, they will need to use a counting strategy. However, before we can determine whether strategies are general or specific, we need to confirm that people use different strategies, and that these involve genuinely distinct procedures.

Criteria for distinguishing between strategies

Strategies can be distinguished conceptually and empirically. Conceptually, a task analysis can identify the potentially different strategies and the processes supposedly involved for each. Such an analysis should then be empirically founded on the basis of at least one of three types of evidence: experimental, pathological, and individual/developmental. Recent developments in neuropsychology have added a fourth possible source. This includes (1) cerebral localisations from neuroimaging studies and (2) time courses of event-related potentials. Of course, such sources of evidence depend upon first either comparing two previously identified strategy types, or creating two different strategy groups by instruction.

Experimental evidence for distinguishing between strategies consists of Factor × Strategy interactions, such that effects of the factor are different when comparing two or more strategy types. Hence, the execution of one strategy may be affected by the factor but not the use of another. For example, when people use the exhaustive-verification strategy to reject false arithmetic problems, they are greatly influenced by problem size, so that they are faster to reject small-number equations such as $8 \times 4 = 31?$ than large-number equations such as $8 \times 9 = 71?$ (e.g., Duverne & Lemaire, 2004; De Rammelaere et al., 2001). When they use the self-terminated strategy, they are equally fast for these. As another example, for single-digit multiplication problems such as $3 \times 4 = ??$, people who use the strategy of retrieving the solution directly from memory are less affected by problem size than people who use repeated addition (i.e., adding 4 three times; see LeFevre, Sadesky, & Bisanz, 1996b; LeFevre, Bisanz, Daley, Buffone, & Sadesky, 1996a).

Observations from pathology, such as double dissociations, are another source of evidence for demonstrating the distinctness of two strategies. A brain-injured patient performing a task may be impaired in the use of one strategy but proficient at another, whereas the reverse may be the case for another. For example, Dehaene and Cohen (1991) reported a case study of severe acalculia. The patient was unable to perform exact calculation correctly on single-digit multiplication, but could use an approximation strategy. Hence, problems such as $2 \times 2 = 9$? were answered correctly, but not problems such as $2 \times 2 = 5$? (see also Warrington, 1982). No case of impaired approximation with preserved exact calculation has yet been reported.

Individual and developmental differences in the use of strategies are a further source of evidence that reinforces distinctions between them. For example, the execution of one strategy may improve faster than another as children develop, or become impaired more quickly than another as adults age. Lemaire & Lecacheur (2002b) instructed adults, 11-year-old, and 9-year-old children to use each of two arithmetical estimation strategies, and found age-related differences in speed of execution. For the *rounding-down strategy* (i.e., finding an approximate sum to problems such as $238 + 786 = ???$ by rounding down both operands to the closest decade: $230 + 780$), latencies were 4.3 s, 7.5 s, and 13.0 s in adults, 11-year-olds, and 9-year-olds, respectively. For the *rounding-up strategy* as applied to the same problems (i.e., $240 + 790$), corresponding latencies were 6.8 s, 12.7 s, and 19.7 s. Hence the rounding-up strategy was harder to apply, and showed greater age-related differences than the rounding-down strategy.

Observing that the use of different strategies activates different brain areas, or results in different electrophysiological time courses, may be viewed as a final source of evidence for confirming the distinction between them. For example, when participants were asked to determine whether the sum of two-digit operands was larger or smaller than 100, El yagoubi, Lemaire, and Besson (2003) found differences in brainwaves on small-split versus large-split problems. As another example, Stanescu-Cosson, Pinel, Van de Moortele, Le Bihan, Cohen, & Dehaene (2000) investigated healthy volunteers performing arithmetic verification problems, either by exact calculation or by approximation strategies. Functional Magnetic Resonance Imaging (fMRI) showed that the approximation strategy activated the bilateral intraparietal, precentral, dorsolateral and superior prefrontal regions, while exact calculation activated the left inferior prefrontal cortex and the bilateral angular regions.

Strategic aspects of cognitive performance

Lemaire and Siegler (1995) proposed a conceptual framework for the investigation of strategic aspects of cognitive performance for a given task. This contained three important components. First, we must know the *strategy repertoire* for the task. In other words, the sum total of all strategies that may be applied to it.[1] Second, we need to investigate *strategy execution* in order to determine the relative performance of the strategies (i.e., how fast and accurate people are with each). Finally, it is important to understand *strategy selection* mechanisms: How do people choose between strategies for a given problem? Insights into strategy selection mechanisms are provided by looking at changes in strategy distributions as a function of different situation parameters (e.g., instructions to be fast versus accurate) and problem parameters (e.g., easy versus hard problems). Individual differences (e.g., age related, skill related) in the awareness of different strategies, and in their execution and selection, can also be investigated.

This conceptual framework has been applied comprehensively to arithmetic problem solving. Here, strategies differ in their relative proportions of use, speed and accuracy, and the task features that determine their use. For example, when people are asked to solve a series of simple multiplication problems such as $8 \times 9 = ??$, the following strategy repertoire has been identified: (1) retrieval (i.e., directly retrieving the correct solution from LTM); (2) repeated addition (i.e., adding one operand the number of times indicated by the other operand); (3) problem transformation (e.g., $8 \times 10 - 8$ to find the solution to $8 \times 9 = ??$); (4) say 'I don't know' without attempting any other procedure (LeFevre et al., 1996b). Considering strategy execution, retrieval is the fastest and most accurate, followed by problem transformation. Repeated addition is less accurate and slower still. Saying 'I don't know' is fast, but this is the least accurate. In terms of strategy selection, adults use retrieval most often, they rarely say 'I don't know', and sometimes use repeated addition or problem transformation. The likelihoods of using repeated addition and of saying 'I don't know' are highly influenced by the sizes of the operands, more so than the likelihoods of using the retrieval and problem transformation strategies.

Strategy selection and execution can also be influenced by participants' characteristics, such as their age or expertise. Developmental studies of arithmetic problem solving (e.g., Geary, 1994; Lemaire, Barrett, Fayol, & Abdi, 1994) have shown (1) that retrieval is used increasingly as children grow older, and (2) that younger adults use repeated addition more often than older adults – who prefer retrieval – (Geary & Wiley, 1991). Retrieval is executed faster and more accurately by more skilled participants (as assessed

---

[1] It is important to note that researchers use the term *strategy repertoire* in different ways. Here, use of this term refers to all possible strategies for a task, irrespective of whether all people are aware of them, or are prepared to use them. Strategy repertoire has also been used to denote the strategies that an *individual* is aware of for performing a particular task. Hence, in the latter context, individuals' strategy repertoires may differ, with the consequence that different people will have different options to choose between during the strategy selection process (e.g., see Roberts & Newton, chapter 6 this volume).

by independent arithmetic paper-and-pencil tests), and proficiency at executing individual strategies improves during childhood but declines during adulthood.

Methods for investigating the strategy repertoire

Before investigating strategy execution and selection, it is necessary to identify the strategies that can potentially be applied to a task (i.e., the strategy repertoire). To this end, two types of method can be used: direct and indirect. *Direct methods* can be applied when strategies are identifiable unambiguously from external behavioural evidence. For example, in human memory, determining that an individual uses rehearsal is easy if he or she vocalises.

Verbal protocols can be an important source of direct evidence. *On-line protocols* are participants' verbalisations during problem solving, whereas *off-line protocols* are collected retrospectively, i.e., after each problem or after a series of problems has been solved. Combined with other sources of data (e.g., latencies, error rates, behavioural indices coded from video recordings of participants), verbal protocol data are a useful means to determine both the strategy repertoire for a task, and an individual's strategy usage. Whenever possible, on-line protocols should be used as, compared with off-line protocols, they are more veridical (i.e., they are more likely to reflect the thought processes actually involved), more reliable (i.e., the same problem solved with the same strategy on different occasions is more likely to produce the same protocol), and their reactivity is acceptably low (i.e., the requirement to verbalise on-line is not too disruptive of the thought processes that people apply).

When the strategy repertoire is being identified for a new task, it is important to collect reliability measures for the classification procedures. For example, where protocols are categorised, strategy classifications should be obtained from two coders independently. High correlations ($r > .90$) are indicative of high reliabilities, and disagreements may be resolved through discussions between coders. Once the repertoire is known, strategy identification during future studies can be facilitated by asking participants, after each trial, to choose from a list of described strategies. Again, converging evidence from latency and accuracy measures, etc. will increase our confidence in these choices.

Whenever possible, psychologists should use direct methods to assess strategy usage, validated by evidence from performance if this is available. This has the advantage of minimising the number of inferences made from performance to processes. Unfortunately, in many areas of cognition, it is not always possible to use direct methods for at least two reasons. First, different strategies may not always be associated with different spontaneous overt behaviours. For example, many tasks are accomplished silently, such as reading (e.g., Stone & Van Orden, 1993). Likewise, certain arithmetic tasks (e.g., Lemaire & Fayol, 1995; Lemaire & Reder, 1999): With verification tasks such as $8 + 4 = 19$? it is impossible from external behavioural evidence to 'see' whether people solve these by exhaustive or by self-terminated strategies. Latencies and percent errors can suggest the use of different strategies, but no external behavioural evidence is available for us to conclude this unambiguously.

The second reason that can preclude the use of direct methods concerns cases of unreliable and unveridical verbal protocols (Ericsson & Simon, 1980; Russo, Johnson, & Stephens, 1989). For some tasks, people are not aware of the strategies that they use because, when the verbal protocols are collected, there are no episodic traces of them in working memory. This happens when tasks are performed relatively quickly or slowly. Rapidly accomplished tasks do not generate episodic traces, and slow tasks may result either in interference between different episodic traces, or their decay. As an example, when people solve problems such as $9 \times 7 = 62$? they are faster than for problems such as $9 \times 7 = 69$? This is despite the fact that 69 is further from the correct product than 62, and that people are normally faster for large-split than small-split problems. This effect has been interpreted on a strategic basis: 62 can be rejected very quickly because it violates the odd/even status of the correct answer; 69 cannot be rejected in this way, and so participants must apply the slightly slower self-terminated strategy in order to reject it. When Lemaire and colleagues (Lemaire & Fayol, 1995; Lemaire & Reder, 1999; Masse & Lemaire, 2001) asked participants how they accomplished these tasks, fewer than 10% mentioned their use of odd/even status of the proposed answers, even though overall performance was consistent with this strategy interpretation.

Inability to use direct methods has led psychologists to focus on indirect methods of strategy identification. These consist of analysing performance variations as a function of different task parameters, and to infer from these the strategies that people use. For example, Zacks (1982) found larger primacy effects (i.e., better performance on the first items in a list) in younger than in older adults, and inferred that a rehearsal strategy was used more often by the younger adults. This interpretation was strengthened when the number of times participants rehearsed out loud was tallied, showing that older people indeed appeared to rehearse less often (Sanders, Murphy, Schmitt, & Walsh, 1980).

When carrying out studies of strategy usage *solely* by using indirect methods, it is important to keep in mind that these have several important limitations. Inferences from performance to process are more numerous with indirect than with direct methods. Consequently, conclusions are less certain and alternative explanations may be proposed to account for patterns of findings (see Marquer & Pereira, 1990 for a detailed discussion on this point). Even though a given account can be accepted as long as no alternative plausible explanation is provided, confidence in our conclusions will always be stronger when direct evidence is also available. Indirect methods applied by themselves will never be as powerful as a combination of direct methods (e.g., verbal protocols) *validated by* indirect methods (e.g., performance). There can also be a problem of circularity, whereby indirect methods by themselves provide both the means of strategy identification, and also the evidence in support of the validity of the strategy classification. Again, a combination of different sources of converging evidence, both direct and indirect, will reduce this problem.

In sum, cognitive strategies may be investigated either directly (by looking at external behavioural evidence such as verbal protocols) or indirectly (by looking at performance variations as a function of task characteristics). Whenever possible, researchers use direct methods. However, when not possible, indirect methods by themselves can shed some light on the strategies that people use. Ideally, evidence from both direct and indirect methods should be combined, and together they are particularly important for furthering our understanding of the different strategies that may be used for a given task.

Methods for investigating strategy execution and selection

Once the strategy repertoire for a task is established, strategy execution and selection can then be investigated. For a number of years, researchers have achieved this by asking people to perform tasks, permitting them to use whatever strategies they wished. Strategy characteristics (i.e., relative frequency, speed, and accuracy) are then examined. As discussed by Siegler and Lemaire (1997), this so-called *choice method* has methodological problems that limit its usefulness. For example, it is impossible to compare strategies for inherent differences in speed and accuracy because different strategies may be used for different types of problems, and perhaps by people with different levels of skill. Furthermore, it is impossible to determine whether having the option to choose between several strategies actually enables participants to perform better than if only one strategy were available. Finally, it is impossible to determine the respective roles of item features (e.g., those that influence difficulty) and strategy characteristics (e.g., relative speed and accuracy) in influencing strategy choices.

To avoid the limitations of the choice method, Siegler and Lemaire (1997) proposed the *choice/no-choice method*. This requires testing every participant under one, or both, of two conditions:[2] (1) the *choice condition*, in which they

---

[2] This method has been used successfully either with the choice/no-choice conditions as a within-subject factor (e.g., Lemaire & Lecacheur, 2001, 2002a; Siegler & Lemaire, 1997) or between-subjects (Lemaire & Lecacheur, 2002b). Either design can be used for reasoning research.

can freely choose which strategy to use for each trial; and (2) the *no-choice* condition, in which they must use a given strategy for all items, with one separately instructed subcondition for each strategy of interest. Using this methodology, unbiased estimates of speed and accuracy are possible for each of the available strategies. This allows an analysis of the extent to which strategy selection is responsible for differences in performance in the choice condition, both overall and between different types of item.[3] Comparing performance between the choice and no-choice conditions will indicate what, if any, benefit participants may gain by having a choice of strategy. Finally, it is easy to assess the effects of item characteristics, both on strategy execution and selection, and to determine whether participants are adaptive in their strategy choices once the relative performance of the strategies has been taken into account. Previous studies using the choice/no-choice method successfully compared (1) younger versus older adults' strategic aspects of multiplication problem solving (Siegler & Lemaire, 1997); (2) younger versus older adults' strategic aspects of between-currency conversion tasks (Lemaire & Lecacheur, 2001); (3) third- versus fifth-grade children's strategy use and execution in (a) spelling single words (Lemaire & Lecacheur, 2002a); (b) solving computational estimation problems (Lemaire & Lecacheur, 2002b). In sum, the choice/no-choice method is important for investigating strategy execution and selection. It provides data that inform us on the speed and accuracy of each strategy, and the determinants of strategy selection.

IMPLICATIONS FOR INVESTIGATING STRATEGIC ASPECTS OF REASONING

If it is true that 'deductive reasoning can, for a large part, be rephrased in terms of problem solving' (Schaeken, De Vooght, Vandierendonck, & d'Ydewalle, 2000, p. 304), then everything that was said about problem-solving strategies in the previous sections can be applied to reasoning research. Moreover, by investigating reasoning strategies, researchers will advance our general knowledge about strategy repertoires, execution, and selection. In the following sections, we will discuss the implications of findings concerning cognitive strategies for issues in reasoning research.

Implications for understanding strategy repertoires in reasoning tasks

As for problem solving, reasoning research is likely to benefit from a consideration of key issues from a strategic viewpoint. This may provide better

---

[3] It is very important to ensure that subjects follow instructions in the no-choice condition, otherwise results can be extremely difficult to interpret (e.g., Sternberg & Weil, 1980).

(i.e., more precise and detailed) accounts of reasoning mechanisms, of individual differences in performance, and of effects of content familiarity and other task features. This will also help to identify whether aspects of strategy usage are specific to particular tasks, or general across a variety of reasoning tasks or domains. Of course, this entails adopting sound methods to investigate the strategic aspects of performance, as well as criteria to distinguish between strategies. This also assumes that people really do use a variety of reasoning strategies.

Do people use different reasoning strategies? Research has recently focused on this question, and multiple-strategy use has been found in a variety of tasks. For example, (1) Johnson-Laird and his collaborators (Bucciarelli & Johnson-Laird, 1999; Johnson-Laird, Savary, & Bucciarelli, 2000) have found that people use several strategies when solving sentential and syllogistic problems; (2) Rauh (2000) observed that people use at least two types of strategy for spatial relational inference tasks; and (3) Girotto and Gonzalez (2000, 2001) have found that probabilistic and statistical reasoning tasks are accomplished by using several strategies. More specifically, when Bucciarelli and Johnson-Laird gave participants 20 syllogisms (i.e., identify the conclusion that follows from premises such as 'Some B are A; All B are C'), they found that the following strategies were used: (1) drawing circles around the end terms (i.e., A and C); (2) using some form of Euler circles; (3) using an idiosyncratic symbol system (such as arrows, lines, and labels to connect terms); (4) using tokens to represent different types of individual. All of these strategies could be used with or without additional annotations. Also interesting was the finding that no individual used a single strategy for all problems: Variability appears to be a central feature of human reasoning, as for problem solving.

As discussed by several authors (e.g., Bucciarelli & Johnson-Laird, 1999; Evans, 1995, 1996; Evans & Over, 1996; Johnson-Laird et al., 2000), verbal protocols have proved useful for investigating the strategy repertoire for a variety of reasoning tasks. Unfortunately, people often cannot explain their thought processes, especially unconscious ones, and so instead they are asked to externalise what they are thinking about while reasoning. However, in this domain, it may be difficult to collect verbal protocols on a trial-by-trial basis, as people may be less likely to verbalise spontaneously. It is therefore important to ensure that participants verbalise for every trial in order to provide the necessary strategy identification data for each type of item. Of course, it is essential to ensure that verbal protocols provide veridical (i.e., valid) information about the strategies that people actually use, and non-reactive (i.e., non-disruptive) data, whose collection has not interfered with the reasoning processes. To date, the very few studies that have collected verbal reports to identify reasoning strategies have revealed similar results for verbal-report and no-verbal-report conditions, suggesting that they are non-reactive

(Bucciarelli & Johnson-Laird, 1999). Further data are needed to establish that verbal reports are veridical, and converging evidence (such as latencies and error rates) will increase confidence still further in conclusions regarding strategy repertoires and individuals' strategy usage.

When using verbal protocols, it is the task of the psychologist to analyse them objectively so as to determine a strategy repertoire. One important consideration is that the grain size with which verbal protocols are coded and analysed may lead to different outcomes. To take an example, at one level, reasoning strategies may include spatial, verbal, and task-specific shortcut strategies (Roberts, 2000). At a finer-grain-level of analysis, it may prove useful to distinguish among different spatial strategies. As for other cognitive domains, this raises the issue of what constitutes a reasoning strategy, and how to distinguish between different strategies.

Regarding definitions of strategy, reasoning researchers have made several proposals. To take just two examples, Evans has suggested that a strategy is a set of 'processes which are relatively slow, goal-directed, systematic, and under explicit conscious control' (Evans, 2000, p. 1). Johnson-Laird has proposed to make a distinction between several levels of analysis, calling a strategy 'the sequence of steps that an individual follows in solving, or attempting to solve, a problem' (Johnson-Laird et al., 2000, p. 210), and furthermore that each step within a strategy is a tactic, that is a mental process inaccessible to conscious awareness. Although these definitions insist on the conscious aspect of strategies – a criterion not necessarily shared by others – they nonetheless echo definitions proposed by problem-solving researchers, so that both research communities conceptualise a strategy as a set of mental processes (or steps, or procedures, or components, or tactics) used to accomplish a task.

Regarding empirical methods of strategy identification, researchers in reasoning may fruitfully use the same sources of evidence as problem-solving researchers. Hence, experimental, pathological, individual/developmental, and neurological evidence are all important. There are a number of item and situation variables that could be manipulated in order to test their consequences for the selection and execution of reasoning strategies. These include the number of mental models required to solve a problem (e.g., one- versus multiple-models problems), types of reasoning (e.g., deductive, inductive, statistical, counterfactual, practical), types of reasoning task (e.g., deriving conclusions from premises versus evaluating conclusions), or other task parameters (e.g., with or without external support such as diagrams, paper-and-pencil, or a computer). In addition, data from patients would be of great interest, particularly if people could be identified who are able to use a given strategy (e.g., verbal) but have difficulty with another (e.g., spatial), along with other patients showing the reverse. Moreover, individual and developmental data would add further support in demonstrating distinctions between strategies. Individual differences in strategy selection or execution may be observed in participants possessing certain characteristics, such as high versus low working-memory span, or high versus low verbal ability. Developmental data might show strategy discovery during the course of learning/development, or different strategy distributions across ages (e.g., younger participants using one strategy more or less often than older participants). Finally, brain imaging studies showing different regions activated by different strategies, or different time courses of event-related potentials for different strategies, would add further support to the argument that there are genuine and important differences in reasoning strategies.

Previous studies in the domain of sentence–picture verification illustrate the use of these different sources of evidence. For this task, participants are asked to determine whether sentences (e.g., 'the star is above the plus') correctly describe subsequently presented pictures (e.g., Clark & Chase, 1972; MacLeod, Hunt, & Mathews, 1978; Marquer & Pereira, 1990; Reichle, Carpenter, & Just, 2000; Roberts, Wood, & Gilmore, 1994). In this task, participants can be divided into two strategy groups, namely linguistic (i.e., the sentence is read and the image is encoded, the meanings of each are represented in a proposition-based format, and both are compared), or visual–spatial (i.e., the sentence is first translated into a visual–spatial format and then compared with the picture). Data have shown that these strategies are (1) differently affected by sentence complexity: The linguistic strategy is more affected by negation than the visual–spatial strategy; (2) selected on the basis of individual differences in ability: Participants with high verbal ability are more likely to use the linguistic strategy, participants with high visual–spatial ability are more likely to use visual–spatial strategy; (3) are supported by partially separable networks of cortical regions: fMRI data have shown that the linguistic strategy produces more activation in language-related cortical regions (e.g., Broca's area), whereas the visual–spatial strategy produces more activation in regions that have been implicated in visual–spatial reasoning (e.g., the parietal cortex). These activations are also related to individual differences in cognitive ability. For people using the linguistic strategy, high verbal individuals have less activation in language-related areas than low verbals. For people using the visual–spatial strategy, high visual–spatial participants have less activation in the left parietal cortex than people with low visual–spatial ability.

In sum, investigating a strategy repertoire in detail is important for understanding how people accomplish a reasoning task. Trial-by-trial verbal protocols provide crucial insights towards this end. In addition, converging evidence from experimental, pathological, individual/developmental difference, and brain imaging studies provide additional support for the conclusions.

Implications for understanding strategy execution and selection in reasoning

Once multiple-strategy use has been acknowledged as an important property of human reasoning, and once a valid and reliable strategy repertoire has been empirically established for a given reasoning task, the next questions concern strategy execution and selection: How does the execution of different strategies compare in terms of speed and accuracy, and how are strategies chosen between on an item-by-item basis?

When investigating strategy execution, it is important that estimates of relative speed and accuracy are not confounded with the item and participant selection artifacts discussed above. Hence, to understand why people obtain better performance when they use one strategy compared with another, it is important that these are compared all else being equal. It is therefore necessary to control for the relative frequency with which each strategy has been used, the types of items for which different strategies tend to be used, and participants' preferences. In other words, relative strategy speed and accuracy should not be contaminated by any selection artifacts. The choice/no-choice method proposed by Siegler and Lemaire (1997) could be used to assess these. As discussed above, this method controls for potential methodological problems and hence enables researchers to address interesting issues that have yet to be investigated in human reasoning.

An example will illustrate the usefulness of the choice/no-choice method as applied to a reasoning task. Suppose we want to investigate strategic aspects of people's performance on conditional reasoning problems similar to the following:

Given that
   (1) There is a red marble in the box if and only if there is a brown marble in the box.
   (2) Either there is a brown marble in the box or else there is a grey marble in the box, but not both.
   (3) There is a grey marble if and only if there is a black marble in the box.
Does it follow that:
   If there is not a red marble in the box then there is a black marble in the box?

Johnson-Laird et al. (2000) showed that four strategies may be used to solve these types of problem: a suppositional strategy, a compound strategy, a chain strategy, and a model strategy (see Johnson-Laird et al., 2000 pp. 214–220). To understand these strategic aspects further, we suggest the following experiment using the choice/no-choice method. Five groups of 20 participants each would be asked to solve at least 60 conditional reasoning problems: A minimum number is necessary to run a sufficiently powerful statistical analyses. One group of participants would be tested under the 'choice condition', in which they would be first trained with all four strategies, and then asked to solve a set of problems using any of these. The second group would be trained to use the suppositional strategy, and then asked to solve an identical set of problems using only this method. The third, fourth, and fifth groups of participants would be trained to use the compound, chain, or model strategies, and then asked to solve the same set of problems using their respective strategies.

Such an experiment would enable us to collect the following data. First, the choice condition would provide the percent use of each strategy. Second, the no-choice conditions would provide speed and accuracy data for each of the four strategies, both overall, and by item type. These performance measures would not be contaminated by strategy choices and would therefore provide unbiased estimates (unless item choice was biased). Third, relative strategy speed and accuracy could be correlated with mean percent use of each strategy in the choice condition, both on item-by-item, and participant-by-participant bases. Finally, the impact of relative strategy performance could be assessed independently of other factors (e.g., problem difficulty), so as to determine the bases on which participants choose between reasoning strategies.

Of even greater interest, this canonical scenario could be adapted to investigate the effects on strategy selection and execution of a number of factors that are known (or not yet known) to affect reasoning performance. Several characteristics of reasoning problems could be manipulated: for example, the number of mental models that a reasoner needs to build for correct solution, familiarity of problem content, presence/absence of negation, availability of counterexamples, order of presentation of information, and response format (e.g., Byrne, Espino, & Santamaria, 1999; Evans & Handley, 1999; Evans, Handley, Harper, & Johnson-Laird, 1999; Favrel & Barrouillet, 2000; Gigerenzer & Hoffrage, 1995; Girotto, Mazzocco, & Tasso, 1997; Hardman & Payne, 1995; Legrenzi, Girotto, & Johnson-Laird, 1993; Schroyens, Schaeken, d'Ydewalle, 2001). Similarly, the choice/no-choice method could be used to determine whether strategy selection or execution (or both) are affected by modes of mental representation and problem solution, or by working-memory constraints (e.g., Barrouillet & Lecas, 1999; Ford, 1995; Gilhooly, Logie, Wetherick, & Wynn, 1993; MacLeod et al., 1978; Stanovich & West, 1998; Sternberg & Weil, 1980; Vandierendonck & De Vooght, 1997). Finally, individual differences in the selection and execution of reasoning strategies, whether age- or skill-related, could be unambiguously documented (e.g., Barrouillet & Lecas, 1998; Barrouillet, Grosset, & Lecas, 2000; Galotti, Baron, & Sabini, 1986; Heit & Hahn, 2001; Lecas & Barrouillet, 1999; Roberts, in press; Roberts, Gilmore, & Wood, 1997; Wood, 1978). In addition to a better understanding of the effects of a number of factors, the choice/no-choice design would enable the same controls in reasoning research as in problem solving and, as a consequence, clearer conclusions would be drawn.

Let me give just one example of a reasoning study whose methodological limitations resemble those known in problem-solving research. Bucciarelli and Johnson-Laird (1999, Exps. 1 and 2) found, like many others, that one-model syllogistic problems were solved more accurately and quickly than either (1) problems in which multiple-models must be constructed in order to identify a valid conclusion, or (2) problems with no valid conclusion. We do not know how people solved each item type (i.e., the percent use of each strategy), and so it is difficult to know whether the number of models required is the only factor to determine difficulty. Suppose participants used an easier-to-execute (i.e., faster and more accurate) strategy more often for one-model problems and a harder strategy for the others. It is therefore difficult to be sure that differences in performance depend on problem characteristics rather than on strategy characteristics. A similar argument can be made concerning participant strategy selection bias (in which efficient strategies are used most often by the best reasoners of the sample, and less efficient strategies are used by the poorest reasoners). By forcing participants to use each strategy on all problems, these selection artifacts are controlled, and unbiased estimates of strategy performance are provided.

More generally, the choice/no-choice method can be used to investigate a variety of strategy issues in reasoning, enabling researchers not only to control for potential artifacts but also to yield firm and unambiguous conclusions with regards to a variety of empirical questions. These include: Is a given strategy faster/more accurate than an alternative for all kinds of reasoning problem, or are there Strategy × Item type interactions for speed and/or accuracy? How do speed and accuracy differences between strategies change with age/learning, and are there execution differences related to other individual differences? Furthermore, the choice/no-choice method can shed light on issues that cannot be addressed by using other methods of strategy assessment. For example: Do people choose their reasoning strategies as a function of problem characteristics, situation characteristics, strategy characteristics, or all three? Do participants have strategy preferences that are not justified by relative strategy effectiveness? If so, what are the sources of these selection biases? As we can anticipate, by looking at reasoning strategies, significant advances can be expected, leading towards a better understanding of what people actually do when they perform such tasks. Note too that, because reasoning is one of the most sophisticated human skills, progress on the cognitive psychology of reasoning would be expected to contribute more generally to a better understanding of human cognition.

ACKNOWLEDGEMENTS

We thank the Cognitique program of the French Ministère de la Recherche and l'Institut Universitaire de France for funding the research reported here. Special thanks go to Vittorio Girotto and to Max Roberts for their insightful comments on a previous version of this chapter. Correspondence about this chapter should be addressed to: Patrick Lemaire, Université de Provence & CNRS, 3 Place Victor Hugo, Case 66, 13331 Marseille (lemaire@up.univ-mrs.fr).

REFERENCES

Ashcraft, M. H., & Battaglia, J. (1978). Evidence for retrieval and decision processes in mental addition. *Journal of Experimental Psychology: Human Learning & Memory, 4*, 527–538.

Barrouillet, P., & Lecas, J. F. (1998). How can mental models theory account for content effects in conditional reasoning? A developmental perspective. *Cognition, 67*, 209–253.

Barrouillet, P. L., & Lecas, J. F. (1999). Mental models in conditional reasoning and working memory. *Thinking & Reasoning, 5*, 289–302.

Barrouillet, P., Grosset, N., & Lecas, J. F. (2000). Conditional reasoning by mental models: Chronometric and developmental evidence. *Cognition, 75*, 237–266.

Bucciarelli, M., & Johnson-Laird, P. N. (1999). Strategies in syllogistic reasoning. *Cognitive Science, 23*, 247–303.

Byrne, R. M. J., Espino, O., & Santamaria, C. (1999). Counterexamples and the suppression of interferences. *Journal of Memory & Language, 40*, 347–373.

Clark, H. H., & Chase, W. G. (1972). On the process of comparing sentences against pictures. *Cognitive Psychology, 3*, 472–517.

Dehaene, S., & Cohen, L. (1991). Two mental calculation systems: A case study of severe acalculia with preserved approximation. *Neuropsychologia, 29*, 1045–1074

De Rammelaere, S., Stuyven, E., & Vandierendonck, A. (2001). Verifying simple arithmetic sums and products: Are the phonological loop and the central executive involved? *Memory & Cognition, 29*, 267–273.

Duverne, S., & Lemaire, P. (2004). Adults' age-related differences in problem verification strategies. *Journal of Gerontology, 59*, 135–142.

El yagoubi, R., Lemaire, P., & Besson, M. (2003). Different brain mechanisms mediate two strategies in arithmetic: Evidence from visual event-related potentials. *Neuropsychologia, 41*, 855–862.

Ericsson, K. A., & Simon, H. A. (1980). Verbal reports as data. *Psychological Review, 87*, 215–251.

Evans, J. St. B. T. (1995). Relevance and reasoning. In S. E. Newstead & J. St. B. T. Evans (Eds.), *Perspectives on thinking and reasoning* (pp. 142–172). Hove, UK: Lawrence Erlbaum Associates Ltd.

Evans, J. St. B. T. (1996). Deciding before you think: Relevance and reasoning in the selection task. *British Journal of Psychology, 87*, 223–240.

Evans, J. St. B. T. (2000). What could and could not be a strategy. In W. Schaeken, G. De Vooght, A. Vandierendonck, & G. d'Ydewalle (Eds.), *Deductive reasoning and strategies* (pp. 1–21). Mahwah, NJ: Lawrence Erlbaum Associates, Inc.

Evans, J. St. B. T., & Handley, S. J. (1999). The role of negation in conditional inference. *Quarterly Journal of Experimental Psychology: Human Experimental Psychology, 52A*, 739–769.

Evans, J. St. B. T., & Over, D. E. (1996). Rationality in the selection task: Epistemic utility versus uncertainty reduction. *Psychological Review, 103*, 356–363.

Evans, J. St. B. T., Handley, S. J., Harper, C. N. J., & Johnson-Laird, P.N. (1999). Reasoning about necessity and possibility: A test of the mental model theory of deduction. *Journal of Experimental Psychology: Learning, Memory, & Cognition, 25,* 1495–1513.

Favrel, J., & Barrouillet, P. L. (2000). On the relation between representations constructed from text comprehension and transitive inference production. *Cognition, 26,* 187–203.

Ford, M. (1995). Two modes of mental representation and problem solution in syllogistic reasoning. *Cognition, 54,* 1–71.

Galotti, K. M., Baron, J., & Sabini, J. P. (1986). Individual differences in syllogistic reasoning: Deduction rules or mental models? *Journal of Experimental Psychology: General, 115,* 16–25.

Geary, D. C. (1994). *Children's mathematical development.* Washington, DC: American Psychological Association.

Geary, D. C., & Wiley, J. G. (1991). Cognitive addition: Strategy choices and speed-of-processing differences in young and elderly adults. *Psychology and Aging, 6,* 474–483.

Gigerenzer, G., & Hoffrage, U. (1995). How to improve Bayesian reasoning without instruction: Frequency format. *Psychological Review, 102,* 684–704.

Gilhooly, K. J., Logie, R. H., Wetherick, N. E., & Wynn, V. (1993). Working memory and strategies in syllogistic-reasoning tasks. *Memory & Cognition, 21,* 115–124.

Girotto, V., & Gonzalez, M. (2000). Strategies and models in statistical reasoning. In W. Schaeken, G. De Vooght, A. Vandierendonck, & G. d'Ydewalle (Eds.), *Deductive reasoning and strategies* (pp. 267–286). Mahwah, NJ: Lawrence Erlbaum Associates, Inc.

Girotto, V., & Gonzalez, M. (2001). Solving probabilistic and statistical problems: A matter of information structure and question form. *Cognition, 78,* 247–276.

Girotto, V., Mazzocco, A., & Tasso, A. (1997). The effect of premise order in conditional reasoning: A test of the mental model theory. *Cognition, 63,* 1–28.

Hardman, D. K., & Payne, S. J. (1995). Problem difficulty and response format in syllogistic reasoning. *Quarterly Journal of Experimental Psychology, 48A,* 945–975.

Heit, E., & Hahn, U. (2001). Diversity-based reasoning in children. *Cognitive Psychology, 43,* 243–273.

Johnson-Laird, P. N., Savary, F., & Bucciarelli, M. (2000). Strategies and tactics in reasoning. In W. Schaeken, G. De Vooght, A. Vandierendonck, & G. d'Ydewalle (Eds.), *Deductive and reasoning and strategies* (pp. 209–240). Mahwah, NJ: Lawrence Erlbaum Associates, Inc.

Lecas, J.-F. B., & Barrouillet, P. L. (1999). Understanding conditional rules in childhood and adolescence: A mental models approach. *Cahiers de Psychologie Cognitive/Current Psychology of Cognition, 18,* 363–396.

LeFevre, J., Bisanz, J., Daley, K. E., Buffone, L., & Sadesky, G. S. (1996a). Multiple routes to solution of single-digit multiplication problems. *Journal of Experimental Psychology: General, 125,* 284–306.

LeFevre, J., Sadesky, G. S., & Bisanz, J. (1996b). Selection of procedures in mental addition: Reassessing the problem-size effect in adults. *Journal of Experimental Psychology: Learning, Memory, and Cognition, 22,* 216–230.

Legrenzi, P., Girotto, V., & Johnson-Laird, P. N. (1993). Focusing in reasoning and decision making. *Cognition, 49,* 37–66.

Lemaire, P., Barrett, S. E., Fayol, M., & Abdi, H. (1994). Automatic activation of addition and multiplication facts in elementary school children. *Journal of Experimental Child Psychology, 57,* 224–258.

Lemaire, P., & Fayol, M. (1995). When plausibility judgments supersede fact retrieval: The example of the odd–even effect on product verification. *Memory and Cognition, 23,* 34–48.

Lemaire, P., & Lecacheur, M. (2001). Older and younger adults' strategy use and execution in currency conversion tasks: Insights from French franc to euro and euro to French franc conversions. *Journal of Experimental Psychology: Applied, 3,* 195–206.

Lemaire, P., & Lecacheur, M. (2002a). Children's strategy use in spelling. *Developmental Science, 5,* 43–48.

Lemaire, P., & Lecacheur, M. (2002b). Age-related differences in children's computational estimation strategy use and execution. *Journal of Experimental Child Psychology*, *82*, 281–304.

Lemaire, P., & Reder, L. (1999). What affects strategy selection in arithmetic? An example of parity and five effects on product verification. *Memory & Cognition*, *22*, 364–382.

Lemaire, P., & Siegler, R. S. (1995). Four aspects of strategic change: Contributions to children's learning of multiplication. *Journal of Experimental Psychology: General*, *124*, 83–97.

MacLeod, C. M., Hunt, E. B., & Mathews, N. N. (1978). Individual differences in the verification of sentence–picture relationships. *Journal of Verbal Learning & Verbal Behavior*, *17*, 493–507.

Marquer, J. M., & Pereira, M. (1990). Reaction times in the study of strategies in sentence–picture verification: A reconsideration. *Quarterly Journal of Experimental Psychology*, *42A*, 147–168.

Masse, C., & Lemaire, P. (2001). How do people choose among strategies? A case study of parity and five-rule effects in arithmetical problem solving. *Psychological Research*, *65*, 28–33

Newell, A., & Simon, H. A. (1972). *Human problem solving*. Englewood Cliffs, NJ: Prentice-Hall.

Rauh, R. (2000). Strategies of constructing preferred mental models in spatial relational inference. In W. Schaeken, G. De Vooght, A. Vandierendonck, & G. d'Ydewalle (Eds.), *Deductive reasoning and strategies* (pp. 177–190). Mahwah, NJ: Lawrence Erlbaum Associates, Inc.

Reichle, E. D., Carpenter, P. A., & Just, M. A. (2000). The neural bases of strategy and skill in sentence–picture verification. *Cognitive Psychology*, *40*, 261–295.

Roberts, M. J. (2000). Individual differences in reasoning strategies: A problem to solve or an opportunity to seize? In W. Schaeken, G. De Vooght, A. Vandierendonck, & G. d'Ydewalle (Eds.), *Deductive reasoning and strategies* (pp. 23–48). Mahwah, NJ: Lawrence Erlbaum Associates, Inc.

Roberts, M. J. (in press). Falsification and mental models: It depends on the task. In W. Schaeken, A. Vandierendonck, W. Schroyens, & G. d'Ydewalle (Eds.), *The mental models theory of reasoning: Refinements and extensions*. Mahwah, NJ: Lawrence Erlbaum Associates, Inc.

Roberts, M. J., Gilmore, D. J., & Wood, D. J. (1997). Individual differences and strategy selection in reasoning. *British Journal of Psychology*, *88*, 473–492.

Roberts, M. J., Wood, D. J., & Gilmore, D. J. (1994). The sentence–picture verification task: Methodological and theoretical difficulties. *British Journal of Psychology*, *85*, 412–432.

Russo, J. E., Johnson, E. J., & Stephens, D. L. (1989). The validity of verbal protocols. *Memory & Cognition*, *17*, 759–769.

Sanders, R. E., Murphy, M. D., Schmitt, F. A., & Walsh, K. K. (1980). Age differences in free recall rehearsal strategies. *Journal of Gerontology*, *35*, 550–558.

Schaeken, W., De Vooght, G., Vandierendonck, A., & d'Ydewalle, G. (2000). *Deductive reasoning and strategies*. Mahwah, NJ: Lawrence Erlbaum Associates, Inc.

Schroyens, W., Schaeken, W., & d'Ydewalle, G. (2001). The processing of negations in conditional reasoning: A meta-analytic case study in mental model and/or mental logic theory. *Thinking & Reasoning*, *7*, 121–172.

Schunn, C. D., & Reder M. (2001). Another source of individual differences: Strategy adaptivity to changing rates of success. *Journal of Experimental Psychology: General*, *130*, 59–76.

Siegler, R. S., & Lemaire, P. (1997). Older and younger adults' strategy choices in multiplication: Testing predictions of ASCM using the choice/no-choice method. *Journal of Experimental Psychology: General*, *126*, 71–92.

Stanescu-Cosson, R., Pinel, P., Van de Moortele, P. F., Le Bihan, D., Cohen, L., & Dehaene, S. (2000). Understanding dissociations in dyscalculia A brain imaging study of the impact of number size on the cerebral networks for exact and approximate calculation. *Brain*, *123*, 2240–2255.

Stanovich, K. E., & West, R. F. (1998). Individual differences in rational thought. *Journal of Experimental Psychology: General*, *109*, 119–159.

Sternberg, R. J., & Weil, E. M. (1980). An aptitude × strategy interaction in linear syllogistic reasoning. *Journal of Educational Psychology, 72,* 226–239.

Stone, G. O., & Van Orden, G. C. (1993). Strategic control of processing in word recognition. *Journal of Experimental Psychology: Human Perception & Performance, 19,* 744–774.

Vandierendonck, A., & De Vooght, G. (1997). Working memory constraints on linear reasoning with spatial and temporal contents. *Quarterly Journal of Experimental Psychology, 50A,* 803–820.

Warrington, E. K. (1982). The fractionation of arithmetic skills: A single case study. *Quarterly Journal of Experimental Psychology, 34A,* 31–51.

Wood, D. J. (1978). Problem solving – the nature and development of strategies. In G. Underwood (Ed.), *Strategies in information processing* (pp. 329–356). London: Academic Press.

Zacks, R. T. (1982). Encoding strategies used by young and elderly adults in keeping track task. *Journal of Gerontology, 37,* 203–211.

Zbrodoff, N. J., & Logan, G. D. (1990). On the relation between production and verification tasks in the psychology of simple arithmetic. *Journal of Experimental Psychology: Learning, Memory, and Cognition, 16,* 83–97.

CHAPTER TWO

Rethinking logical reasoning skills from a strategy perspective

Bradley J. Morris
Grand Valley State University and LRDC, University of Pittsburgh, USA

Christian D. Schunn
LRDC, University of Pittsburgh, USA

The study of logical reasoning has typically proceeded as follows: Researchers (1) discover a response pattern that is either unexplained or provides evidence against an established theory; (2) create a model that explains this response pattern; then (3) expand this model to include a larger range of situations. Researchers tend to investigate a specific type of reasoning (e.g., conditional implication) using a particular variant of an experimental task (e.g., the Wason selection task). The experiments uncover a specific reasoning pattern, for example, that people tend to select options that match the terms in the premises, rather than derive valid responses (Evans, 1972). Once a reasonable explanation is provided for this, researchers typically attempt to expand it to encompass related phenomena, such as the role of 'bias' in other situations like weather forecasting (Evans, 1989). Eventually, this explanation may be used to account for all performance on an entire class of reasoning phenomena (e.g., deduction) regardless of task, experience, or age. We term this a unified theory.

Some *unified theory* theorists have suggested that *all* logical reasoning can be characterised by a single theory, such as one that is rule based, which involves the application of transformation rules that draw valid conclusions once fired (Rips, 1994). Other theorists believe that all logical reasoning can be described as model based, creating veridical representations of premises, and searching them for possible conclusions (Johnson-Laird, 1999). Others still have suggested yet additional approaches (e.g., matching rules, pragmatic schemas) that may unify all aspects of performance. It seems possible, however, given the range of problem types, task demands, and experience and cognitive resources of reasoners, that there may be more than one way for solving an entire class of reasoning problem.

Consider the case of deduction. This involves a wide variety of tasks, from simple statement evaluation (e.g., 'Is my cat black?') to more complex tasks such as evaluating predicate syllogisms (e.g., Some A are not B, Some B are C, therefore Some A are not C; TRUE or FALSE) (Roberts, 2000; Johnson-Laird, 1999). There is no evidence that deduction occupies a particular region of the brain (Goel, Buchel, Frith, & Dolan, 2000; Osherson, Perani, Cappa, Schnur, Grassi, & Fazio, 1998). This suggests that deduction is not a special process separate from the rest of cognition, and hence it is not likely to be unified across tasks or situations. Likewise, there is no *behavioural evidence* that deduction is a coherent distinct process (Johnson-Laird, 1999). Moreover, cognitive psychology has identified a variety of general processes (e.g., analogy, retrieval, guessing) that could, in theory, be used. Thus, it should not be controversial to suggest that several types of process might be used to solve reasoning problems in at least some situations.

In contrast to unified theories, we propose an alternative, in which many possible strategies may be used to solve a deductive problem, rather than always the same single type of reasoning process. Thus, this is a new framework for explaining reasoning performance, incorporating simplified versions of existing theories as possible *strategies* (see also Roberts, 2000). We list a variety of such strategies that seem likely to be used in at least some situations. It is not crucial to the argument that all of these are actually used. However, we will propose conditions under which various strategies are particularly likely to manifest themselves, thereby developing a framework through which these can be distinguished theoretically and empirically.

It should be noted that recent research from mental models theorists (Van der Henst, Yang, & Johnson-Laird, 2002) suggests that there are individual differences in the application of mental models, for example, when solving syllogisms. Although this work suggests that reasoners use various approaches (classified as strategies), all of these are derived from the same inferential mechanism: mental models. While we agree that we should investigate individual differences in approaches to reasoning, we suggest not only that there are differences in how people apply the same inferential mechanism, but also that several different mechanisms are used.

STRATEGY USE IN LOGICAL REASONING

What does it mean, as a cognitive researcher, to think in terms of strategies? A glance at the literature suggests that unified theories have difficulty accounting for differences in performance, both between individuals, and across tasks/situations (for a review see Rips, 1994; Johnson-Laird, 1999). We suggest that these differences are due to the selection of different strategies, and that this is a function of (1) the history of success with each strategy, and (2) the match between the processing demands of the strategy and the task demands. Together, these form the *situational niche*.

As stated earlier, unified theories posit a single account for the range of human performance, although there are disagreements as to which single theory is correct. We suggest a strategy selection theory to explain the same phenomena, proposing a series of specified strategies, each relegated to explaining a subset of the total range of human deductive performance. This is closely related to other models that focus on individual differences (Roberts, 1993, 2000). For example, Roberts (2000) suggests that deductive perform-ance can be better accounted for by three strategies (spatial, verbal, task specific) than any single theory (e.g., mental models; Johnson-Laird, 1999).

What do we gain from this *logical strategy model* (LSM)? It allows for a wide range of findings – patterns of variability across problems, tasks, individuals, and different points of development – to move from theoretical embarrassment to core, theoretically relevant phenomena that not only can be explained, but are also crucial to understanding the cognition of logical reasoning. It also allows a variety of established theories to be incorporated into a single framework, in which all form strategies that are possible explan-ations of behaviour, differing only in the extent to which each particular strategy has been used in similar situations, and their matches to current task demands.

The match between a particular strategy and its situational niche may not be rational, but may help to explain individual and situational differences. For example, it is well established that familiar content tends to improve performance on the Wason selection task (Wason & Johnson-Laird, 1972). Hundreds of experiments have been used to investigate this phenomenon, and these have led to a variety of explanations (e.g., pragmatic reasoning schemas). These differ widely in their range of applicability: Some are specific to a particular set of materials, while others seek to explain a broader range of behaviour. What has rarely been investigated is the influence of the situ-ational niche on performance, or, more specifically how is the *task itself* con-tributing to the response pattern? For example, take two contrasting theories: in one, specific knowledge is required to solve a problem; in the other, abstract rules (excluding the influence of knowledge) are needed. Problem A is given in which a substantial amount of relevant content knowledge is provided. In this case, we would expect the knowledge-based strategies to be best suited. If however, Problem B were given in which no background information is sup-plied, then we would predict that a different solution strategy is more likely to be used. Hence the logical strategy model (LSM) permits flexibility in explan-ation by allowing for an individual to display a range of possible solution strategies.

The influence of processing and task demands has been examined in the literature on expert/novice performance (for a review see Leighton & Sternberg, 2003). In terms of processing demands, experts tend to have greater, better organised knowledge, that allows superior access to relevant concepts, and a more extensive repertoire of strategies for solving problems than novices (Chi, Glaser, & Farr, 1988; Stanovich, 1999; Leighton & Sternberg, 2003). This leads to the creation of more useful problem representations and greater awareness of the strategies they use to accomplish problem solving. In terms of task demands, experts better attend to relevant problem details, select appropriate strategies, and better evaluate their own performance than novices (Chase & Simon, 1973; Leighton & Sternberg, 2003). Yet, the expert/novice literature provides little explanation as to the nature of reasoning mechanisms underlying these differences, nor how reasoning strategies are acquired or selected.

The logical strategy model (LSM) is in stark contrast to unified theories, in which explanations of processing logical statements are confined to one type of strategy. A possible criticism at this point is that a unified theory is more parsimonious: Why suggest that individuals possess a collection of competing strategies when a single type would suffice? We provide two responses.

First, current unified theories have been unable to account for a range of performance without many ad hoc additions. For example, mental logic theory posits that logical inferences are derived by the application of a set of near-automatic, content-free inference rules (Braine & O'Brien, 1998; Rips, 1994). In order to explain the effect of familiar content, this theory has incorporated an additional step in the reasoning process, a 'pragmatic filter', which determines whether a statement is to be considered logical or conversational. In the former, logical inference rules are applied, while in the latter case, less formal conversational rules are applied. The result is that the theory postulates an approach to reasoning that undermines its own primary thesis. As another example, mental models theory suggests that logical inference is achieved by the creation and search of models of a problem's premises (Johnson-Laird, Byrne, & Schaeken, 1992). This theory does not specify how models of ambiguous or metaphorical premises can be constructed without exceeding working memory capacity (Braine & O'Brien, 1998). Similar problems can be found with the universal application of all unified theories.

Second, the logical strategy model (LSM) does not require a set of resources specific to logical reasoning, which is an ad hoc component of some theories. Instead, it assumes a variety of general-purpose cognitive mechanisms. Within this framework, a series of strategies can be derived, with minimal effort on the part of the cognitive system, as a result of experience with the environment. Let us return to the example given earlier. To account for reasoning in situations in which either statements are presented (1) with familiar content, or (2) without familiar content, our framework can account for empirical findings in terms of two strategies. The first situation does not trigger the use of formal rules. Instead, specific content is used to derive a plausible conclusion. In the second situation, inference rules are used because the most salient property of the problem is the *relations* between elements, not the *content* of the elements. The use of each strategy is specific to the situation.

In the sections that follow we will outline eight types of strategy, examining each on eight dimensions: general processing demands, task demands, influence of context, efficacy/solution time (accuracy and cost), possibility of transfer (i.e., will a solution be usable in a different context?), type of memory activated (e.g., declarative), representational form (e.g., propositional), and change in strategy as a function of experience. The results are also summarised in Table 2.1, p. 44.

These eight strategies do not reflect prescriptive norms, but represent the range that naive or untrained subjects may use when they are given deduction tasks. Note that this is not yet an exhaustive list, and we are merely suggesting the most plausible core set. After describing the strategies, we will examine the influence of task demands on strategy selection and use. Space limitations preclude a description of the full range of possible applications. However, our model is reasonably articulated for the purposes of this chapter.

Strategy 1: Token-based (mental models)

Overview

The token-based reasoning strategy has the following characteristics: (1) information is represented as tokens derived from natural language, which correspond to perceptual or verbal instantiations of possible states; (2) reasoning is achieved not through the application of formal rules but by the creation, inspection, and manipulation of tokens (Johnson-Laird, 1983; Johnson-Laird et al., 1992). This strategy is similar to Roberts (2000) spatial strategy.[1]

Processing demands

There are three steps in applying token-based processes: (1) *propositional analysis* refers to language processing, and is largely analogous to representing the surface structure of a statement, requiring sufficient verbal/spatial working memory to encode and parse language; (2) *model generation* refers to the creation of tokens derived from the propositional analysis, and any other relevant information in the existing knowledge base and the environment.

---

[1] It is important to note that the 'tokens' need not be represented via a visual or spatial image (see Johnson-Laird, 1999).

This requires sufficient verbal/spatial working memory to create and hold tokens; (3) *model use* is the process of searching and evaluating the set of models created, and requires sufficient processing capacity to maintain these while searching for counterexamples, and evaluating truth values. The primary limitation on processing is the working memory required to create and search models for a solution. One particular difficulty is that ambiguous premises may require multiple mental models, thus leading to a dramatic increase in the use of working memory capacity and processing time.

The token-based strategy seems particularly useful in the solution of problems in which there are spatial relations because token-based representations can encode these more easily than can proposition-based ones (Johnson-Laird, 1983, 1999). For example, in the transitive problem 'Bill is to the right of Fred, Fred is to the right of Sam, Is Sam to the right of Bill?' the relevant dimension is easily encoded as follows:

[Sam]   [Fred]   [Bill]

Summary

The token-based strategy is content/context dependent, in that the type of semantic information influences the tokens created. However, there should be consistency in the treatment of logical connectives based on their meaning (requiring the activation of procedural memory). There should be transfer between problem isomorphs, though success will vary by the degree of similar semantic content (and hence the activation of declarative elements in memory). This is an algorithmic strategy, in that under optimal conditions, processing should result in a valid/correct conclusion. Processing costs (defined as solution time) should be high because of the procedures involved in creating and searching models.

Strategy 2: Verbal (mental logic)

Overview

Verbal theories explain logical reasoning as the result of content-free, logical transformation rules applied to linguistically derived mental structures (Rips, 1994; Braine & O'Brien, 1998).

Processing demands

The core elements of verbal theories share basic characteristics. Input is represented and processed in a verbal form (e.g., predicate-argument structures; Braine & Rumain, 1981, 1983). Sufficient verbal working memory is required to hold formal elements and represent them. The action of transformation rules is content free, and these are implemented as either condition–action pairs (Rips, 1994) or as inferential schemas (Braine & O'Brien, 1998). The output of a rule is either in the form of a conclusion, a statement that will be operated upon by additional rules, or a statement that does not trigger additional rules. Errors may be explained either by (1) a failure in the activation, or failure in the output of one (or several) rules or (2) the failure to apply an inferential rule, instead applying a pragmatic rule. As problem complexity increases, there will be an increase in the number of rules to fire, thus increasing the possibility of overall error, and hence problem difficulty.

The verbal strategy is most useful in solving abstract problems in which the focus is on relationships between elements (e.g., *If A is tweeky, then B is zop*). For example, the original version of the Wason selection task (Wason, 1961) is specified only by formal structure, not by content.

Summary

The verbal strategy is context-independent, algorithmic, and should transfer between isomorphic problem types. Processing costs should be low, because inference takes place via compiled rules that fire automatically as a result of a match to syntactic relationships. Thus the action of rules is dependent on the activation of procedural rather than declarative memory.

Strategy 3: Knowledge-based heuristics

Overview

Heuristics are rules that do not utilise logically valid algorithms. Such a strategy need not generate a valid conclusion but may result in 'logic-like' performance (Cheng & Holyoak, 1985; Cosmides, 1989). Knowledge-based heuristics are easily implemented processing rules that use content as the basis for deriving a conclusion. Unlike algorithmic procedures (e.g., a verbal strategy), these conclusions are not necessarily valid (often violating logical inference rules), yet are often pragmatically supported. An example is the *pragmatic reasoning schema* (Cheng & Holyoak, 1985) in which social (permission rules) and physical (causality) regularities form the basis of inference schemata.

Processing demands

There are three steps in the use of knowledge-based heuristics: *sentence parsing, detection of relations*, and *solution output*. Sentence parsing refers to comprehension and utilises implicit and explicit information. The detection of relations occurs when the present content is similar to content for which there are available rules. For example, in permission relations, there are established rules (typically phrased as conditionals) that suggest appropriate responses. Activating content allows these rules to be accessed. Cues such as temporal sequence may suggest obligatory or causal relations between elements. For example, in the statement 'Mow the lawn and I will give you five dollars' the condition is set in the first clause while the consequent is set in the second clause. Once the rules are accessed, they are applied to the specific situation of the content and a solution is produced. Previous knowledge of other exchanges (e.g., in which transactions are made on the basis of obligations) form the basis of these heuristics.

Summary

Use of a knowledge-based heuristic does not necessarily lead to a valid response. This is a context-dependent strategy that requires activation of declarative memory, through which conclusions are drawn. Thus there should be little transfer away from the domain of applicability. Processing cost should be low because little is required other than activating and applying appropriate rules.

Strategy 4: Superficial heuristics

Overview

Superficial heuristics are selective processing strategies in which solutions are derived from surface details, such as terms or common elements, rather than on content (as in knowledge-based heuristics). Two well-known examples lead to *matching biases* (Evans, 1989) and *atmosphere effects* (Woodworth & Sells, 1935).

Processing demands

Superficial heuristics lead to selective processing, but differ from all previous strategies in that the focus is on the presence of surface elements; no specific content is accessed. They operate as follows: (1) surface structure is encoded; (2) key elements are identified; (3) rules applied to them. For example, in the Wason selection task, subjects prefer to choose cards named in the rules rather than cards that are not named (Evans, 1972). Given '*If there is an odd number on one side, then there is a vowel on the other side*' the subject may focus on 'odd number' and 'vowel' as key elements. Then, when searching possible solutions, the subject will attend to those states that contain the key elements. Hence, a card with an odd number and a card with a vowel are selected because these match the elements in the rule. A similar processing model applies to the heuristics that lead to atmosphere effects.

Summary

Superficial heuristics are context-independent strategies that do not necessarily produce valid conclusions. Their use depends upon the activation of procedural memory. We should see transfer between tasks, but with low solution accuracy, due to focusing on surface elements. Processing cost should be low because little is required beyond matching surface content, thus solution times should be fast.

Strategy 5: Analogy

Overview

Analogical reasoning utilises knowledge of existing situations to derive solutions to novel problems (Holyoak & Thagard, 1989). This is typically distinguished as a separate process from deduction. However, we suggest that analogical mapping may provide resources for solving such problems. Analogies enable solution by mapping meaningful links between one already in memory (source) and the new problem (target). As an illustration, we recount the results for a 10-year-old girl enrolled in a gifted program. On a version of the Wason task framed with *abstract* materials (e.g., thogs, merds), she produced the correct responses, which is surprising given that few adults do so. When we asked her to explain her reasoning, she said that the question was like a chemistry experiment she had recently completed in her class. She outlined the procedure – including allusions to confirming and disconfirming evidence – and explained how each 'card' in the Wason task was like one of these options. She proceeded to explain the need for both correct options.

Processing demands

Analogical mapping takes place in three steps: (1) accessing a suitable source from memory, or current perception, that is meaningfully related to the new problem (target); (2) adapt this analog to the demands of the target; (3) induce useful commonalities between the source and the target (Gentner, 1983; Holyoak & Thagard, 1995). The first step may entail a range of possible information including solutions to previously solved problems, identification of similar problem elements, or partial solutions for the problem at hand. Once a suitable source is found, equivalences between this and the target must be identified, which form the basis of the solution.

Summary

Unlike superficial heuristics, in which there is a focus on common terms (low cost), or knowledge-based heuristics, in which there is a focus on semantic or thematic relations between elements (low cost), the analogy strategy focuses on relations between structural elements, such as similarities in the problem space (or in regions of the total problem space). Analogy is a heuristic, context-independent strategy that should have a high processing cost due to processing high-level similarities, e.g., the Waitresses and Oranges problem versus the Tower of Hanoi (Zhang & Norman, 1994). Analogies should transfer, and depend upon the activation of either declarative or procedural memory, or both.

Strategy 6: Task-specific procedures

Overview

Like superficial heuristics, task-specific procedures are non-logical, but can achieve correct solutions without the need for long sequences of formal inference rules, or the consideration of multiple mental models. They are reasoning 'short-cuts' that produce solutions without the need for a declarative understanding, although some insight may be required to induce them. By necessity, the solution cannot represent the total problem space, and must result from an incomplete or partial search, otherwise these would be of no benefit compared with algorithmic strategies (i.e., token based or verbal). One limitation of task-specific procedures is that they do not generalise beyond the specific type of task in which they were induced. Logical training may include instruction in the use of such procedures, but this will lead to an 'understanding' analogous to that attributed to the occupant of the Chinese Room (Searle, 1984, 1990).

Processing demands

Once a task-specific procedure has been induced and added to memory, processing demands are due to three steps: (1) encoding relevant, but necessarily incomplete, problem features; (2) activating an appropriate procedure; (3) implementing this. For example, in a syllogism evaluation task, some subjects concluded that any syllogism with two 'somes' in the premises was invalid (Galotti, Baron, & Sabini, 1986). Implementing a solution requires *only* sufficient working memory to hold the encoded premises and to fire the appropriate procedure.

Summary

Task-specific procedures are context dependent, do not necessarily yield a valid conclusion, and do not transfer. The processing cost should be relatively low once a procedure has been induced, due to this being relatively short and/or compiled. Once stored, use depends upon activation of procedural memory by familiar problem elements.

Strategy 7: Pragmatic acquiescence

Overview

The preceding six strategies are all traditional cognitive problem-solving methods through which responses are produced. However, another possibility is that social elements may influence solutions. Consider the following scenario: A student is asked by his professor to draw a conclusion from two written premises. The student hastily draws a conclusion. The professor begins to talk about other possible interpretations and begins to build a case for another conclusion. When she asks the student if he agrees with her reasoning, the student replies 'yes'. Pragmatic acquiescence refers to response patterns that are attempts to match the expectations of the questioner. In a situation in which someone has little prior knowledge, he or she may be inclined to seek social cues from the questioner as to how to respond. Rather than using the surface features of the problem, as in superficial heuristics, these solutions are derived from the pragmatics of the problem/testing situation. This type of strategy is used when (1) the pragmatic cues are most salient, (2) subjects lack motivation, or (3) other strategies fail to produce an acceptable solution.

Processing demands

Pragmatic acquiescence is likely to require at least two steps: encoding relevant cues, and selecting a solution from these. We suggest at least four types of cue: speaker status, language, intonation, gesture. These cues should demonstrate developmental and cultural effects. For example, children tend to be deferential to adults. Similarly, people in 'collective' cultures tend to defer to authority more than those in 'individual' cultures (Akimoto & Sanbonmatsu, 1999).

Speaker status should be directly related to the probability of acquiescence. That is, the likelihood of matching the expectations of the questioner should increase as the authority of the speaker increases. One implication is that we would expect that suggestions from experts would be more likely to influence behaviour than non-experts. This also suggests an informal metric for calculating the status of self and speaker. Language cues may be the most obvious for suggesting the type of response that is expected (e.g., 'don't you agree?'). Intonation and gesture cues may trigger the use of pragmatic knowledge, and together may suggest the type of responses expected. For example, increasing pitch at the end of a sentence, or holding an outstretched hand, are both pragmatic cues. Once the reasoner has encoded and interpreted relevant cues, these can determine a response.

Pragmatic acquiescence can occur under a variety of conditions: (1) if no other strategy is identified; (2) if a strategy produces a solution that is in conflict with the pragmatically cued response and fails to override this solution; or (3) if the cued response is so highly activated that it overrides all other strategies. In all cases, this suggests that the reasoner lacks the knowledge or motivation (e.g., being uninterested, polite, political) necessary to solve the problem at hand.

Summary

Pragmatic acquiescence is a heuristic strategy that is context independent and should transfer across tasks. The cost is relatively low in that it may completely circumvent processing and is, by itself, relatively inaccurate.

Strategy 8: Retrieval

Overview

Retrieval involves accessing a previous solution from long-term memory (LTM). Because there is no processing, this should be the lowest cost strategy with the highest accuracy. The solution in this case is a declarative element (the answer), rather than procedural (a method for finding an answer). No processing is required, but the solution could be the result of previous processing on the part of the reasoner, or by other means (e.g., observing the processing of someone else). In contrast, the retrieval of *procedural elements* (e.g., context-sensitive schemas in knowledge-based heuristics) requires additional processing to derive a solution.

Retrieval differs from all other proposed strategies in that it is the only one that does not create a solution on-line, instead a solution is accessed directly from memory. For example, we suspect that many cognitive psychology students (and faculty) solve the Wason four-card task by retrieving the textbook presented solution. While this may seem an atypical case, logical reasoning problems in the real world often do repeat themselves, and solutions are often socially transmitted.

The tendency to access solutions will vary as a function of the time interval between discovery and access (recency), the number of times the solution is accessed (frequency), and the degree to which the current problem state is similar to the problem state associated with the solution (fit). Guessing could be a loosely constrained form of retrieval in which a response is produced on the basis of inaccurate or irrelevant information.[2]

---

[2] Guessing might also resemble other strategies. For example, a guess may be based on surface elements (superficial heuristics), social pressure (pragmatic acquiescence), or the activation of related information (knowledge-based heuristics).

Processing demands

Retrieval of previous solutions depends on a variety of factors. The most crucial is the number of possible matches to the current problem. If there is only one match, then retrieval is simple. Because there are often several possible solutions to a particular problem, in order to retrieve one, there must be a mechanism to determine which of these will be accessed at any given time, or to perform conflict resolution. We suggest the three common memory mechanisms (recency, frequency, and fit) described above (see Anderson & Lebiere, 1998).

Summary

Retrieval is a context-dependent strategy that requires simply the activation of declarative memory. Because there is no processing, this should be the lowest cost strategy with the highest accuracy.

TASK CHARACTERISTICS AND SITUATIONAL NICHES

The previous section outlined the key processing steps for each of eight types of strategy. The probability that each strategy will be used is a function of its processing demands and its situational niche. The following section will outline how these factors may be related so as to influence the likelihood of application of specific strategies.

The situational niche is similar to Todd and Gigerenzer's (1999) notion of ecological rationality. Both notions are derived from Simon's (1957) concept of bounded rationality, in which reasoning proceeds on the basis of limited processing capacity, and both notions are content/context sensitive, in that the type of process is a function of the task demands. However, while a system with ecological rationality seeks the most adaptive decision/ judgement within an open system (i.e., one in which the most appropriate decision need not result in a favourable outcome), a situational niche represents the current context in which reasoning is occurring, and within this there is a need to match the processing demands of the strategy with the current task demands, but within a closed reasoning system.

The degree to which a problem is familiar will influence the use of a particular strategy. This is expressed on two dimensions: (1) the familiarity of the content and context; (2) the degree of experience with a particular problem type. Increased familiarity in the first sense should raise the probability of knowledge-based heuristic, analogy, and retrieval strategies. For example, it is a well-documented finding that an invalid syllogism with a believable conclusion is more likely to be accepted than an invalid syllogism with an unbelievable conclusion (Evans, Barston, & Pollard, 1983). In this

TABLE 2.1
Summary of predicted strategy properties

Strategy	Processing demands	Task properties match	Context dependent?	Efficacy/solution time	Transfer?	Memory activation	Form of representation	Change with experience
Token-based	High: Verbal and spatial memory	Spatial: Contextual relevance	Yes	Algorithmic Slow	Yes	Procedural Declarative	Linguistic Spatial	Increase
Verbal	Low: Verbal memory	Abstract materials	No	Algorithmic Medium	Yes	Procedural	Schemas; Match to syntax	Increase
Knowledge-based heuristic	Low: Semantic or thematic relations	Semantic and thematic relations	Yes	Heuristic Fast	No	Declarative	Schemas; Match to context	Decrease
Superficial heuristics	Low: Superficial features	Surface structure relations	No	Heuristic Fast	No	Procedural	Surface	Decrease
Analogy	High: Deep structure relations	Structural relations; Isomorphic areas in problem space	No	Heuristic Slow	Yes	Procedural Declarative	Propositional or spatial	No change
Task-specific	Low: Inducing regularities	Previous experience	Yes	Heuristic Fast	No	Procedural	Schemas; Match to task	Increase
Pragmatic acquiescence	Low: Social cues	Social situation	No	Heuristic Fast	Yes	???	???	Decrease
Retrieval	Low: Match to solution	Previous experience	No	Algorithmic Fast	No	Declarative	Propositional	Increase

case, the familiarity of the conclusion may be the most salient element, and thus most likely to elicit a strategy choice (e.g., retrieval, or a knowledge-based heuristic). In the case of less familiar content, for example a syllogism with two 'somes' in the premises, a reasoner may recognise that a task-specific procedure can be used to derive a conclusion (Galotti et al., 1986). When given a series of unfamiliar, abstract materials, a reasoner may rely strictly on the formal elements of inference, applying a mental models or a mental logic strategy. In each of these cases the familiarity of content changes the problem's situational niche, resulting in different probabilities of triggering a given strategy.

In the second sense of familiarity, strategy selection may also depend on the degree of experience a reasoner has with a specific problem type. If a reasoner has a great deal of experience, he or she is more likely to use analo-gies, or use the same strategy as used on previous trials. Strategy selection will be influenced by previous experiences and outcomes, and these will be associ-ated with the further use of prior strategies. As experience decreases, strategy selection is more likely to be a function of other factors in the situational niche. For example, presentation can be an important influence: Formats may be verbal, written, or visual, and may illustrate or obscure problem characteristics crucial to a correct solution (Larkin & Simon, 1987).

In order to illustrate the possible links between strategy selection and situational niche, we present the following example. Imagine a transitivity problem in which the basic instructions are given as follows:

Five people are waiting in line at a movie theatre with a new seating policy. This states that in order to allow everyone to see the screen, all patrons have to be seated by height. That is, shorter patrons are seated near the front while taller patrons are seated near the back. The five people are Homer, Marge, Bart, Lisa, and Maggie. Based on their relative height (including hair), place them in proximity to the screen.

Knowledge of the source material may influence the type of strategy used. A reasoner with a great deal of knowledge of The Simpsons® may simply retrieve a solution due to the high content familiarity. Those with no knowl-edge of the television show will need to solve the problem using a different strategy, and its selection may depend on the format of additionally presented information. If presented pictorially, the format directly mimics a token-based representation and allows a solution to be derived from scanning the relative heights from the visual array. If presented in writing, task format can influence both difficulty and strategy usage. For example, with an ordered list (as in Example 1), a simple scan of relations may allow a partial solution to be derived. In this case, a task-specific procedure can be used in which the tallest person appears only on the left side of the text, and the shortest person only on the right. From here, the remaining relations must be inferred by using a different strategy. Example 1:

Homer is taller than Lisa.
Marge is taller than Bart.
Homer is taller than Bart.
Bart is taller than Lisa.
Lisa is taller than Maggie.
Marge is taller than Homer

When terms are randomly distributed in text (i.e., ordering is not aligned with task demands), each element must be encoded and compared to all other components, requiring greater working memory resources (see Example 2). Such a format may best match a token-based strategy, in which the entities are represented spatially as a series of tokens. Example 2:

Homer is taller than Lisa. Bart is taller than Lisa. Marge is taller than Bart.
Homer is taller than Bart. Lisa is taller than Maggie. Marge is taller than Homer

These examples suggest a link between task demands, task presentation, strategy processing demands, and individual's processing resources. In particular, differences in task demands and formatting will lead to differences in the salience of problem elements. In addition, previous strategy use will influence the probability that a given strategy will be used in the future. Using this framework, we may be able to explain both inter- and intra-individual differences.

To illustrate further the competition between strategies, consider performance differences due to conclusion believability (belief bias effects). For verbal strategies, errors in processing are attributed to a failure in applying an appropriate rule. There are at least two conditions under which a rule is unavailable: (1) *Failure to retrieve* a rule may occur temporarily even though it is present in long-term memory (LTM).[3] (2) *Failure to apply* a rule can occur because of content effects (Braine & O'Brien, 1998). That is, when the content is either familiar, or supports an inference beyond that of the statement's form, then the application of a rule is either suppressed or an incorrect rule may be triggered (Rips, 1994). Although this suppression has been cited as a condition under which abstract rules fail to apply, it is plausible that instead knowledge-based heuristics are more likely to be applied. Conversely, knowledge-based heuristics often fail to fire when given abstract elements (e.g., If A then B) and their use is restricted to situations where relations such

---

[3] Note that this use of (rule) retrieval is different than our proposed (answer) retrieval strategy.

as obligation and permission can be readily identified (Cheng & Holyoak, 1985; Rips, 1994).

EXPERIMENT

We tested three general predictions (detailed below) of the logical strategy model (LSM) using a web-based experiment in which subjects were given a series of deduction problems: (1) to evaluate conclusions as valid or invalid; (2) to produce correct responses. After producing a response to each problem, subjects were asked to report how they solved each by selecting one from five strategy descriptions. To keep the set of alternatives manageable, we focused on those that were most likely to be used for the chosen tasks: token based; verbal; superficial heuristics; knowledge-based heuristics, and analogy.

The experiment examines three general predictions of the logical strategy model:

(1) Individuals should use a variety of strategies across a range of logic problems. We predict that no individual will use only one strategy across the entire problem set.

(2) Strategy use should be related to problem type such that each strategy's processing demands, in conjunction with a problem's task demands, lead to particular patterns of strategy selection. We particularly predict that (a) problems with familiar content should be associated with knowledge-based heuristics, unfamiliar problems with token-based strategy use; difficult problems with token-based strategies and superficial heuristics, and abstract problems with verbal strategies, because this form is the closest match to the inferential schemas and should be less likely to activate pragmatic schemas (Braine & O'Brien, 1998). We also predict that (b) each strategy has a cost, operationalised as reaction time, and in particular that superficial heuristics and knowledge-based heuristics have a lower cost than analogies, token-based, and verbal strategies.

(3) Strategy use should be related to performance: Algorithmic strategies (e.g., token-based, verbal) should be associated with more correct responses than heuristic strategies (e.g., superficial and knowledge-based heuristics).

Method

Subjects

The subjects were 45 university students (mean age 20.8) enrolled in an upper level psychology course. Subjects were given extra credit for participating.

Materials

Twenty-four deductive problems were selected from well-known studies of reasoning (> 100 citations). There were two problem types: syllogisms and conditionals. The syllogisms and most conditionals each consisted of a series of premises (or antecedents) and a conclusion, and subjects were asked to evaluate the conclusion as valid or invalid. In a small subset of the conditionals (Wason-type problems), subjects were presented with a rule in the form of a conditional, and given a series of possible evidence states. Subjects were asked to select those that were necessary to test the validity of the rule.

For each problem type, there were different subtypes in which one element of the problem content was manipulated: abstract versus concrete, familiar versus unfamiliar, and simple versus difficult. Abstract problems used letters only, while concrete items used elements that were related either causally or by permission/obligation. Familiar elements were well known (e.g., dogs, cats), while unfamiliar items had nonsensical terms (e.g., thogs, merds). Simple and difficult problems were taken from Braine and O'Brien (1998, chapter 7) based on subject difficulty ratings of conditional and syllogism problems.[4] Examples of problems are provided in the Appendix at the end of this chapter.

Subjects were also asked to reflect on how they solved each problem. They were presented with five strategy descriptions, each corresponding to the processing operations in one of the aforementioned strategies. For example, with superficial heuristics, subjects are expected to focus on the surface structure and try to maintain consistency between the terms in the premises and conclusions. The verbal strategy was presented as shown in Table 2.2 because the implementation of verbal rules is described as being automatic and not

TABLE 2.2
Examples of strategy descriptions for the web experiment

Tell us how you solved that last problem. Select the description below that best describes how you solved that last problem

Verbal	I didn't really have to think it through. My choice just seemed right.
Token-based	I imagined a variety of situations with various letters and looked to see if the conclusion matched what I was imagining.
Superficial heuristic	I looked to see if the key words in the argument (e.g., *some, A*) were also in the conclusion.
Knowledge-based heuristic	This is the kind of situation in which these items have to be related and I just looked to see if the situation was true.
Analogy	This reminded me of another situation. I thought through the other situation and that allowed me to answer this problem.

---

[4] No information was given on actual difficulty ratings, thus there is no comparison between subject and actual difficulty ratings for these problems.

requiring conscious processing (Braine & O'Brien, 1998). Each strategy description was tailored to match the content in the problem. Examples are presented in Table 2.2.

Procedure

Subjects were given a web-link in class and asked to log on and complete the experiment at some point during a one-week period. When subjects logged on they were asked to select their birth date from a range of eight periods. These links took subjects to one of four orders (syllogism first/forward, syllogism first/backward, conditional first/forward, conditional first/backward). The next page gave a brief description of the study. Two further pages asked subjects to give demographic information including major, GPA, SAT scores (verbal, math), and the number of logic, math, and science classes they had taken. The remainder of the experiment consisted of the logic problems and strategy self-reports. The final pre-experimental page presented a brief description of the procedure.

The subjects were asked to solve a series of logic problems for which they (1) evaluated the given conclusion as either valid or invalid, or (2) (for half of the conditionals) selected the correct cases that would test a given rule in Wason tasks (Cheng & Holyoak, 1985, Cosmides, 1989, Wason, 1961; Wason & Johnson-Laird, 1972). The web pages were constructed so that only one response was possible for the former, while up to four responses were acceptable for the latter problems. After selecting their response(s), subjects clicked on the 'Continue' button that took them to the strategy self-selection page. On this page, they were asked to think about how they had solved the immediately previous problem. They were asked to select one description from five (see Table 2.2) – only one response was possible. After completing all 24 problems, subjects were directed to a final page with a short debriefing, thanking them for their participation.

Results

We conducted this experiment to test three predictions of the logical strategy model (LSM): (1) subjects should report using a variety of strategies across the problem set; (2) strategies have costs and that strategy use should be related to the demands of the problem type; (3) strategy use should be closely associated with performance. Unless otherwise mentioned, alpha levels are $p < .01$.

(1) Variation in strategy use

As predicted, the subjects used a variety of strategies – all five were endorsed by at least some subjects (see Table 2.3). Subjects differed in which strategies

TABLE 2.3
Strategy selection by problem type

	Verbal %	Token-based %	Knowledge-based %	Superficial heuristic %	Analogy %
All items	13	21	27	**31**	8
Familiar	13	21	**38**	22	7
Unfamiliar	14	23	17	**37**	8
Simple	13	24	25	**30**	8
Difficult	12	24	25	**33**	6
Abstract	10	29	18	**33**	11
Concrete	12	20	26	**32**	10
Syllogisms	10	25	24	**31**	11
Conditionals	14	24	23	**33**	6
Wason	14	**36**	21	20	8
Non-Wason	12	22	22	**36**	8

they preferred. The most common modal strategy was superficial heuristics (23), followed by knowledge-based heuristics (11), token-based (9), verbal (2), and analogy (0). The great majority of subjects used several strategies. None of the subjects used only one strategy. Only two subjects used a single strategy for more than 75% of the problems. Two-thirds of the subjects used all five strategies at least occasionally, endorsing each for at least 10% of trials.

(2) The relationship between strategy use and problem type

(a) Is strategy use associated with a particular type of problem? To investigate this possibility, we calculated strategy frequencies for each problem type. For each problem there was one strategy that was used most frequently. Superficial heuristics were the most frequently selected strategy for 13 problems (3 conditionals, 10 syllogisms), knowledge-based heuristics were most frequently selected for 8 problems (6 conditionals, 2 syllogisms), while token-based were most frequently selected for 3 conditionals, verbal for 1 conditional, and analogy was never the most frequently selected. Table 2.3 displays strategy choices by problem type (conditional vs. syllogism), by type of conditional (Wason-type vs. non-Wason-type), and by problem content (e.g., familiar).

We predicted specific relationships between problem types and strategy use: That familiar problems would be particularly associated with knowledge-based heuristics, unfamiliar problems with token-based strategies, difficult problems with token-based strategies and superficial heuristics, and abstract problems with verbal strategies.

Knowledge-based heuristics were most commonly used on three of four familiar problems. By contrast, superficial heuristics and token-based strategies were the most frequently selected for all four unfamiliar problems. Superficial heuristics were most frequently selected for all four difficult problems. However, contrary to our predictions, verbal strategies were not selected the most frequently for abstract problems, where there was no clear preference. These results generally confirm our predictions that problem types should be associated with particular strategies, because each strategy's processing demands should be associated with particular task demands/features.

(b) Cost: Strategy use and solution time. We next examined whether strategies had different processing costs as measured by solution times.[5] There were significant differences in solution times related to the type of strategy chosen in the self-report question. The differences in the overall mean solution times were compared in a 2 (item type: conditional vs. syllogism) × 5 (strategy) ANOVA. The results are displayed in Figure 2.1. There was a main effect of item type, $F (1, 44) = 10.7$, as syllogism solution times (mean = 11 seconds) were significantly longer than conditional solution times (mean = 8.8 seconds).

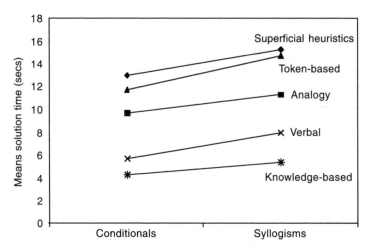

Figure 2.1   Solution times associated with self-reported strategies for conditional and syllogistic reasoning problems.

---

[5] The solution time was measured as the difference in the time stamp on the designated problem and the strategy selection page that preceded it. Once each solution time was calculated, it was labelled by the strategy self-report that followed. For example, a subject responds to the familiar conditional in 3.4 seconds. After responding to this question, the subject then chooses superficial heuristics for the self-report. The datum is entered as 'superficial heuristics 3.4 seconds'.

There was a main effect for strategy, F (4, 44) = 19.3. Tukey HSD tests indicated that knowledge-based heuristics (ST = 4.8 sec) and verbal strategies (ST = 6.8 sec) had significantly shorter solution times than token-based (ST = 14.2 sec) and superficial heuristics (ST = 13.2 sec). The solution times for superficial heuristics were much longer than we had predicted and may have interesting implications for our model of strategy choice. In particular, we suspect that subjects, in the course of trying to solve a difficult problem, tried a more accurate strategy first, failed, and then switched to superficial heuristics. This multi-strategy process would hence yield surprisingly long times for the superficial heuristics.

There were no interactions for solution times between item type and strategy, despite some necessary differences in the wording of the strategy questions across tasks types, indicating a stability of these processing differences between strategies.

(3) The relationship between strategy use and performance

Is strategy choice related to performance? As suggested earlier, algorithmic strategies (e.g., verbal, token based) should be associated with more correct responses while heuristic strategies (e.g., knowledge based, superficial) should be associated with more errors. A correlational analysis between the number of correct responses on syllogisms, standard conditionals, Wason-type conditionals, and strategy choices found several significant values. There was a significant positive relationship between the use of algorithmic strategies and correct responses on syllogisms ($r = .47$), while there was a significant negative relationship between the use of heuristic strategies and the number of correct responses on syllogisms ($r = -.29$). A similar relationship was found for Wason-type conditionals: The overall number of correct responses was significantly, positively correlated with the use of algorithmic strategies ($r = .51$) and significantly, negatively correlated with heuristic strategies ($-.31$).

Conclusions

The logical strategy model (LSM) suggests that deductive performance is not the result of a specialised system, but results from the application of numerous general strategies. These compete, and ultimately selection is made on the basis of the fit between the unique costs and benefits of the strategy (processing demands) and the salient properties of the problem (task demands). This situational niche (processing and task demands) specifies a task-sensitive strategy selection mechanism on the basis of the 'best fit' between available strategies and problem type.

Similar multi-strategy models have been suggested for judgement and decision-making (see Bettman, Johnson, Luce, & Payne, 1993; Todd &

Gigerenzer, 1999). Like the logical strategy model (LSM), these suggest competition between various strategies in which selection is accomplished, in part, from an evaluation of effort–accuracy trade-offs. However, the logical strategy model (LSM) differs from these models in its function and goals: (1) the function of the LSM is the creation and evaluation of knowledge (inference) rather than selection and evaluation of which knowledge is needed for decision making; (2) the goal of LSM is to explain reasoning performance within a closed system (i.e., definable correct/incorrect responses) while the goal of other related models is to explain how the most adaptive decision is taken in an open system (i.e., no definable correct/incorrect responses; Todd & Gigerenzer, 1999); (3) the details of the particular strategies proposed also vary between these accounts.

The results of the experiment provide evidence to support three predictions of the logical strategy model (LSM): (1) Individuals used multiple strategies over the problem set. Most subjects reported using multiple strategies and no individual reported using one strategy on more than 75% of trials. (2a) Strategy use was related to problem type. Subjects reported using knowledge-based heuristics when familiar content was present, used superficial heuristics for more difficult and less familiar problems, and reported using token-based strategies for Wason-type tasks. (2b) Strategies had different costs as measured by processing time. Token-based and superficial heuristics were associated with the longest processing times, while knowledge-based heuristics and verbal strategies were associated with the shortest processing times. We had predicted that the use of superficial heuristics would be relatively low cost, and the higher than expected cost may suggest that either each processing step is costly or that superficial heuristics may be used after unsuccessful attempts with other strategies (e.g., knowledge-based heuristics). (3) Strategy use was associated with accuracy. As predicted, the use of heuristic strategies was associated with a larger number of incorrect responses, while the use of algorithmic strategies was associated with a larger number of correct responses.

As stated earlier, the LSM may allow for explanation of previous findings. Recent research such as Stanovich and West (1998, 2000) has also focused on individual differences. They have shown that individual variability in logical reasoning performance correlates with intelligence for certain types of task but not others. Our model would predict how strategy choice could vary with intelligence (higher capacity strategies for higher capacity individuals), and also that choice could vary independently of intelligence (given the large variety of applicable strategies and relevant background experiences that influence strategy choice).

Our work with the LSM is just in the beginning stages, and there are several obvious next steps to strengthen the empirical basis for our model: (1) We will examine the effect of strategy descriptions on self-report to show that subjects are not confused by the definitions (thereby producing variability) or simply selecting based on social desirability of options (thereby selecting strategies they in fact do not use); (2) we will do more work to triangulate other indicators of strategy use with self-reports of strategy use; (3) we will investigate the possibility of multiple strategies being used on a single problem (as a possible explanation for why superficial heuristic solution times were so long); (4) we will more closely examine the dimensions on which processing and task demands may influence strategy selection.

ACKNOWLEDGEMENTS

The authors would like to thank Corinne Zimmerman, Max Roberts, Elizabeth Newton and Walter Sá for their comments on a previous draft.

APPENDIX: EXAMPLE PROBLEMS

(1) Syllogism (abstract)

You are given the following argument:

No A are B
Some C are B
Conclusion: Some C are not A
Is the conclusion valid or invalid?

(2) Wason-type conditional (abstract)

You are given the following rule:

If a card has a vowel on one side, then it has an even number on the other side.
Four cards are placed on a table as follows: (A, D, 6, 7).
Which card or cards would be turned over to determine whether the rule is true or false?

Select all that you would need to turn over

A   D   6   7

(3) Conditional (familiar)

You are given the following argument:

If Bill is here, then Sam is here
If Sara is here, then Jessica is here
Bill is here or Sara is here
Conclusion: Sam or Jessica is here
Is this conclusion valid or invalid?

REFERENCES

Akimoto, S. A., & Sanbonmatsu, D. M. (1999). Differences in self-effacing behaviors between European and Japanese Americans: Effect on competence evaluations. *Journal of Cross-Cultural Psychology, 30*, 159–177.

Anderson, J. R., & Lebiere, C. (1998). *The atomic components of thought.* Mahwah, NJ: Lawrence Erlbaum Associates, Inc.

Bettman, J. R., Johnson, E. J., Luce, M. F., & Payne, J. W. (1993). Correlation, conflict, and choice. *Journal of Experimental Psychology: Learning, Memory and Cognition, 19*, 931–951.

Braine, M. D. S., & O'Brien, D. P. (Eds.), (1998). *Mental Logic.* Mahwah, NJ: Lawrence Erlbaum Associates, Inc.

Braine, M. D. S., & Rumain, B. (1981). Development of comprehension of 'or': Evidence for a sequence of competencies. *Journal of Experimental Child Psychology, 31*, 46–70.

Braine, M. D. S., & Rumain, B. (1983). Logical reasoning. In J. H. Flavell & E. Markman (Eds.), *Handbook of Child Psychology: Vol. 3. Cognitive Development* (pp. 263–339). New York: Wiley.

Chase, W. G., & Simon, H. A. (1973). Perception in chess. *Cognitive Psychology, 4*, 55–81.

Cheng, P. W., & Holyoak, K. J. (1985). Pragmatic reasoning schemas. *Cognitive Psychology, 17*, 391–416.

Chi, M., Glaser, R., & Farr, M. J. (1988). *The nature of expertise.* Hillsdale, NJ: Lawrence Erlbaum Associates, Inc.

Cosmides, L. (1989). The logic of social exchange: Has natural selection shaped how humans reason? Studies with the Wason selection task. *Cognition, 31*, 187–276.

Evans, J. St. B. T. (1972). On the problems of interpreting reasoning data: Logical and psychological approaches. *Cognition, 1*, 373–384.

Evans, J. St. B. T. (1989). *The psychology of deductive reasoning.* London: Routledge.

Evans, J. St. B. T., Barston, J. L., & Pollard, P. (1983). On the conflict between logical and belief in syllogistic reasoning. *Memory and Cognition, 11*, 295–306.

Galotti, K. M., Baron, J., Sabini, J. P. (1986). Individual differences in syllogistic reasoning: Deduction rules or mental rules? *Journal of Experimental Psychology: General, 115*, 16–25.

Gentner, D. (1983). Structure-mapping: A theoretical framework for analogy. *Cognitive Science, 7*, 155–170.

Goel, V., Buchel, C., Frith, C., & Dolan, R. J. (2000). Dissociation of mechanisms underlying syllogistic reasoning. *Neuroimage, 12*, 504–514.

Holyoak, K. J., & Thagard, P. R. (1989). A computational model of analogical problem solving. In S. Vosniado & A. Ortony (Eds.), *Similarity and analogical reasoning.* Cambridge: Cambridge University Press.

Holyoak, K. J., & Thagard, P. R. (1995). *Mental leaps: analogy in creative thought.* Cambridge, MA: MIT Press.

Johnson-Laird, P. N. (1983). *Mental models.* Cambridge, MA: Harvard University Press.

Johnson-Laird, P. N. (1999). Deductive reasoning. *Annual Review of Psychology, 50*, 109–135.

Johnson-Laird, P. N., Byrne, R. M. J., & Schaeken, W. (1992). Propositional reasoning by model. *Psychological Review, 99*, 418–439.

Larkin, J. H., & Simon, H. A. (1987). Why a diagram is (sometimes) worth ten thousand words. *Cognitive Science, 11*, 65–100.

Leighton, J. P., & Sternberg, R. J. (2003). Reasoning and problem solving. In A. F. Healy & R. W. Proctor (Eds.), *Handbook of psychology: Experimental psychology, Vol. 4.* (pp. 623–648). New York: Wiley.

Osherson, D., Perani, D., Cappa, S., Schnur, T., Grassi, F., & Fazio, F. (1998). Distinct brain loci in deductive versus probabilistic reasoning. *Neuropsychologica, 36*, 369–376.

Rips, L. J. (1994). *The Psychology of Proof.* Cambridge, MA: MIT Press.

Roberts, M. J. (1993). Human reasoning: deduction rules or mental models, or both? *Quarterly Journal of Experimental Psychology, 46A*, 569–589.

Roberts, M. J. (2000). Individual differences in reasoning strategies. In W. Schaeken, G. DeVooght, A. Vandierendock, & G. d'Ydewalle (Eds.), *Deductive reasoning and strategies* (pp. 23–48). Mahwah, NJ: Lawrence Erlbaum Associates, Inc.

Searle, J. R. (1984). *Minds, brains, and science.* Cambridge, MA: Harvard.

Searle, J. R. (1990). Consciousness, explanatory inversion, and cognitive science. *Behavioral & Brain Sciences, 13*(4), 585–642.

Simon, H. A. (1957). *Models of man: Social and rational; mathematical essays on rational human behavior in society setting.* New York: Wiley.

Stanovich, K. E. (1999). *Who is rational? Studies of individual differences in reasoning.* Mahwah, NJ: Lawrence Erlbaum Associates, Inc.

Stanovich, K. E., & West, R. F. (1998). Individual differences in rational thought. *Journal of Experimental Psychology: General, 127*(2), 161–188.

Stanovich, K. E., & West, R. F. (2000). Individual differences in reasoning: Implications for the rationality debate? *Behavioral & Brain Sciences, 23*(5), 645–726.

Todd, P. M., & Gigerenzer, G. (1999). Precis of simple heuristics that make us smart. *Behavioral and Brain Sciences, 23*, 727–780.

Van der Henst, J., Yang, Y., & Johnson-Laird, P. N. (2002). Strategies in sentential reasoning. *Cognitive Science, 26*, 425–468.

Wason, P. C. (1961). Response to affirmative and negative binary statements. *British Journal of Psychology, 52*, 133–142.

Wason, P. C., & Johnson-Laird, P. N. (1972). *The psychology of reasoning: Structure and content.* London: Batsford.

Woodworth, R. S., & Sells, S. B. (1935). An atmosphere effect in syllogistic reasoning. *Journal of Experimental Psychology, 18*, 451–460.

Zhang, J., & Norman, D. A. (1994). Representation in distributed cognitive tasks. *Cognitive Science, 18*, 87–122.

CHAPTER THREE

Working memory and strategies in reasoning

K. J. Gilhooly
School of Psychology, University of Hertfordshire, UK

The study of thinking and problem solving is organised into fairly broad areas such as reasoning, planning, and decision making, and within each area into families of tasks such as syllogistic reasoning, decision making under uncertainty, and planning in move problems. Even within specific tasks it is clear that individuals vary in how they tackle them, and that individuals vary over time. Virtually every task of interest to the study of thinking and problem solving, I suggest, is open to a variety of approaches, or strategies, for solution. For example, given the task of finding the sum of the digits 1 to 100, an obvious approach is to begin adding the numbers in sequence. However, a better approach is possible if the person notices that the digits 1 to 100 form 50 pairs each of which add to 101 i.e., (1 + 100), (2 + 99), (3 + 98), (4 + 97) and so on. This second 'grouping and multiplying' procedure readily gives the correct answer (5050). It is reported that the famous mathematician Gauss used the second procedure when given the above task as a young child in school (Hall, 1970) enabling him to produce the correct answer very quickly while his classmates struggled with the 'simple summing' procedure. Intuitively, it would seem that the 'grouping and multiplying' method is better because it produces the answer with less load on memory. This chapter will be discussing work which relates to the link between strategies in reasoning tasks and memory load and, in particular, working memory load.

The relationship between strategies and working memory first seems to have been addressed by Bruner, Goodnow, and Austin (1956) in their classic study of a concept learning task, *A Study of Thinking*. In the context of this task, in which a person has to identify a rule for classifying objects on the basis of combinations of features, Bruner et al. defined a strategy as 'a pattern of decisions in the acquisition, retention, and utilization of information that serves to meet certain objectives' (1956, p. 54). Among the objectives were (1) to attain the concept with the minimum number of examples and (2) to 'minimize the amount of strain on inference and memory capacity while at the same time insuring that a concept will be attained' (p. 54). This is an early statement of the importance of minimising cognitive load when solving problems.

On the basis of a task analysis, Bruner et al. (1956) identified alternative strategies which varied in their cognitive loading and efficiency of information use. These idealised strategies specified information processing steps, and could be used to predict expected behaviour. For example, consider a selection paradigm in which an array of 81 cards is presented bearing figures varying in shape, number of figures, colour, and size, with three possible values per attribute. The participant is shown a positive example of a concept that the experimenter has in mind and it is explained that the target concept is conjunctive (i.e., one or more features must be present together for a card to be a correct exemplar). For example, the participant might be shown a card with *two large red squares*, and be told that this is a positive example. The participant can then ask about the status of further cards in order to identify the conceptual rule.

One possible strategy is labelled 'simultaneous scanning'. For this, the card presented by the experimenter is used to eliminate 240 of the possible 255 rules. (This is always logically possible whatever the conjunctive rule.) For the card presented in the earlier example, this leaves the following:

(1) cards with two shapes   (2) cards with red shapes
(3) cards with squares   (4) cards with large shapes
(5) cards with two red shapes   (6) cards with two squares
(7) cards with two large shapes   (8) cards with red squares
(9) cards with large red shapes   (10) cards with large squares
(11) cards with two red squares   (12) cards with two large red shapes
(13) cards with two large squares   (14) cards with large red squares
(15) only the card with two large red squares

Next, a person following this strategy would determine which card would be expected to eliminate the greatest number of remaining possibilities, or hypotheses, and inquire about the card's status, and so on, until only one hypothesis remains. This last hypothesis will be the correct one. An alternative method is 'conservative focussing'. For this, the participant starts with the initial positive instance as a focus and makes a sequence of choices which change just one attribute value of the first positive card (e.g., a card showing *one* large red square). Changed attribute values which yield a negative instance are part of the correct answer. Attributes which when changed still yield a positive classification are irrelevant and are not part of the correct hypothesis. Intuitively, it seems compelling that 'conservative focussing' is much less cognitively loading than 'simultaneous scanning', and indeed 'conservative focussing' was observed much more commonly. Bruner et al. (1956) noted that participants altered their strategies to take into account problem difficulty and sometimes chose methods that were less than ideal, but which lightened pressures imposed by the tasks. Thus, there was a tendency to adopt strategies which minimised cognitive load. (N.B., people will not necessarily use the most efficient strategies in this respect if they are not aware of them and cannot discover them, see Newton & Roberts, chapter 7 this volume; Roberts & Newton, chapter 6 this volume.)

Bruner et al. used a fairly broad notion of cognitive load or 'strain'; for example, as Bruner et al. (1956, p. 84) describe it, 'simultaneous scanning' would involve inferring the 255 possible rules, storing them in long-term memory, then retrieving each in turn into working memory to check against the first correct instance to mark 240 as eliminated and 15 as still possible solutions. Even if participants only explicitly generated the 15 hypotheses consistent with the first positive instance, this modified simultaneous scanning strategy would still make heavy demands on working memory. After the candidate hypotheses have been identified, the next stage is to determine the optimum card to select in order to eliminate as many of these as possible. This involves extended and complex computations. The load or strain caused by such a strategy bears on multiple components of the cognitive system. Each of the many steps required are open to errors, any of which would derail the whole procedure.

More recent research has attempted to focus specifically on working memory loading and its influence on strategy application and selection. Subsequent to Bruner et al., progress has been made in developing detailed models of working memory, and a number of investigators have attempted to relate such models to strategies in a detailed way, particularly in the area of reasoning. It will be useful to first outline the main approaches to working memory currently prevalent. I will then discuss possible links between working memory and strategies, and go on to consider the results from studies of reasoning.

WORKING MEMORY

A useful starting definition of 'working memory' is as follows: 'Working memory is those mechanisms or processes that are involved in the control, regulation, and active maintenance of task-relevant information in the service of complex cognition.' (Miyake & Shah, 1999, p. 450). Currently, there are two main approaches to specifying the mechanisms of working memory. For the first, this involves a single pool of resources (e.g., 'activation') which can be flexibly allocated between storage and processing within a single task (e.g., Daneman & Carpenter, 1980; Just & Carpenter, 1992) and which varies between individuals. The second approach proposes that working memory consists of multiple components (e.g., Baddeley & Logie, 1999) which have specialised storage and processing roles.

The 'single pool of resources' approach focuses on correlations between individual differences in working memory capacity and performance on a variety of tasks. Working memory capacity has been measured by a number of span tasks involving both storage and processing. For example, in the sentence span task of Daneman and Carpenter (1980) participants are given a series of sentences to read. After these sentences, participants are asked to recall the last word of each in the correct sequence. The longest sequence of sentences for which all the final words can be recalled correctly is the sentence span. This has been found to be correlated with other span measures, using different materials, such as digit strings (Yuill, Oakhill, & Parkin, 1988), simple equations (Turner & Engle, 1989) and a counting span task (Baddeley, Logie, Nimmo-Smith, & Brereton, 1985). Working memory span measures have been found to be correlated with performance on a range of other complex tasks, such as: reading comprehension (Daneman & Carpenter, 1980); following directions (Engle, Carullo, & Collins, 1991); reasoning (Kyllonen & Chrystal, 1990), and complex learning (Kyllonen & Stephens, 1990). It would appear then that working memory span taps a general capacity which underlies many more complex cognitive tasks.

In the influential model developed by Baddeley and colleagues (Baddeley, 1992; Baddeley & Hitch, 1974; Baddeley & Logie, 1999), a three-part working memory system was originally proposed. This comprised a *central executive* which co-ordinated the activities of two subsidiary or 'slave' storage systems, the *visuo-spatial sketchpad* and the *phonological loop*. The role of the phonological loop is to hold a limited amount of phonological or speech-based information. The visuo-spatial sketchpad was seen as holding a limited amount of visually or spatially coded information. This fractionation is supported by dual task studies, which have shown selective interference from visuo-spatial and verbal secondary tasks on memory for visuo-spatial and verbal information respectively, as well as differential patterns of impairment in neuropsychological patients (for reviews see Baddeley & Logie, 1999; Della Sala & Logie, 1993). Subsequently, it has been proposed that the central executive has no storage function, but rather operates as an attentional controller. The phonological loop has been fractionated into a passive *phonological store* and an active *rehearsal process*. Logie (1995) has proposed that the visuo-spatial sketchpad might be fractionated into two temporary memory systems, a passive *visual cache* which stores static visual patterns and an active spatially based system that stores dynamic information, an *inner scribe*. The inner scribe has been particularly linked to temporary memory for movement sequences (Logie, Englekamp, Dehn, & Rudkin, 2001). The central executive is also open to fractionation into a number of functions (e.g., focusing attention, switching attention, activating representations in long-term memory (LTM), co-ordinating multiple task performance). Baddeley (2000) has proposed a further component, the *episodic buffer*, for temporarily holding multi-modal information. However, as yet, this component has not been sufficiently specified to lead to experimental investigations.

Dual task methods have been widely used to determine the contribution of working memory components in various tasks. For example, if a primary task is disrupted by concurrent articulatory suppression (such as, repeating aloud 'the, the, the . . .' continuously) but not by concurrent spatial activity (such as moving one hand in a simple pattern), then the inference would be that the primary task involves the phonological loop but not the visuo-spatial sketchpad. Central executive involvement is generally tested by concurrent random generation of items from a well-defined set (e.g., digits from 1 to 5; keys 1 to 9 on a numeric pad). Many studies have found these and related methods to be useful in assessing the involvement of working memory components in a variety of tasks (Andrade, 2001; Baddeley & Logie, 1999).

STRATEGIES AND WORKING MEMORY

Theoretically, the information-processing approach assumes that responses to complex tasks, such as concept learning, reasoning, or planning, result from the execution of underlying strategies which, in interaction with the problem materials, determine the sequence of specific information processing actions and decisions. Ideally, we would like to specify such strategies in detail. However, in practice, strategy specification spans a continuum from broad characterisations (e.g., the use of a 'verbal strategy' in a task might be inferred from brain scanning data showing activation of the left temporal cortex, say, but otherwise be left undefined) to descriptions specific enough to run as computer programs. Even with strategy descriptions which are specific enough to predict responses to any given input, implementation details, such as how information is temporarily stored, are often lacking. Consider the case of syllogistic arguments (e.g., 'All of the painters are golfers. Some of the golfers are not tall people. Therefore, what follows?') for which the 'Atmosphere' strategy (Woodworth & Sells, 1935) is in one sense well specified. It states that if one or both premises are negative, a negative conclusion is given (otherwise a positive conclusion is given); and if one or both premises are particular (i.e., contain the word 'some'), a particular conclusion is given, otherwise a universal conclusion is given. However, this strategy could be implemented in alternative ways which would place more or less load on working memory (Gilhooly, 1998). A 'pattern recognition' version would be based on ten rules in long-term memory (LTM) giving the answer for each possible pair of premises: (e.g., 'If premises are "All, All" then response is "All" '; 'If premises are "All, Some" then the response is "Some" '; 'If premises are "All, Some not" then the response is "Some not" '; and so on.) Such an implementation would not load working memory at all. A 'sequential' implementation would go through a series of steps to search for particulars and negatives before reaching a conclusion, and this implementation would be more loading of working memory. Both implementations would deliver the same pattern of responses over a set of syllogisms, and discrimination between them would require other measures, such as latencies, think aloud protocols, etc.

What might the results from dual task studies tell us regarding reasoning strategies? If loading a slave system – such as using articulatory suppression to load the phonological loop – leads to changes in performance on the target task, then it may be inferred that the commonly used strategies are implemented in such a way as to draw on the phonological loop. In other words temporary phonological storage is required. Similar inferences can be drawn regarding the role of the visuo-spatial sketch pad from studies involving the loading of that component. However, caution is required when two or more working memory components appear to be implicated by dual tasks in a standard group experiment. Such results might arise (1) because all commonly occurring strategies load the same two or more components or (2) because different commonly occurring strategies actually load different components.

A more powerful dual task methodology can be used where there is an attempt to compare different strategy groups, either (1) by training participants in different strategies, or (2) by selecting participants through the use of pre-tests designed to separate them into different strategy groups. Participants differentiated in these ways should generally show different effects of dual tasks.

Individual difference studies in which capacities of working memory components are assessed can also be informative. For example, if visuo-spatial working memory capacity measures correlate well with performance on a particular task, then this suggests that the typical strategies load the visuo-spatial sketch pad. In addition, performance of strategies which load onto different working memory components should be correlated with different working memory measures.

In principle then, it seems that a combination of task analysis (to yield possible strategies), analysis of response patterns (to identify typical strategies), training and selection (to produce strategically homogeneous groups), analyses of latencies, verbal protocols, dual tasks, brain scanning, and individual difference measures (to narrow down implementation possibilities), should be informative about strategies and their interactions with working memory.

REASONING: THEORETICAL APPROACHES

The focus here will be on *deductive reasoning*, i.e., tasks which could be successfully tackled by the application of a set of processes specified by a formal deductive theory. Deductive reasoning allows the derivation of new true statements with certainty from given true statements (premises). There are currently three broad approaches to explaining how people perform such tasks. Two approaches propose 'unified theories' of reasoning, which postulate that particular ways of processing reasoning tasks are universal (Roberts, 1993). These are the *mental models* approach of Johnson-Laird (e.g., Johnson-Laird, 1983; Johnson-Laird & Byrne, 1991) and the *mental rules* approach associated with Braine, O'Brien, and Rips (e.g., Braine & O'Brien, 1998; Rips, 1994). The third approach stresses the role of *strategies*, which vary depending on task demands, training, and individual differences (Roberts, 2000). The strategy approach can include mental models and rules approaches as special cases, viewing them as optional strategic choices, rather than universal and obligatory (see also Morris & Schunn, chapter 2 this volume).

The main assumptions of the mental models approach are that people form representations of the presented information (premises) in terms of tokens linked together to exemplify the stated relationships. The premise representations are then combined into integrated representations from which it should be possible to identify conclusions directly. The main stages proposed are as follows (Evans, Newstead & Byrne, 1993). First, a model is formed representing one possible state of the world in which the premises would be true. Next, a proposed conclusion is formed by discovering a proposition which is true in the model and is informative. If there is more than one way of combining premise models, then the remaining combinations should be formed and checked against the proposed conclusion until either a counter-example to the proposed conclusion is found, or all possibilities have been considered without the discovery of a counter-example. Only conclusions that hold for all combinations of premise models are valid deductions. If the proposed conclusion is falsified, then a new proposed conclusion compatible with all model combinations should be sought. If no such conclusion can be found, there is no valid conclusion. The mental models theory proposes that all participants follow the same basic approach and the only allowance for individual differences lies in the completeness of executing the mental models procedure. Errors are due to failure to consider all possible ways of combining premise information, perhaps because of working memory limitations.

Indeed, Johnson-Laird (1983) specifically proposed a role for working memory in reasoning. In discussing figural effects in syllogistic reasoning (which are effects due to different ways of arranging the terms in syllogistic arguments), Johnson-Laird wrote:

> The effects of both number of models and figure arise from an inevitable bottleneck in the inferential machinery: the processing capacity of working memory, which must hold one representation in a store, while at the same time the relevant information from the current premise is substituted in it. This problem is not obviated by allowing the subjects to have the written premises in front of them throughout the task: the integration of premises has to occur in working memory, unless the subjects are allowed to use pencil and paper so as to externalise the process.
>
> (Johnson-Laird, 1983, p. 115)

The *mental rules* (or *mental logic*) approach also proposes that all participants follow one general method, with more or less completeness due to working memory limitations. For this, reasoning requires the use of inference rules drawn from a set available to all normal adults, and which is a subset of those available in formal logic (Braine, 1978; Rips, 1994). For example, the *modus ponens* rule (given that both 'if p then q', and 'p' are true, then 'q' must also be true) is almost always followed, and would be regarded as part of normal adult competence. When an inference requires use of a rule that is not possessed, chains of available rules must be applied instead. Working memory limitations are involved in that the more steps required to reach a conclusion, the larger the load on working memory, and so the more errors that are expected. Braine, Reiser, and Rumain (1984) report latency results consistent with this expectation.

The third broad approach does not propose universal mechanisms, but rather argues that people can use many different *strategies* which vary both across participants, and within participants, depending on abilities, task format, experience and training (Roberts, 2000). On this approach, both mental models and mental rules are optional strategies which can be adopted or not, rather than invariable approaches followed by all participants in all reasoning tasks. A range of heuristic strategies for reasoning tasks has also been proposed, and although superior to guessing, these are typically not completely equivalent in accuracy to logical rule application. The use of heuristic strategies is consistent with the observation that participants are liable to error in many abstract reasoning tasks; for example, the modal answer to most syllogisms is an error (Erickson, 1978).

WORKING MEMORY IN PROPOSITIONAL
REASONING: EMPIRICAL RESULTS

Given premises, 'If p then q' and 'p', what follows? The valid (modus ponens) inference is 'q'. Given, 'If p then q' and 'not-q', 'not-p' follows validly (modus tollens). Given, 'If p then q' and 'not-p' (denial of the antecedent), or 'q' (affirmation of the consequent), nothing validly follows (i.e., no conclusion is definitely true). These problems are examples of conditional reasoning and represent basic problems in propositional logic. A number of studies have used dual tasks with conditional reasoning in order to explore the role of working memory, and the salient results will now be outlined.

Experimental manipulations: dual tasks and training

Early studies using dual task methods (Evans & Brooks, 1981; Toms, Morris, & Ward, 1993) found little evidence of working memory involvement in conditional reasoning. Toms et al. concluded that conditional reasoning did not involve the visuo-spatial sketchpad or the articulatory loop, but required some abstract representation in working memory which could be provided by the central executive. However, these early studies did not check for possible trade-offs: Participants may have maintained inference performance at the cost of concurrent articulation and/or tapping performance. A further difficulty with Toms et al.'s conclusions regarding the central executive is that secondary tasks which clearly load this, such as random generation, were not used to test directly for central executive involvement.

Klauer, Stegmaier, and Meiser (1997) remedied the limitations of the earlier studies and also used a training method in some studies. They used a number of propositional reasoning tasks including conditionals (*if p then q*), biconditionals (*if and only if p then q*), exclusive disjunctions (*either p or q*) and inclusive disjunctions (*at least p or q*) with a range of secondary tasks, and examined possible trade-offs. With untrained participants, small interfering effects of articulatory suppression, and marked interference of verbal random generation were found, together with no interference from a visual tracking task. Examining possible trade-offs, propositional reasoning interfered with random generation, did not disrupt articulatory suppression, but did have a mildly impairing effect on visual tracking. Overall it seems that propositional reasoning strongly involves the central executive, with lesser roles for the articulatory loop and visuo-spatial sketchpad. Klauer et al. suggested that untrained participants tend to apply heuristics which place a low load on working memory. They proposed that training people to consider the possible truth values of the terms in the premises would lead to an analytic approach similar to that proposed by mental models theory (Johnson-Laird

& Byrne, 1991), and that applying such a strategy would increase working memory load.

A truth-table training method was developed as follows. Participants were given statements involving the four possible connectives, and were then asked to evaluate whether given situations made the statements true or false. A pilot study found that such truth table training did improve subsequent reasoning. Truth table pre-training was then given in a study which used tapping as a secondary task. As predicted, the propositional reasoning of participants with pre-training was more disrupted by tapping than was that of untrained participants. However, it was not determined whether performance declined because the truth table strategy was performed badly, or because other strategies were adopted instead. No trade-offs were found between primary and secondary tasks. It was concluded that application of a mental model-like strategy leads to loading of the visuo-spatial sketchpad. Further, the results indicated that the pattern of loading of working memory in a task depends on the strategy applied to the task.

The role of working memory components in executing different strategies was examined further by Meiser, Klauer, and Naumer (2001). This study involved the training of participants in three strategies: (1) a truth table strategy (as in Klauer et al., 1997), which was intended to induce a mental models-like approach; (2) a mental logic strategy; (3) a pragmatic reasoning schema strategy. Mental logic training involved participants working through inference problems, the solutions to which were presented using the limited set of mental logic rules proposed by Braine and other mental logic theorists (e.g., modus ponens). Training in the pragmatic reasoning schema strategy involved applying schemata such as a social obligation rule (Cheng et al., 1986) and permission rules (Cheng & Holyoak, 1989) to a number of questions about a fictitious company described in a story as having a number of such rules. The training methods had been assessed by Klauer, Meiser, and Naumer (2000) and were found to have differential benefits, such that the truth table and pragmatic reasoning training produced more benefit than mental logic training, which was no more effective than a neutral 'pseudo-training' condition. In an initial study, Meiser et al. (2001) found that propositional reasoning was disrupted by concurrent spatial tapping, as in Klauer et al. (1997). However, the amount of spatial interference was the same over all training methods, which is counter to the assumption that mental models strategies should be especially susceptible to spatial interference (since mental models seem to lend themselves to a spatial representation). Further studies found that random number generation and concurrent articulation caused more disruption of reasoning after truth table training than after the other training methods. It was concluded that the mental model strategy is relatively demanding of working memory resources in propositional reasoning with abstract materials. However, the generally assumed special role of the visuo-spatial sketchpad for a mental models strategy was not established, given that the effects of visuo-spatial loading by tapping were equivalent over the different strategies.

Individual difference studies

Larger working memory spans would be expected to facilitate the execution of strategies. Assuming that most strategies are in principle capable of supporting a good, if not necessarily perfect, level of performance, then measures of working memory span should correlate with performance. Studies of this issue with regard to propositional reasoning have been carried out by Barrouillet and Lecas (1999) and Markovits, Doyon, and Simoneau (2002).

Barrouillet and Lecas (1999) start by pointing out that according to the mental model approach, the construction and manipulation of mental models are carried out in a limited capacity working memory. They suggest that participants may reduce working memory load by constructing *simplified* initial models, which leave implicit some of the information. These models can then be expanded or *fleshed out* if the need arises. Thus, the initial model for the conditional *if p then q* would correspond to:

$$[p] \qquad q$$
$$\cdots$$

The first row is a model that represents the joint occurrence of antecedent (p) and consequent (q). The second line (the three dots) is an implicit model. The brackets, [p], indicate an exhaustive representation so that p cannot occur without q. Fleshing out the model could produce the biconditional interpretation, i.e., the two states of affairs that are compatible with the interpretation *if and only if p then q*:

$$[p] \qquad q$$
$$\neg p \qquad [\neg q]$$
$$\cdots$$

or the conditional interpretation:

$$[p] \qquad q$$
$$\neg p \qquad q$$
$$\neg p \qquad [\neg q]$$

Note: '¬p' means 'not-p'.

According to Barrouillet and Lecas, more working memory capacity is required to construct and hold the three-model representation of the conditional than the two-model (biconditional) representation, or the one-model (conjunction) representation. Because working memory span in children increases with age, the interpretation of conditional statements should develop with age from one-model at early ages to two-model and three-model at older ages. A study in which children had to identify cases which violated *if p then q* (Barrouillet & Lecas, 1998) found that the dominant interpretation changed as expected. In a follow-up study, Barrouillet and Lecas (1999) gave participants a rule, such as 'If you wear a white shirt, you wear green trousers' and a set of cards reading 'White shirt', 'Blue shirt', 'Green trousers' and 'Red trousers'. Participants were instructed to generate as many combinations as possible of trouser and shirt cards that fitted the rule. As expected, the older children produced more combinations which indicated conditional and biconditional representations, i.e., representations based on a larger number of models. The children were also given a counting span task as a measure of working memory. It was found that this was a good predictor of the number of models used when representing a conditional. The results are as expected for the mental models approach which assumes that reasoning involves constructing and manipulating mental models in working memory. Barrouillet and Lecas's results favouring the use of mental models may seem counter to Klauer et al.'s initial finding that most participants appeared to use more superficial heuristics. However, Barrouillet and Lecas's tasks are rather different from those of Klauer et al., and seem to require generation of models that could fit the situation described by the rule, while Klauer et al.'s tasks of drawing conclusions from propositions are open to a number of approaches, including mental models and superficial heuristics.

Markovits, Doyon, and Simoneau (2002) assessed verbal working memory span and visual span measures as predictors of conditional reasoning, using both concrete and abstract conditionals. In the verbal span task (Baddeley et al., 1985), participants first had to judge whether sentences were sensible or not, and were then asked to recall either the subject or the object of each sentence in the order of presentation. The visual span task required participants to recall the positions of five small black circles which appeared at random positions within a square shape for 1 sec each. There was a positive correlation between verbal working memory span and reasoning with both concrete and abstract premises. Visual span was positively correlated with accuracy of reasoning from concrete premises but not from abstract premises. It could be argued that since the verbal span test required both storage and processing, it would load more on the central executive than would the more passive visual span test, which required storage only. On this argument, the results indicate a role for the central executive in both abstract and concrete conditional reasoning, but the visuo-spatial sketchpad is only involved in conditional reasoning with concrete materials. It is plausible that concrete materials would induce imagery based strategies which would implicate the visuo-spatial sketchpad.

Summary of results on working memory in propositional reasoning

Apart from some early studies, research has generally found strong evidence for a major role of the central executive in propositional reasoning (Klauer et al., 1997; Meiser et al., 2001; Toms et al., 1993). Most of the studies reviewed above have also reported evidence of a role for the visuo-spatial sketchpad for both trained and untrained participants (Klauer et al., 1997; Markovits et al., 2002; Meiser et al., 2001). However, although involvement of the visuo-spatial sketchpad has been taken as an indicator of the use of mental models, Meiser et al. (2001) found that participants trained in this approach were *not* more affected by spatial suppression than were participants trained in mental rules or pragmatic schema approaches. Studies of the phonological loop in conditional reasoning using dual tasks (Klauer et al., 1997; Meiser et al., 2001) found positive results for untrained participants and for participants trained in a mental models approach, but not for participants trained in mental logic or pragmatic reasoning schemas. Training in a mental models approach appears to produce a high-load strategy which draws on all components of working memory.

WORKING MEMORY IN SYLLOGISTIC REASONING: EMPIRICAL RESULTS

The area of *syllogistic reasoning*, (for a review see Evans et al., 1993) has attracted considerable research, and many theorists have specifically proposed that working memory has an important role in such tasks (Fisher, 1981; Johnson-Laird, 1983; Johnson-Laird & Byrne, 1991; Sternberg & Turner, 1981). However, until recently, few studies addressed the detailed involvement of working memory in syllogistic reasoning.

Categorical syllogistic arguments invite reasoning about relationships given in two statements (premises) assumed true; for example, 'All men are mammals' and 'All monks are men'. One premise relates the subject of the argument (monks) to the middle term (men) and the other premise relates the middle term to the predicate (mammals). The types of relationships used to link these terms utilise set inclusions, overlaps and exclusions. The task is to indicate what conclusion, if any, can be validly drawn relating the subject and predicate terms. In the example above, it can be validly inferred that 'All monks are mammals'. Despite a long history of experimental and theoretical study (e.g., Chater & Oaksford, 1999; Ford, 1995; Johnson-Laird & Bara,

1984; Wetherick & Gilhooly, 1995; Wilkins, 1928; Woodworth & Sells, 1935) there is no single accepted explanation of how people tackle syllogisms.

Experimental manipulations: Dual tasks and training

Gilhooly, Logie, Wetherick, and Wynn (1993) examined the role of working memory in syllogistic reasoning using abstract materials. In the first study, working memory load was varied by presenting syllogisms either verbally (causing a high memory load) or visually (so that the premises were continuously available for inspection and memory load was low). Participants were asked to generate conclusions rather than select them from a menu. Performance accuracy with the high memory load was significantly impaired, supporting the hypothesised role of working memory. Because the responses were self-generated, it was possible to examine types of errors made as a function of memory load. These could be classified into three types: (1) errors of forgetting, in which the conclusion included the middle term; (2) errors of incomplete analysis, in which definite conclusions were offered to arguments having no valid conclusions; (3) errors of information integration, in which incorrect conclusions were drawn from valid arguments. The only significant difference in error category scores was a higher rate of errors of forgetting in the high-load condition. This suggests that the effect of working memory loading was on retention of the terms and their roles in the argument, rather than on the process of combining premises.

In the second experiment, premises were simultaneously presented visually on a computer screen for a participant-determined time. Participants indicated when they had drawn a conclusion by pressing the space bar; responses were then indicated by choosing from a menu of possible conclusions. Times taken to process the premises and to indicate conclusions were recorded, along with the responses made. Dual task methods were applied in order to assess the role of working memory components. Syllogistic performance was disrupted by concurrent random number generation. However, concurrent articulatory suppression and concurrent tapping in a pre-set pattern did not affect performance. Examining trade-offs, the syllogism task interfered with random generation and with articulatory suppression but not with tapping. Overall, the results indicated that the central executive played an important role in syllogistic task performance, the phonological loop had a lesser role, and the visuo-spatial sketchpad did not appear to be involved (contrary to expectations based on the mental models approach).

Strategies were also examined in this study and the following alternatives were identified:

(1) the atmosphere strategy (Woodworth & Sells, 1935; see earlier).

(2) the matching strategy (Wetherick & Gilhooly, 1995) according to which the conclusion is a proposition of the same logical form as the more conservative of the premises, where the logical forms are ordered for conservatism, from most to least: 'No'; 'Some not'; 'Some'; and 'All'. (This is related to the Probability Heuristics Model more recently proposed by Chater & Oaksford, 1999.)

(3) logic equivalent strategies – these were not specified in detail but are strategies which lead to logically correct answers.

(4) guessing – in which participants simply guess among the alternative conclusions presented on each trial.

The categorical syllogisms used were such that the use of atmosphere, matching, and logic equivalent strategies could be assessed from the patterns of responses. Participants were classified on the basis of the strategy that best fitted their response patterns. Participants having ties in goodness of fit between two strategies were classed as exhibiting mixed strategies. Response patterns that did not give at least a 55% fit to one of the main strategies and led to low correct rates were classed as guessing. In control conditions, and in the articulatory suppression and tapping conditions, strategy usage did not differ, but the matching strategy predominated. With random number generation there was a significant increase in the incidence of guessing from 4% to 38% of participants. However, even in this high-load situation average accuracy (43%) was significantly above chance levels (20%). From these results it was concluded that high secondary loads bring about changes in strategy, typically from matching to guessing, to avoid overloading working memory. These results complement those of Klauer et al.'s (1997) study of propositional reasoning, which found that changing strategy, so as to increase working memory load, affected the impact of a fixed secondary load (tapping).

Gilhooly, Logie, and Wynn (2002) presented syllogistic premises briefly in a sequential visual display, rather than the simultaneous participant controlled premise presentation of their earlier study (Gilhooly et al., 1993). Sequential presentation should cause a greater memory load, and so it was expected that the slave systems would show more involvement in these circumstances in order to maintain relevant information not available from external displays. No effects from concurrent tapping on accuracy or latencies in the reasoning task were found, but there were impairments of average tapping speed and of consistency of tapping rate. These results indicate difficulty in performing both syllogistic reasoning and tapping simultaneously when sequential premise presentation is used. Thus, with sequential presentation there seems to be some involvement of the visuo-spatial sketchpad in the categorical syllogism task even with abstract materials. The articulatory suppression conditions showed impairment of syllogistic accuracy and speed of conclusion reporting. Checking trade-offs indicated slowing down and greater variation in articulation rates in the dual condition. These results suggest that the phonological loop is heavily involved in categorical syllogistic reasoning with sequential presentation. Finally, there was a highly significant impairment of reasoning task performance under conditions of random generation. Also, random generation rate was significantly slower and more variable in the dual condition, and randomness of generation as measured by the Evans (1978) RNG index was impaired in the dual conditions.

In terms of strategies, the atmosphere strategy was most common both in the control condition, and with dual tasks loading the slave memory systems. Comparison of control strategy data in this sequential presentation study with control data from the previous simultaneous presentation study indicated that sequential presentation significantly raised the rate of guessing (from 4% to 19%). Random generation, as in our earlier simultaneous premise presentation study, produced a significant increase in the percentage of participants classed as guessing (56% versus 15% in control conditions). However, average accuracy, even under conditions of random generation (37%), was significantly above chance levels (20%). As in the simultaneous premise presentation study, increasing the working memory load by using dual tasks produced a shift toward less demanding strategies.

When premises are displayed continuously throughout the processing period, as in Gilhooly et al. (1993), there is a relatively light load on the working memory components, with participants able to use the display to 'refresh' their memory while attempting to draw a conclusion. Sequential premise presentation brings about a heavier load on the slave systems, and this leads to (1) mutual interference between reasoning and articulatory suppression and (2) interference from reasoning to tapping. Considerable central executive capacity is likely to be taken up by the random generation task, and the mutual impairment of syllogistic reasoning and random generation in the sequential presentation study is as expected from the findings in our previous simultaneous presentation study. The results of these experiments (Gilhooly et al., 1993, 2002) indicate that the central executive is heavily involved in syllogistic reasoning tasks, both with simultaneous and sequential presentation of premises. With sequential presentation, dual task methods suggest a marked involvement of the phonological loop and some involvement of the visuo-spatial sketchpad. With simultaneous presentation, the slave components of working memory, especially the visuo-spatial sketchpad, are less involved. Overall, it would appear that the roles of working memory components depend on the task environment (e.g., sequential vs. simultaneous premise presentation) and on the strategies adopted by participants (e.g., guessing, matching, atmosphere, or a more logical strategy).

The studies of categorical syllogistic reasoning discussed above used unselected, untrained participants, and they varied markedly in the strategies exhibited. Gilhooly, Logie, and Wynn (1999) reported two experiments using groups that were intended to be relatively homogeneous in strategy use. In one of the studies participants were pre-selected as low or high skill by means of a pencil-and-paper screening test that favoured logic-equivalent strategies and penalised the common heuristics of atmosphere and matching. High skill participants scored an average of 50% on the screening test while the low skill group scored an average of 18%. In the second study, low skill participants, identified by the same screening test, were trained to follow a systematic strategy for solving categorical syllogisms. In both studies, patterns of interference from secondary tasks were obtained in order to assess the roles of working memory components. Both studies involved simultaneous presentation of the premises for participant determined times.

In the first study, six high and six low skill groups carried out syllogistic tasks in control conditions and under one of the following dual task conditions: (1) articulatory suppression; (2) unattended speech (to load the phonological store but not the loop); (3) verbal random generation; (4) spatial random generation; (5) simple pattern tapping; (6) unattended pictures (to load the passive visual store or visual cache but not the inner scribe). Strategies were identified as in our other studies (Gilhooly et al., 1993, 2002). It appeared that the more skilled participants were using a relatively high demand strategy (most commonly, the atmosphere strategy) which loaded the central executive, phonological loop and passive visual store subsystems (suggesting the possible use of imagery). Lower skill participants were typically using a less demanding strategy (most commonly, matching) which did not load any aspect of working memory so heavily.

In the second study, participants were selected on the basis of a screening test as being of low skill at syllogisms but still performing above guessing level. A training booklet was devised which aimed to increase their understanding and improve performance. This showed 20 example syllogisms on separate pages for participants to attempt, and then check their answers on a following page. If they were correct they proceeded to the next problem. If they were incorrect, they were invited to turn to a third page in order to examine the correct answer and try to understand a verbal interpretation of why it was correct. The general method of solution, as explained in the booklet, was to attempt to convert problems into the form subject-middle, middle-predicate (i.e., syllogistic figure 1) and then to reason in terms of set membership. To achieve the desired figure, the order of premises may need to be changed and premises may need to be re-ordered internally by conversion, e.g., from 'All P are M' to 'Some M are P'. This training scheme had been validated by pilot studies as transferring to new problems, having lasting effects, and improving the understanding of statements of category relationships. Trained participants subsequently scored an average of 72% on the screening test which compares favourably with the 50% average of the high skill group in the previous study. Following training, separate groups of trained participants carried out syllogistic tasks with and without one of the following four secondary tasks (which had shown interference with the skilled group in the first study): (1) articulatory suppression; (2) unattended pictures; (3) spatial random generation; (4) verbal random generation. Assessment of strategy use indicated that training had led to use of high demand strategies (most commonly, logic equivalent). Dual task results showed that the typical strategy brought about by training heavily loaded the central executive and also, but to lesser extent, the phonological loop and the inner scribe sub-system of the visuo-spatial sketchpad. The training regime emphasised reordering of premises and of terms within premises, and it may well be that such reordering involves spatial mental manipulations. Dual tasking led to greater frequencies of less demanding strategies. In particular, verbal random generation led to an increase in guessing as the likely strategy from 6% of participants in the control condition to 37% in the dual condition.

Overall, it seems clear that the three groups of participants in Gilhooly et al. (1999), that is the trained, the high skill and the low skill groups, tended to use different strategies, and that these were associated with different patterns of working memory loading. The low skill participants' modal matching strategy mainly loaded the central executive, with little load on the slave subsystems; the high skill participants' modal atmosphere strategy loaded the central executive, phonological loop, and passive visual store or cache, and the trained participants' modal logic-equivalent strategy loaded the central executive, phonological loop and spatial subsystems.

Individual difference studies

Scores on measures of central executive functioning, such as sentence span and random generation, seem to be particularly affected by aging in later life, while measures of slave system capacities show less effect (Fisk & Warr, 1996; Van der Linden, Bregart, & Beerton, 1994). Thus it is plausible to suppose that aging would lead to poorer syllogistic performance due to declines in central executive capacity. Gilinsky and Judd (1994) tested 278 adults ranging in age from 19 to 96 years on three verbal measures of working memory span, namely, Baddeley and Hitch's (1974) Auditory Digit Span, Salthouse's (1991) Computation Span, and Daneman and Carpenter's (1980) Reading Span. The span tasks all involved both processing and storage requirements. These measures were fairly well correlated and were combined to give a composite measure of working memory capacity. The participants' scores on syllogistic reasoning showed a steady decline in accuracy, especially after 40 years of age. (Similar age-related deficits in syllogistic performance have also been reported by Fisk & Sharp, 2002.) Gilinsky and Judd carried out regression analyses which indicated that variance in working memory capacity scores explained a significant portion of the age related variance in syllogistic performance.

Capon, Handley, and Dennis (2003) examined individual differences in syllogistic performance as a function of short term and working memory span for visuo-spatial and verbal materials. Syllogistic performance using concrete materials was significantly correlated with all the span measures. This suggests that the participants were using strategies drawing on both verbal and visuo-spatial resources. Gilhooly et al. (1993) did not find evidence of use of the visuo-spatial sketchpad in their dual task study. However, the materials in that study were abstract. It is plausible that concrete materials as used by Capon et al. would be more likely to evoke imagery and hence use of the visuo-spatial sketchpad.

WORKING MEMORY AND STRATEGIES IN REASONING: OVERVIEW

All approaches to reasoning would agree that central executive involvement is to be expected in such tasks (with the possible exception of very highly prac- tised tasks which may become automated). Apart from early studies, which have methodological limitations, all studies have found strong evidence for a major role of the central executive in propositional reasoning, irrespective of particular strategies which seem to be employed (Klauer, et al., 1997; Meiser et al., 2001; Toms et al., 1993). Similar findings regarding the invariable role of the central executive also emerge from dual task studies of syllogistic reasoning. In addition, an individual differences study (Gilinsky & Judd, 1994) found that aging impaired syllogistic performance. This was attributed to a decline in central executive functioning with age and is consistent with the general finding in dual task studies of central executive involvement in reasoning. These results are what would be expected given that, typically, the reasoning tasks are unpractised and evoke strategies requiring executive control so as to be applied successfully.

Widespread interest in the mental models approach has led to a number of studies addressing the possible role of the visuo-spatial sketchpad in reason- ing. Mental models are generally assumed to be spatially represented and so this approach would suggest a strong role for the visuo-spatial sketchpad. Most of the propositional reasoning experiments reviewed above reported positive findings with both abstract and concrete materials and also with participants who had been trained in particular strategies, as well as untrained participants (Klauer et al., 1997; Meiser et al., 2001). In the case of syllogisms with abstract materials, Gilhooly et al. (1993, 1999, 2002) found some involvement of the visuo-spatial sketchpad for participants using more demanding strategies (atmosphere and logic equivalent), whether induced by training or occurring naturally, but not for participants following the less demanding matching strategy.[1] Capon et al. (2003) found evidence for the role of the visuo-spatial sketchpad with concrete materials and untrained participants. Although involvement of the visuo-spatial sketchpad has sometimes been assumed to be a key indicator of a mental models approach being followed, it should be noted that Meiser et al. (2001) did not find that participants trained in a mental models approach were affected more by spatial suppression than were participants trained in mental rules or pragmatic schema approaches.

Studies of the role of the phonological loop in conditional reasoning using dual tasks (Klauer et al., 1997; Meiser et al., 2001) found positive results for untrained participants and for participants trained in a mental models approach, but not for participants trained in mental logic and pragmatic reasoning schemas. Training in a mental models strategy would seem to induce a high-load strategy which draws on all components of working memory. In the case of syllogisms, Gilhooly et al.'s dual task studies found general involvement of the phonological loop although this was only weakly so for the low demand 'matching' strategy. For untrained participants the role of the phonological loop was increased when sequential presentation of premises was employed.

To sum up the work reviewed here (see also Table 3.1), we can conclude that reasoning tasks evoke a number of different strategies (from superficial heuristics to 'deeper' strategies based on the underlying logic of the tasks), and these bring about a variety of loading patterns over the components of working memory. Central executive loading seems to be invariable in the strategies induced by reasoning tasks. The types of strategies induced (e.g., loading on phonological loop or visuo-spatial sketchpad) are affected by the task material (abstract or concrete). Premise presentation (in sequence, or simultaneously and continuously available) affects the degree of use of the 'slave' or 'cache' memories, presumably to compensate for loss of stimulus support.

For future work in this area I suggest that the following issues could be usefully addressed.

(1) The development of better validated procedures for assessing strategy use would be helpful. For example, although the methods used in our syllogistic studies have produced plausible results, their psychometric

---

[1] One question that arises is why atmosphere might be more demanding to apply than matching? I suggest that matching is simpler, in that the matching response is based on information from one premise, while atmosphere requires information in both premises to be combined. Gilhooly et al. (1999) found that groups assessed as predominantly using atmosphere were more susceptible to dual task interference than were predominantly matching groups. This also indicates that atmosphere is the more demanding to apply.

TABLE 3.1
Summary of key studies investigating the role of working memory in reasoning

Study	Notes	WM Subsystem		
		CE	P	V
Propositional reasoning studies				
Klauer et al. (1997)	No training	✔✔	✔	✔
Meiser et al. (2001)	Truth-table training	✔✔	✔✔	✔
	Mental rules training	✔	✔	✔
	Pragmatic reasoning schema training	✔	✔	✔
Markovits et al. (2002)	Abstract material, correlational study	✔	✔	✘
	Concrete material, correlational study	✔	✔	✔
Categorical syllogism studies				
Gilhooly et al. (1993)	Simultaneous presentation	✔✔	✔	✘
Gilhooly et al. (2002)	Sequential presentation	✔✔	✔	✔
Gilhooly et al. (1999)	Simultaneous presentation, high skill	✔✔	✔	✔
	Simultaneous presentation, low skill	✔	✘	✘
	Simultaneous presentation, trained	✔✔	✔	✔
Capon et al. (2003)	Concrete materials, correlational study	✔	✔	✔

Notes: Working memory subsystems are as follows: CE central executive; P phonological; VS visuo-spatial. Two ticks indicates strong involvement, one tick indicates some involvement, a cross indicates no involvement.

properties are unknown: Methods of known reliability and validity would be very useful.

(2) Typically, different individuals have been assigned to different dual task groups. It would be useful to assess individual differences in susceptibility to different dual tasks by testing people under a range of dual task conditions and to relate differences in their susceptibility to the strategies being used. In addition, results from independent group studies indicating involvement of two slave memories can be ambiguous in that significant interference results could arise from two separate subgroups each using one slave memory only in their strategy implementations. Having all participants tested with a range of dual tasks would help determine whether typical strategies draw on two or more working memory components.

(3) A general problem for the study of working memory in complex tasks is to clarify relationships between the multi-component approach and the individual difference approach. The individual difference approach has typically used working memory span measures which give a single global indication of capacity for storage and processing tasks. However, such single measures are ambiguous regarding the relative contributions of central executive and slave components to overall performance. There is a need for more differentiated (and well-validated) measures which assess executive and slave capacities

separately. Such measures could be used in individual difference studies to test conclusions from dual task experiments from a different angle. For example, they could determine whether individual differences in working memory capacity overall, and for individual components, are linked to the use of different strategies.

REFERENCES

Andrade, J. (2001). The contribution of working memory to conscious experience. In J. Andrade (Ed.), *Working memory in perspective* (pp. 60–78). Hove, UK: Psychology Press.
Baddeley, A. D. (1992) Is working memory working? *Quarterly Journal of Experimental Psychology, 44A*, 1–32.
Baddeley, A. D. (2000). The episodic buffer: A new component of working memory? *Trends in Cognitive Sciences, 4*, 417–423.
Baddeley, A. D., & Hitch, G. J. (1974). Working memory. In G. H. Bower (Ed.), *Recent advances in learning and motivation* (Vol. VIII, pp. 47–89). New York: Academic Press.
Baddeley, A. D., & Logie, R. H. (1999). Working memory: The multiple component model. In A. Miyake & P. Shah (Eds.), *Models of working memory: Mechanisms of active maintenance and executive control* (pp. 28–61). Cambridge: Cambridge University Press.
Baddeley, A. D., Logie, R. H., Nimmo-Smith, I., & Brereton, N. (1985). Components of fluent reading. *Journal of Memory and Language, 24*, 119–131.
Barrouillet, P., & Lecas, J-F. (1998). How can mental models account for content effects in conditional reasoning: A developmental perspective. *Cognition, 67*, 209–253.
Barrouillet, P., & Lecas, J-F. (1999). Mental models in conditional reasoning and working memory. *Thinking and Reasoning, 5*, 289–302.
Braine, M. D. S. (1978). On the relation between the natural logic of reasoning and standard logic. *Psychological Review, 85*, 1–21.
Braine, M. D. S., & O'Brien, D. P. (1998). *Mental logic*. Mahwah, NJ: Lawrence Erlbaum Associates, Inc.
Braine, M. D. S., Reiser, B. J., & Rumain, B. (1984). Some empirical justification for a theory of natural propositional logic. In G. H. Bower (Ed.), *The psychology of learning and motivation: Advances in research and theory* (Vol. 18, pp. 313–371). New York: Academic Press.
Bruner, J. S., Goodnow, J. J., & Austin, G. A. (1956). *A study of thinking*. New York: Wiley.
Capon, A., Handley, S. J., & Dennis, I. (2003). *Working memory and individual differences in reasoning*. Paper presented at the 4th International Conference on Thinking, Durham, September.
Chater, N., & Oaksford, M. R. (1999). The probability heuristic model of syllogistic reasoning. *Cognitive Psychology, 38*, 191–258.
Cheng P. W., & Holyoak, K. J. (1989). On the natural selection of reasoning theories. *Cognition, 31*, 61–83.
Cheng P. W., Holyoak, K. J., Nisbett, R. E., & Oliver, L. M. (1986). Pragmatic versus syntactic approaches to training deductive reasoning. *Cognitive Psychology, 18*, 293–328.
Daneman, M., & Carpenter. P. A. (1980). Individual differences in working memory and reading. *Journal of Verbal Learning and Verbal Behavior, 19*, 450–466.
Della Sala, S., & Logie, R. H. (1993). When working memory does not work: The role of working memory in neuropsychology. In F. Boller and H. Spinnler (Eds.), *Handbook of neuropsychology* (Vol. 8, pp. 1–63). Amsterdam: Elsevier.
Engle, R. W., Carullo, J. J., & Collins, K. W. (1991). Individual differences in working memory for comprehension and following directions. *Journal of Educational Research, 84*, 253–262.

Erickson, J. R. (1978). Research in syllogistic reasoning. In R. Revlin & R. E. Meyer (Eds.), *Human reasoning* (pp. 39–50). Washington, DC: Winston.

Evans, F. J. (1978). Monitoring attention deployment by random number generation: An index to measure subjective randomness. *Bulletin of the Psychonomic Society, 12*, 35–38.

Evans, J. St. B. T., & Brooks, P. G. (1981). Competing with reasoning: A test of the working memory hypothesis. *Current Psychological Research, 1*, 139–147.

Evans, J. St. B. T., Newstead, S. E., & Byrne, R. (1993). *Human reasoning: The psychology of deduction.* Hove, UK: Lawrence Erlbaum Associates, Ltd.

Fisher, D. L. (1981). A three-factor model of syllogistic reasoning: The study of isolable stages. *Memory and Cognition, 9*, 496–514.

Fisk, J. E., & Warr, P. (1996). Age and working memory: The role of perceptual speed, the central executive, and the phonological loop. *Psychology and Aging, 11*, 316–323.

Fisk, J. E., & Sharp, C. (2002). Syllogistic reasoning and cognitive ageing, *Quarterly Journal of Psychology, 55A*, 1273–1294.

Ford, M. (1995). Two modes of mental representation and problem solution in syllogistic reasoning. *Cognition, 54*, 1–71.

Gilhooly, K. J. (1998). Working memory, strategies and reasoning tasks. In R. H. Logie & K. J. Gilhooly (Eds.), *Working memory and thinking* (pp. 7–22). Hove, UK: Psychology Press.

Gilhooly, K. J., Logie, R. H., Wetherick, N. E., & Wynn, V. (1993). Working memory and strategies in syllogistic reasoning tasks. *Memory and Cognition, 21*, 115–124.

Gilhooly, K. J., Logie, R. H., & Wynn, V. (1999). Syllogistic reasoning tasks, working memory and skill. *European Journal of Cognitive Psychology, 11*, 473–498.

Gilhooly, K. J., Logie, R. H., & Wynn, V. (2002). Syllogistic reasoning tasks and working memory: Evidence from sequential presentation of premises. *Current Psychological Research, 21*, 111–120.

Gilinsky, A. S., & Judd, B. B. (1994). Working memory and bias in reasoning across the life span. *Psychology and Aging, 9*, 356–371.

Hall, T. (1970). *Carl Friedrich Gauss: A biography.* (A. Froderberg, Trans.). Cambridge, MA: MIT Press.

Johnson-Laird, P. N. (1983). *Mental models.* Cambridge: Cambridge University Press.

Johnson-Laird, P. N., & Bara, B. (1984). Syllogistic inference. *Cognition, 16*, 1–62.

Johnson-Laird, P. N., & Byrne, R. (1991). *Deduction.* Hove: Lawrence Erlbaum Associates, Ltd.

Just, M. A., & Carpenter, P. A. (1992). A capacity theory of comprehension: Individual differences in working memory. *Psychological Review, 99*, 122–149.

Klauer, K. C., Stegmaier, R., & Meiser, T. (1997) Working memory involvement in propositional and spatial reasoning. *Thinking and Reasoning, 3*, 9–48.

Klauer, K. C., Meiser, T., & Naumer, B. (2000). Training propositional reasoning. *Quarterly Journal of Experimental Psychology, 53A*, 868–895.

Kyllonen, P. C., & Chrystal, R. E. (1990). Reasoning ability is (little more than) working memory capacity?! *Intelligence, 14*, 389–433.

Kyllonen, P. C., & Stephens, D. L. (1990). Cognitive abilities as determinants of success in acquiring logic skill. In Special Issue: *Frontiers of learning and individual differences: Paradigms in transition.* MOE-Project Learning Abilities Measurement Program. Brooks Air Force Base, TX: US Air Force Human Resources Lab.

Logie, R. H. (1995) *Visuo-spatial working memory.* Hove: Lawrence Erlbaum Associates, Ltd.

Logie, R. H., Englekamp, J., Dehn, D., & Rudkin, S. (2001). Actions, mental actions, and working memory. In M. Denis, R. H. Logie, C. Cornoldi, M. De Vega, & J. Engelkamp (Eds.), *Imagery, language and visuo-spatial thinking* (pp. 161–184). Hove, UK: Psychology Press.

Markovits, H., Doyon, C., & Simoneau, M. (2002). Individual differences in working memory and conditional reasoning with concrete and abstract content. *Thinking and Reasoning, 8*, 97–164.

Meiser, T., Klauer, K. C., & Naumer, B. (2001). Propositional reasoning and working memory: The role of prior training and pragmatic content. *Acta Psychologica, 106*, 303–327.

Miyake, A., & Shah, P. (1999). Toward unified theories of working memory. In A. Miyake & P. Shah (Eds.), *Models of working memory: Mechanisms of active maintenance and executive control* (pp. 442–482). Cambridge: Cambridge University Press.

Rips, L. J. (1994). The psychology of proof: Deductive reasoning in human thinking. Cambridge, MA: MIT Press.

Roberts, M. J. (1993). Human reasoning: Deduction rules or mental models, or both? *Quarterly Journal of Experimental Psychology, 46A*, 569–589.

Roberts, M. J. (2000). Individual differences in reasoning strategies: A problem to solve or an opportunity to seize? In W. Schaeken, G. De Vooght, A. Vandierendonck, & G. D'Ydewalle (Eds.), *Deductive reasoning and strategies* (pp. 23–48). Mahwah, NJ: Lawrence Erlbaum Associates, Inc.

Salthouse, T. A. (1991). *Status of working memory as a mediator of adult age differences in cognition.* Paper presented at the 99th Annual Convention of the American Psychological Association, San Francisco.

Sternberg, R. J., & Turner, M. E. (1981). Components of syllogistic reasoning. *Acta Psychologica, 47*, 245–265.

Toms, M., Morris, N., & Ward, D. (1993). Working memory and conditional reasoning. *Quarterly Journal of Experimental Psychology, 46A*, 679–699.

Turner, M. L., & Engle, R. (1989). Is working memory capacity task dependent? *Journal of Memory and Language, 28*, 127–154.

Van der Linden, M., Bregart, S., & Beerton, A. (1994). Age related differences in updating working memory. *British Journal of Psychology, 84*, 145–152.

Wetherick, N. E., & Gilhooly, K. J. (1995). 'Atmosphere', matching and logic in syllogistic reasoning. *Current Psychology, 14*, 169–178.

Wilkins, M. C. (1928). The effect of changed material on the ability to do formal syllogistic reasoning. *Archives of Psychology, 102*.

Woodworth, R. J., & Sells, S. B. (1935). An atmosphere effect in formal syllogistic reasoning. *Journal of Experimental Psychology, 18*, 451–460.

Yuill, N., Oakhill, J., & Parkin, A. J. (1988). Working memory, comprehension ability and the resolution of text anomaly. *British Journal of Psychology, 80*, 351–361.

CHAPTER FOUR

Verbal and spatial strategies in reasoning

Alison M. Bacon, Simon J. Handley, and Stephen E. Newstead
Centre for Thinking and Language, University of Plymouth, UK

A considerable body of research has attempted to determine the nature of reasoning processes. Two major and opposing schools of thought have emerged. Rule-based theories (e.g., Braine & O'Brien, 1998; Rips, 1994) suggest that individuals possess an inherent mental logic. Reasoning involves transducing premises into an abstract logical form (based on the syntactic structure of a given problem) and applying formal deduction rules to generate a new proposition. This is then converted into a conclusion appropriate for the task. As such, errors can be accounted for by the number and complexity of rules required.

In contrast, proponents of the mental models theory (e.g., Bucciarelli and Johnson-Laird, 1999; Johnson-Laird & Byrne, 1991) suggest that reasoning involves the construction of specialised mental representations, composed of elements analogous to possible states of the world. These models are constructed not from the syntactic structure of information, but from its semanticity: the meanings and background knowledge associated with premise information. As such, deductions are 'guided by more than logic' (Johnson-Laird & Byrne, 1991, p. 21). In general terms, the theory proposes that the deduction process has three stages: (1) construction of an initial model, enriched by context-dependent information and background knowledge; (2) generation of a putative conclusion based on the model; (3) a search for counter-examples which may refute the putative conclusion, i.e., models where the premises are true but the conclusion is false. If no such counter-example is found, the conclusion is accepted. Mental models theory does not presume the use of formal inference rules, but does suppose an implicit understanding of basic logical principles, for instance, that for a conclusion to be valid, it must be true given that the premises are true. Errors occur as a function of the number of models required to make an inference (see for instance, Bucciarelli & Johnson-Laird, 1999). For a review of mental models theory see Johnson-Laird (2001).

Recently however, some researchers have begun to acknowledge that these approaches may not be as universal as once accepted and that there may be individual differences in the strategies that people use. It is these individual differences which are the focus of the present chapter. Johnson-Laird, Savary, and Bucciarelli (2000, p. 210) present a useful working definition of strategy as 'the sequence of steps that an individual follows in solving or attempting to solve a problem'. Each step in the strategy is referred to as a *tactic*. As such, their definition echoes that of earlier work by Sternberg (for instance, 1982) who described the execution of a reasoning strategy as comprising a combination of processes which he termed *components*. Evans (2000) adds that strategy use is dynamic and flexible. Individuals can therefore choose whether or not to adopt a particular strategy, or can change strategy as task demands differ. Hence, he claims, strategies do not result from the operation of hardwired mechanisms, nor are they constrained by the demands of earlier learning.

SYLLOGISTIC REASONING

First let us look at evidence for individual differences in strategies for one of the most widely studied reasoning tasks, syllogistic reasoning. A syllogism is an argument comprising three propositions: two premises and a conclusion. They may be presented with either abstract content, for example:

> All B are A
> Some C are B
> Therefore, Some C are A

or thematic content:

> All teachers are psychologists
> Some writers are teachers
> Therefore, some writers are psychologists.

Each syllogism contains three terms (A, B and C, or psychologists, teachers and writers in the above examples) one of which, the middle term, B (teachers), is common to both premises. The classic syllogistic inference is to determine, from the information given in the premises, the relationship which is not explicitly stated, i.e., that between the two end terms, A and C. This forms the conclusion. Each proposition contains one of four possible quantifiers (*All, Some, None, Some . . . not*) which describe the relationship between the terms. The *mood* of the syllogism is described in terms of the combination of quantifiers present and is given the designation shown in Table 4.1. Syllogism structure is also described in terms of one of four *figures* based on the arrangement of the terms (see Table 4.1).

As there are four possible quantifiers, there are 16 distinct premise combinations (moods) associated with each figure, and hence 64 possible syllogistic forms. Given that each conclusion will contain one of the four quantifiers, and its terms may follow the order A-C or C-A, this gives a total of 512 possible syllogisms. However, of these relatively few have logically valid conclusions (Garnham & Oakhill, 1994, chapter 6, discuss in some detail methods of determining syllogistic validity). For the present purposes we will restrict our discussion to the 27 syllogisms described as valid by Johnson-Laird and Byrne (1991).

Theories of syllogistic reasoning

The rule-based and mental model theories have been applied to syllogisms, but a number of other theories have tried to explain syllogistic inference in terms of various non-logical heuristic processes. Wetherick and Gilhooly (1990) claim that when the logic of a problem is not immediately apparent, reasoners generate a response by choosing a conclusion where the quantifier *matches* one of those in the premises. Where there is a choice of quantifier, they select that which is the most conservative, i.e., that which makes an assertion about the smaller proportion of whatever is represented by the subject term. As such, for the syllogism quoted previously, the matching theory would predict the conclusion *Some C are A*. Similarly, Chater and

TABLE 4.1
The four syllogistic moods, and the four syllogistic figures
(Johnson-Laird and Bara, 1984)

Quantifier	Mood description		Designation
All	Universal affirmative		A
Some	Particular affirmative		I
None	Universal negative		E
Some . . . not	Particular negative		O
Figure 1	Figure 2	Figure 3	Figure 4
A–B	B–A	A–B	B–A
B–C	C–B	C–B	B–C

Oaksford (1999) propose the *probability heuristics model* of syllogistic reasoning within which probability-based heuristics allow for the generation of the most informative valid conclusion. The most important of these is the *min*-heuristic which suggests that the quantifier for the conclusion will be the same as that for the least informative premise (the min-premise). For some syllogisms, the min-conclusion may *probabilistically entail* (p-entail) further logical conclusions of a form different to either premise, i.e., if the min-conclusion is *No X are Y*, then it is probable that *Some X are not Y*. Overall, reasoning about the likely relationship between terms is based on the relative informativeness of the premises and this theory claims that such simple, but 'rational' strategies are justified by probability theory rather than formal logic.

Strategies in syllogistic reasoning

Although one of the categories of theory discussed earlier may indeed underpin all syllogistic reasoning, differences have been observed whereby some individuals appear to use strategies based on mental models, whilst others employ strategies that are rule based. Ford (1995) asked subjects to generate conclusions to the 27 valid syllogisms (as per Johnson-Laird & Byrne, 1991). She presented extensive verbal and written protocol data to show that of the 20 subjects all but four appeared to display one of two types of behaviour. Those which Ford termed *spatial reasoners* used shapes such as circles or squares placed in different spatial configurations to represent the relationships between the terms in the premises. They provided written protocols illustrating such procedures diagrammatically, and their verbal reports frequently described these relationships in terms of group membership, sets and subsets. Ford likens the spatial diagrams to traditional Euler circles: diagrammatic models representing set membership and the relationships between sets. Interestingly, this is a strategy which Polk and Newell (1995) claim is unlikely to be employed by untrained individuals. Erickson (1978) has also proposed that reasoners use a mental analogue of Euler circles in syllogistic tasks, representing each premise in turn and then combining the two sets of diagrams to represent the relationship between all three terms in the syllogism. However, Ford describes how spatial reasoners represent the relationship between terms in the first premise and then add information about the third term to that representation in a way which reflects its relationship with the common term.

Ford identified six syllogisms where she claimed there was just one way in which this relationship could be represented. These largely correspond to the single-model syllogisms identified by mental model theory (Johnson-Laird & Byrne, 1991). Ford described these as having *totally constrained* representations, and claimed that spatial reasoners perform best on these. The remaining syllogisms Ford described as being *less constrained*, and she identified multiple ways in which the premises might be represented. The majority of these would be categorised as *multiple model* according to Johnson-Laird and Byrne, with just four (those containing *All–Some* premises) classed as single model. Ford presents data to show that her spatial reasoners performed less well on less-constrained problems though, interestingly, the difference was not significant when only the single model problems (totally constrained versus less constrained) were compared.

The other main strategy group Ford identified was referred to as *verbal reasoners*. Ford claimed these showed no evidence of using mental models at all. Rather, they displayed various types of substitution behaviour: To reach a conclusion, they replaced the middle term from one premise with the end term from the other, as if solving an algebraic problem. Although Ford does highlight cases of what she termed 'naive substitution' (p. 25), where terms were replaced literally and without regard for quantifiers or logical relationships, she claims that the majority (7 out of 8 verbal reasoners in her sample) showed awareness of logical principles, for instance, that *All A are B* is not logically equivalent to *All B are A*. Ford concluded that the substitution strategy involved the application of logical inference rules which she likened to modus ponens and modus tollens – inference rules recognised by logicians for centuries.[1] Much research has shown that modus tollens is more difficult to apply (see for instance, Evans, Newstead, & Byrne, 1993), and Ford reports a significant detriment in verbal reasoners' performance on syllogisms which she claims require this type of rule. Where the logical form of the problem made the application of these rules difficult, she proposed that verbal reasoners use 'sophisticated substitution' – a process which involves the modification or reformulation of one of the premises in order that the simple rules can be applied (for instance, realising that the premise *All A are B* implies that there are some B who are A, and hence 'rewriting' the premise as *Some B are A*). Again, problems with this requirement were associated with poorer performance. Interestingly, Ford described only these two strategy types, and does not explicitly suggest that any of her subjects used simple heuristic processes such as matching.

Ford's sample was small (N = 20) and her argument relied heavily on verbal protocols. Ericsson and Simon (e.g., 1993) have written at length about the implications of this, and Chater and Oaksford (1999) claim that

---

[1] Modus ponens, or affirming the antecedent, describes the use of a rule in which one given entity entails another. Hence given the conditional premise *If p then q*, and the condition *p*, then the reasoner can deduce *q*. Modus tollens (denying the consequent) is the inference that may be made where the condition presented is *not q*. The correct response is *not p*. In syllogistic terms, applying modus ponens to the premise *All A are B*, for example, leads to the supposition *If there are things which are A, then there are things which are A and B*. (Manktelow, 1999, presents an explanation of the application of these logical rules in syllogistic reasoning).

individual differences such as those described by Ford may have been invoked by employing verbal protocol methodology. Nevertheless, her findings seem to suggest that individual differences are present and that these should be taken into account by mental model and rule-based theories. Such a view has been echoed elsewhere, for instance by Roberts (1993, 2000). However, earlier work by Johnson-Laird and Bara (1984) did suggest a possible implementation of mental models theory which involved the supposedly verbal process of substitution. In addition, Bucciarelli and Johnson-Laird (1999) have shown that people can construct external models of premises and use multiple models to evaluate putative conclusions where necessary. A purely verbal strategy cannot account for this. However, whilst maintaining that even the verbal strategy may be formulated so as to involve the manipulation of mental models, they agree with Ford that the strategies remain underspecified and are a matter for investigation. As Roberts (2000) points out, the number of individual differences studied in reasoning is very small, and replications are desirable. Hence, Experiment 1 aimed to replicate and extend Ford's (1995) study.

EXPERIMENT 1

Our motivation for Experiment 1 was twofold: first to determine whether the verbal and spatial strategies which Ford describes are robust; second, whether it is possible to identify and differentiate between strategy users without the need for concurrent verbal reports. In one experimental condition (N = 20) we carried out a direct replication of Ford's study. In the second (N = 32) we asked subjects to work through the syllogisms just once, writing down their working, and these individuals provided no verbal reports. In addition, all subjects completed a short questionnaire which was intended independently to elicit evidence of the use of different strategies. Its 13 items were developed in line with the behaviours which Ford associated with verbal and spatial strategies. Questionnaires were scored such that a high score represented a high degree of spatial reasoning and a low score indicated a high degree of verbal reasoning. Reliability analysis suggested the elimination of five items with low item to total correlations, resulting in an optimum Cronbach's Alpha of .68. The questionnaire items are presented in Table 4.2.

The findings largely fulfilled the aims of the experiment (see also Bacon, Handley, & Newstead, 2003). The descriptions of verbal and spatial strategies presented by Ford (1995) suggested that written protocols should show very distinct characteristics. Using these as classification criteria, highly consistent verbal (N = 28) and spatial reasoners (N = 18), who used just one strategy for all trials, could easily be identified. However, five subjects produced mixed protocols, for instance, using what appeared to be propositional

TABLE 4.2
The final eight items of the reasoning behaviour questionnaire

1	To what extent did you attempt to reverse the position of the occupations within the statements?
2	To what extent did you use mental images of shapes (e.g., circles/other shapes) in spatial relationships in deciding on a conclusion?
3	To what extent did you attempt to substitute terms/occupations from one statement to another (i.e., switch the occupations around between statements)?
4	To what extent did you think about the words used in the statements?
5	To what extent did you attempt to combine the two statements into one to form a single, longer, verbal description?
6	To what extent did you represent the information in linguistic form (e.g., sentences/words) in deciding on a conclusion?
7	Did you develop a rule, or set of rules, to help you which you then re-applied to each subsequent problem? YES/NO
8	Did you think about sets/Venn diagrams (similar to that shown below) either using circles or any other shape? YES/NO

Note: For items 1–6 above, subjects were asked to indicate their responses to each item on a 5-point scale from 'not at all' to 'a lot'.

notation (arrows, mathematical symbols, etc.), but also presenting the information spatially, or producing verbal-style protocols for some problems and spatial ones for others. As there were so few of these mixed reasoners, we will concentrate on the two main strategy groups, verbal and spatial. Protocols 1 and 2 present examples of their written protocols (see Figure 4.1).

Responses to the questionnaire appeared to provide converging evidence for the presence of verbal and spatial strategies. Interestingly, subjects allocated to the mixed strategy group generally provided mixed or conflicting responses to the questionnaire items. Analysis of variance comparing mean questionnaire scores for the three strategy groups indicated a significant difference between verbal ($M = 18.2$ out of 32) and spatial reasoners ($M = 24.8$), with the mixed group falling between ($M = 22.2$), $F(2, 48) = 10.35$, $p < .01$. Scheffé post-hoc comparisons indicated that the difference between scores for the verbal and spatial groups was highly significant ($p < .01$). When the mixed strategy group was removed, K-means cluster analysis applied to the questionnaire items revealed two distinct clusters. Pearson's Chi square suggested a highly significant association between strategy type and questionnaire response, $\chi^2(1) = 12.3$, $p < .01$.

Protocols 1 and 2 are typical of those observed both by ourselves and Ford, but do they actually represent differences in underlying reasoning processes, or just in how reasoners have chosen to represent the premises on paper? Examination of verbal protocol data suggests the former. The 28 verbal reasoners frequently referred to actions such as replacing, substituting and cancelling terms, and their features are typical of those which Ford

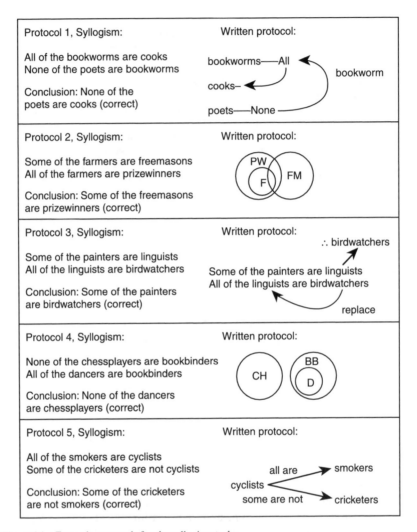

Figure 4.1   Example protocols for the syllogism tasks.

claims describe the behaviours exhibited by verbal reasoners. For example, Protocol 3 (Figure 4.1) was accompanied by the following verbal protocol:

Verbal protocol given in conjunction with Protocol 3 (Figure 4.1): 'Some of the painters must be birdwatchers, because again you know that all linguists are birdwatchers, you can just replace there. You can just replace linguists with birdwatchers. So you can just put arrows there and some of the painters are birdwatchers.'

For many of the verbal reasoners, examination of the protocols suggests similar procedures to Protocol 3, and which Ford termed *naive substitution*, that is, they obtain a value for the B term from the first universal affirmative premise they encounter, whatever the presentation order, then simply substitute that value for B in the other premise to obtain a conclusion with the same quantifier as that premise. This substitution seems to be made literally by term and position, irrespective of the quantifier in the premise where the substitution is made, and frequently produces the correct conclusion, as the example shows.

Eighteen spatial subjects produced verbal reports in which they described the terms and their interrelationships as groups or subsets, along with written protocols which suggest, according to Ford's criteria, that they were using a spatial reasoning strategy. These protocols typically represented terms within circles placed in differing spatial relationships to represent the relationship of the terms within and between the premises. For instance, Protocol 4 (Figure 4.1) was accompanied by the following verbal protocol:

> *Verbal protocol given in conjunction with Protocol 4 (Figure 4.1)*: 'So now we have the chessplayers and the bookbinders as two completely separate groups . . . and all of the dancers are bookbinders so we have the dancers as a subset of bookbinders . . . and dancers . . . none of the dancers are chessplayers.'

Spatial reasoners appear to begin by constructing a representation of the first premise they are presented with, irrespective of mood, and even when the later premise is universal affirmative. Information from the second premise regarding the C term is then added to this representation in a manner which describes its relationship with the common term B.

Are verbal and spatial strategies equally effective?

In terms of overall percentage of accurate conclusions, we found no significant difference in performance between verbal (44.4%) and spatial reasoners (50.4%), $t(44) = 1.4$, $p > 0.05$. Ford does not directly compare the overall performance of her verbal and spatial groups, but the data she presents for individual syllogisms suggests that her subjects performed similarly to ours (48.5% for verbal reasoners; 49.1% for spatial reasoners). In the current study, for both strategy groups, there was no significant difference in performance between the verbal protocol and no protocol conditions ($p > 0.05$ in both cases).

When individual syllogisms are considered, some performance differences become apparent. Ford makes the distinction between what she terms same-form and different-form syllogisms. *Same-form* problems are those where the quantifier of the valid conclusion matches that of at least one of the premises.

For verbal strategy users, the naive substitution described previously can be successfully applied to all same-form syllogisms (Protocols 1 and 3 are examples, see Figure 4.1) and hence these are easy for them. *Different-form* syllogisms are those where the conclusion quantifier is different to that of either premise. Because the verbal strategy relies entirely on premise quantifiers in generating conclusions, it can lead to difficulty for this type of problem. Of the 27 valid problems used, 14 are same form and 13 different form. On same-form problems, verbal (73%) and spatial reasoners (71.8%) perform comparably, $F(1,44) = 0.03$, $MSE = 408.9$, $p > .05$. However, not so for different-form syllogisms (13.7% and 27.4% respectively), $F (1,44) = 5.0$, $MSE = 408.9$, $p < .05$. In fact, 72.3% of conclusions generated by verbal strategy users to different-form problems were incorrect by virtue of containing the *same* quantifier as one of the premises. This figure was 60% for spatial strategy users. In mental-model terms, the different-form syllogisms are three-model, and hence the most difficult of all (Johnson-Laird & Byrne, 1991), and these are also described by Ford as less constrained. However, unlike Ford, we found very little evidence of spatial reasoners attempting to represent multiple models of the premises, and this seemed to be a major factor in their difficulty with different-form syllogisms.

A more meticulous examination of syllogisms along the lines of Ford's analysis reveals that our reasoners differed from hers in other ways. For instance, Ford makes a distinction between problems which require the modus ponens and modus tollens forms of her rules, and shows that her verbal reasoners found the latter more difficult. However, in no instance did we find any equivalent difference. Rather than attempting the more formal or sophisticated substitution process that Ford describes for more difficult syllogisms, our verbal reasoners appeared to use naive substitution throughout. On more difficult problems containing an *All* premise, they frequently made precisely the type of conversion errors that Ford claims her reasoners eschew (assuming that *All A are B* is equivalent to *All B are A*). Similarly, for spatial reasoners, we found none of the performance differences as a function of premise constraint that Ford presented. For both types of syllogism, our spatial strategy users tended to represent a single model of the premises and show little evidence of considering alternative representations on less-constrained problems. For a more thorough exposition of Experiment 1, see Bacon et al. (2003).

Variations in tactics within strategies

Not all verbal reasoners apply substitution in the pure sense described above. In a follow-up study to Experiment 1 (N = 66), subjects produced concurrent written protocols but no verbal reports. They were also asked to complete a questionnaire comprising the eight items from Experiment 1 (see Table 4.2) plus an additional item requiring them to a write a brief narrative describing their strategy usage. From the written protocols, we identified 25 subjects who drew flowchart type diagrams, typically showing the middle term as central, with the other terms linked to it by lines or arrows and the quantifiers indicated by words. For an example, see Protocol 5 (Figure 4.1). According to Ford's descriptions, such protocols are indicative of verbal reasoning and hence any subject presenting such data were allocated to the verbal group in Experiment 1. However, the additional descriptive data revealed that similar diagrams were used by subgroups of both verbal and mixed reasoners. The majority who used such representations also presented a typical verbal strategy questionnaire profile and their responses to the open narrative suggested that, for these people, the diagram provided a way of simplifying and integrating the premises in propositional form. After drawing the diagram, they frequently cancelled out the middle term (literally on paper, or mentally) and linked the other two terms together according to their quantifiers in order to form a conclusion. Several individuals described the application of an informal rule for the linking of quantifiers and production of a conclusion along the lines of:

all + some = some
all + none = none
all + some-not = some-not
none + some = none

Such rules present similarities to the principles highlighted for the matching strategy (Wetherick and Gilhooly, 1990, 1995) described earlier, and make similar predictions. As the linking rules shown above clearly result in a conclusion containing a quantifier corresponding to that from one of the premises, their application leads to errors for different-form syllogisms. Hence, many of these people presented a similar error profile to those using substitution. This approach is clearly verbal-propositional in nature and related to substitution, though not as effective: Comparison of performance revealed that people using substitution performed significantly better (65% correct) than those who employed the linking rule strategy (36.5%); $t(31) = 4.9$, $p < .01$.

It could be argued that there is also a spatial element to the use of flowchart diagrams, and indeed a minority of subjects who presented such data appeared to use a mixed reasoning strategy. For them, the strategy appeared to involve two stages, first spatial *then* verbal: These subjects first constructed a spatial layout which helped them to clarify information and organise the occupation groups in their mind in the same way as Euler circles might for a more conventional spatial strategy user. But then they either applied a propositional rule to link the A and C parts of the model and draw a conclusion according to the quantifiers, or they applied substitution. Hence the inference process itself, i.e., drawing a conclusion, is propositional, even though the information may be classed as represented spatially. A similar description of the relationship between spatial representations and rule-based reasoning has been suggested by Rips (1986).

THE ROLE OF WORKING MEMORY IN REASONING STRATEGIES

As we have seen, individuals have a strong tendency to use either visuo-spatial or verbal-propositional representations when reasoning syllogistically. What is it about these individuals that leads them to prefer one strategy over another? Part of the answer may relate to working memory capacity – a factor long associated with reasoning performance (see for instance Gilhooly, 1998; chapter 3 this volume; Johnson-Laird, 2001).

Working memory and reasoning

Baddeley (1986) describes a tripartite model of *working memory* comprising a controlling attentional system, termed the *central executive* which oversees and co-ordinates the operation of two slave systems: The *phonological loop* is concerned with processing linguistic material and comprises a phonological store served by an articulatory control process which allows for the mainten-ance of memory traces by means of subvocal rehearsal. The other system, the *visuo-spatial sketchpad* is responsible for the construction and manipulation of visuo-spatial images. It can be fed directly through visual perception or indirectly through the generation of a visual image. Hence, information pre-sented in non-visual modalities can be converted into a spatial code through imagery. Storage is maintained by a spatial control process thought to involve eye tracking. However, these slave systems are thought to play a rather more passive role in higher cognitive tasks, which involve processing as well as storage of information. For instance, simple measures of phonological loop capacity, such as digit recall span, do not predict accuracy in reading com-prehension, whereas more complex measures, which are assumed to also reflect the role of the central executive, do predict this (e.g., Daneman & Carpenter, 1980; Gilhooly, 1998; Shah & Miyake, 1996). For a discussion of recent developments in the working memory model, see Baddeley and Logie (1999).

A number of studies have investigated the involvement of the three com-ponents of working memory in reasoning, primarily through the use of dual-task methodology, whereby secondary tasks are used to reduce available capacity for particular subcomponents. The phonological loop is typically loaded by secondary tasks which suppress subvocal articulation (such as concurrent repetition of a given word or number) and the visuo-spatial sketchpad by concurrent spatial tasks, such as moving the non-preferred hand in a set spatial pattern. Gilhooly, Logie, Wetherick, and Wynn (1993) found that such secondary tasks did not significantly reduce syllogistic reasoning performance. However, small but consistent interference by articulatory suppression was observed. Another secondary task, random number generation, did significantly affect performance and latencies for premise processing. This task was intended to interfere with the working of the central executive. These findings suggest that the central executive plays a major role in syllogistic reasoning with some minor involvement of the phonological loop (see also Gilhooly, Logie, & Wynn, 2002, in which overall working memory load of the task was raised). However, no evidence was found for a visuo-spatial sketchpad contribution. Gilhooly et al. note that this goes against some model-oriented theories such as Euler circles, which have suggested the use of mental imagery. However, many subjects in their studies used superficial heuristics, and Gilhooly et al. suggest that greater involvement of the visuo-spatial sketchpad might be observed if subjects were induced to employ other strategies.

Verbal and spatial strategies and working memory

If the working memory model is considered in conjunction with differences in the use of strategies, the propositional nature of our verbal strategy suggests at least some involvement of the phonological loop. The research reviewed above suggests minimal (if any) involvement of the visuo-spatial sketchpad in reasoning. However, some of the reasoners in our studies clearly use a visuo-spatial approach which suggests that the visuo-spatial sketchpad may be important for these people. Certainly, tasks which are thought to have a very strong spatial component, such as linear syllogisms containing spatial adjectives, *are* affected by secondary tasks which load the visuo-spatial sketchpad, though again the central executive also seems to play a major role (e.g., Vandierendonck & De Vooght, 1997). Shah and Miyake (1996) postulated a fractionated central executive with resources for spatial and linguistic information. To demonstrate this, they employed a series of simple and complex measures of verbal and spatial working memory span, the simple measures drawing on one or other of the slave systems and the complex measures drawing on either of these plus the central executive. Using similar methodology, Handley, Capon, Copp, and Harper (2002) presented evidence that two systems for dealing with spatial and verbal representations were involved in both conditional reasoning and spatial problem solving.

Capon, Handley, and Dennis (2003) extended this research to syllogistic reasoning. They argued that if Shah and Miyake's thesis was correct, and verbal and spatial central executive resources are dissociable, then established theories of reasoning would offer differing predictions regarding the role of working memory in reasoning. Rule-based theories, which emphasise the role of propositional or language-based representations (hence likewise the verbal strategy), would suggest that syllogistic tasks would draw preferentially on verbal resources. In contrast, model theories (which encompass the spatial strategy) would predict a more important role for spatial working memory. Subjects completed two syllogistic reasoning tasks (with visual versus verbal presentation of the premises) plus a series of working memory span measures. Correlational analysis indicated that syllogistic reasoning performance was predicted by both spatial and verbal working memory span. Furthermore, a confirmatory factor analysis showed that an orthogonal three-factor model, comprising a verbal, spatial and general factor, fitted the data well, χ^2 (61) = 69, p = .23; CFI = .97. Table 4.3 shows the factor loadings of all the experimental measures. Interestingly, Capon et al. (2003) have since tested this three-factor model on Shah and Miyake's data and found it to be an excellent fit χ^2 (17) = 10.7, p = .87, CFI = 1. Overall, syllogistic reasoning performance (irrespective of presentation modality) loaded significantly, and to a similar degree, on *both* verbal and spatial working memory resources, and also on a third, general factor.

Capon et al. (2003) offer two explanations: either that syllogistic reasoning involves both verbal and spatial forms of representation or, and perhaps more importantly for the present discussion, that individual differences exist. Loadings on the two factors may in fact reflect different groups of individuals. In terms of the verbal and spatial strategies described earlier, for visually presented material, we would expect a degree of phonological loop involvement for all reasoners. However, spatial reasoners may also draw on visuo-spatial sketchpad resources. Further work by the present authors suggests this may indeed be the case.

TABLE 4.3
Loadings for a three-factor model (Capon et al., 2003)

Task	Factor 1 (verbal WM resource)	Factor 2 (spatial WM resource)	Factor 3 (general resource)	R^2
Simple spatial span		.53**	.35**	.41
Simple verbal span	.58**		.58**	.66
Complex verbal span	.51**		.59**	.61
Complex spatial span 1		.32*	.68**	.56
Complex spatial span 2		.14	.54**	.31
Syllogisms – verbal pres.	.33**	.54**	.35**	.52
Syllogisms – visual pres.	.51**	.70**	.16	.78

Notes: Significance of factor loadings: * p < .05; ** p < .01

EXPERIMENT 2

Experiment 2 aimed to investigate the relative role of the three working memory components for verbal and spatial reasoners. Given that individuals seem to possess a predilection towards one or other strategy, we made two possible predictions:

(1) The strategy groups differ in their verbal and spatial working memory abilities
(2) Their abilities are similar but different strategies draw differentially on verbal and spatial working memory resources

In an individual differences study ($N = 155$) subjects completed a short syllogistic task to determine their preferred strategy. They also completed a visually presented syllogistic reasoning task and the two simple and two complex verbal and spatial working memory measures used by Capon et al. (2003).

Once again the verbal ($N = 93$) and spatial strategies ($N = 48$) were clearly identifiable from subjects' written reports. A further 14 were classed as either mixed reasoners or indeterminate. As previously, no significant difference in syllogistic reasoning performance was observed between verbal (46.6% correct) and spatial (50.1%) reasoners, $t(74.6) = 0.09$, $p > 0.05$. Moreover, as Table 4.4 indicates, there were also no significant differences in scores on any of the working memory measures ($p > .05$ in every case). Hence the strategy groups have similar working memory abilities and prediction (1) above can be discounted.

A correlational analysis is also presented in Table 4.4. For the simple verbal span, the correlation was stronger for verbal reasoners compared with spatial strategy users. This did offer some evidence that spatial versus verbal

TABLE 4.4

Mean numbers of items correct for the working memory span measures, by strategy group, and correlations between scores on the working memory span measures and performance at the syllogistic reasoning task, by strategy group

Strategy group	Simple verbal span	Complex verbal span	Simple spatial span	Complex spatial span
Performance at the span tasks by strategy group				
Verbal	47.3	27.8	21.9	18.1
Spatial	47.7	26.3	23.7	18.2
Correlations with the span tasks by strategy group				
Verbal	.36**	.37**	.30*	.20
Spatial	−.05	.37**	.37**	.19

Notes: * $p < .05$; ** $p < .01$

reasoners' performance might not be predicted by wholly the same factors. In order to test whether the two strategy groups draw differentially on different working memory resources, a multi-population confirmatory factor analysis was conducted. For technical reasons, we were unable to utilise Capon et al.'s (2003) three-factor model. Instead we tested a correlated two-factor model, in which we constrained the spatial measures to load on one factor and the verbal measures on the other (as in Handley et al., 2000 mentioned earlier). Syllogistic performance was allowed to load on both factors and the models were run separately on each strategy group. The model fitted well: χ^2 (24) = 29.8, p = .19, CFI = .96 and Table 4.5 shows the standardised loadings for each strategy group.

The findings provide evidence consistent with the notion that, during syllogistic reasoning, verbal and spatial reasoners draw on different working memory resources. As Table 4.5 shows, for the verbal strategy group, syllogistic performance loaded significantly on the verbal working memory resource factor whereas that of the spatial reasoners loaded significantly on the spatial working memory resource factor. However, although this clearly suggests some difference in the working memory resources that verbal and spatial reasoners draw upon, these are preliminary findings only and need to be treated with some caution. The R^2 values in Table 4.5 indicate that much of the variance in performance is not explained. Hence, there may be cognitive style or other ability determinants of performance which are unaccounted for, and which may also be related to strategy choice. In addition, the sample

TABLE 4.5
Loadings for a two-factor model for both strategy groups

Task	Strategy group	Factor 1 (Verbal WM resource)	Factor 2 (Spatial WM resource)	R^2
Syllogisms	Verbal	.43*	.10	.26
	Spatial	.28*	.31*	.22
Simple verbal span	Verbal	.75**		.56
	Spatial	.53**		.28
Complex verbal span	Verbal	.73**		.53
	Spatial	1.00**		1.00
Simple spatial span	Verbal		.55**	.30
	Spatial		.92**	.85
Complex spatial span	Verbal		.68**	.46
	Spatial		.65**	.42

Notes: Significance of factor loadings: * p < .05; ** p < .01

size was quite small for this type of analysis (especially in the spatial strategy group).

VERBAL AND SPATIAL STRATEGIES IN TRANSITIVE INFERENCE

Transitive inference is a form of relational reasoning in which terms are ordered in a single dimension. For instance, if A is above B and B is above C, A must therefore be above C, and the identification of this relationship is a transitive inference. Such inferences have usually been studied in the form of three-term series problems, i.e., linear syllogisms.[2] For example, if three terms can be arranged in a linear sequence – A B C – according to their relative properties, and given that the property is height, this can be expressed as a linear syllogism:

A is taller than B	or alternatively,	B is not as tall as A
B is taller than C		C is shorter than B

Both describe the same array of objects unambiguously. Experimental tasks typically present such problems and ask subjects to determine the relation-ship between A and C, or to state which is the taller/shorter of A and C (see also Dierckx & Vandierendonck, chapter 5 this volume).

Again, universal strategies have been proposed for this task. For instance, De Soto, London, and Handel (1965) proposed a spatial strategy whereby individuals construct a mental image comprising the relative properties of the terms in a spatial array. Others, notably Clark (1969), posited a verbal-propositional strategy whereby information was encoded linguistically as given in the premises. In a review of these theories, Evans (1982) concluded that both made similar predictions regarding the relative difficulty of differ-ent forms of linear syllogism, and hence both were well supported by the evidence (see also Evans et al., 1993). However, Egan and Grimes-Farrow (1982) found evidence for individual differences in reasoning strategies. They suggested two strategy types for this task which they identified from written and verbal protocols. Some of their subjects established a scale or continuum onto which the three terms/objects were placed and then compared according to their relationship. This same process occurred whatever the relational adjective in the problem, and the representation of the terms/objects remained abstract throughout, usually as a simple token such as the initial

---

[2] The tasks that have been described for Experiments 1 and 2 are traditionally known as 'syllogisms', but technically should be referred to as *categorical syllogisms*. Where the word *syllogism* is used unqualified in subsequent sections, this should be taken to continue to refer to the categorical task.

letter. These people were termed *abstract directional* thinkers. Other subjects attributed physical properties to the terms according to the relational adjectives, and explicitly represented the objects as having these properties (large, small, light, dark, etc.). They then compared the relative properties visually to reach a conclusion. These individuals were termed *concrete properties* thinkers. Although both of these strategies might be said to possess a visuospatial element, they differ in the extent to which they rely on explicit representations of the properties indicated by the relational adjectives. Similarly, in syllogistic reasoning, spatial reasoners rely on representations which display the explicit relationships between terms, whilst verbal reasoners are able to manipulate simple linguistic tokens on a more abstract, syntactic basis.

EXPERIMENT 3

As we have seen, for syllogisms, individuals differ in whether they use visuospatial or verbal-propositional representations. In addition, performance at this task varies as a function of strategy usage in conjunction with working memory span measures. A further question to investigate is whether there is cross-task consistency in strategy usage. A positive finding would show that strategy usage may be a stable and consistent factor in reasoning, rather than an artefact of the syllogistic task. In this study (N = 62) we aimed to examine the association between the strategies used on syllogistic reasoning and transitive inference tasks. It was predicted that verbal syllogistic reasoners would prefer a more abstract strategy for transitive inference whilst spatial syllogistic reasoners would present a more visual, properties-based strategy. No verbal reports were taken, but subjects were asked to write down their working for both tasks. Task presentation was counterbalanced. The findings of Experiment 1 were replicated for the syllogistic task. Clear evidence of verbal (N = 38) and spatial reasoners (N = 17) was apparent in the written reports. Five subjects were classed as mixed and a further two as indeterminate. For transitive inference, the characteristics described by Egan and Grimes-Farrow were clearly evident. For convenience, we have retained the terms *abstract directional* and *concrete properties* here. All but six subjects could be easily classified as belonging to one of these two strategy groups. However, the two strategies were less exclusive than Egan and Grimes-Farrow suggested.

Thirty-four subjects yielded written protocols which clearly showed the characteristics of abstract directional reasoning as described above. Protocol 6 (see Figure 4.2) is typical. Twenty-two subjects showed evidence of using a concrete properties strategy. Their protocols clearly showed representations of these properties but, unlike the subjects in the Egan and Grimes-Farrow study, they also tended to put the letters on a continuum or in the order of their linear relationship. Protocol 7 (see Figure 4.2) is typical. Only two of the

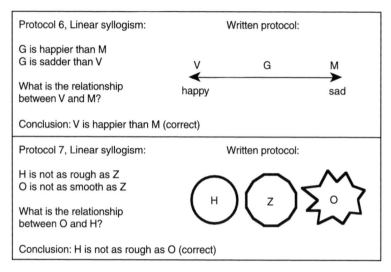

Figure 4.2   Example protocols for the linear syllogism task.

people who used the concrete properties approach included no directional element in their protocol. In terms of the theories of transitive inference outlined earlier, only a small minority of subjects overall (N = 5) used a purely non-directional propositional strategy (such as that advocated by Clark) and presented evidence of reformulating premises to simplify difficult relationships (e.g., rewriting *X is not as tall as Y* as *Y is taller than X*). The remainder all used some kind of spatial or dimensional array. What discriminates between abstract directional and concrete properties strategy groups is the degree of reliance on explicit representation of the physical properties of the terms. Abstract directional thinkers can use the letters to denote the terms, but concrete properties thinkers seem to require a more explicit visual comparison – rather as do spatial reasoners for syllogisms. The relationship between strategy groups across the two tasks is interesting in light of this. Table 4.6 illustrates the comparison. All mixed and indeterminate strategy users have been omitted from this analysis.

TABLE 4.6
Cross-tabulation showing strategy selection across the two reasoning tasks

| Syllogistic strategy | Transitive inference strategy | | |
	Abstract directional	Concrete properties	Propositional
Verbal	26	8	4
Spatial	4	12	1

As Table 4.6 shows, verbal syllogistic reasoners are most likely to adopt a abstract directional strategy on transitive inference whereas spatial syllogistic reasoners are most likely to use a concrete properties strategy (non-directional propositional reasoners were similar to abstract directional reasoners in this respect). This is fully in line with our prediction. Pearson Chi square indicates a strong association between the two main strategies adopted across the two tasks; χ^2 (1) = 12.0, p < .01. The abstract directional strategy for transitive inference and the verbal strategy for syllogisms are alike in that semantic meaning does not seem to play as great a role. In the former, the differing relational adjectives presented are immaterial and the terms are represented in an abstract form. Consequently, identification of the conclusion is straight-forward and this process is identical for all problems. However, error rate (6.7%) was comparable with that for concrete properties thinkers (5.9%), $t(48)$ = 0.2, p > 0.05. Hence, both strategies are similarly effective, but reas-oners who think more concretely prefer to visualise the semantics of the physical properties for each problem in order to draw a conclusion. This must involve additional processing steps for solution, and informal observation of subjects during the experiment suggests that the abstract directional strategy is efficient in terms of processing speed (latencies were not directly measured). Overall, it would seem that a tendency to employ abstract/syntactic versus concrete/semantic strategies remains constant across two reasoning domains.

GENERAL DISCUSSION AND CONCLUSIONS

The aim of this chapter was to identify evidence which challenges the prevail-ing ideology of a single fundamental mechanism for human reasoning. The verbal and written reports collected in Experiment 1, and replicated in Experiments 2 and 3, clearly suggest the presence of at least two distinct strategies for syllogistic reasoning (and also for linear reasoning in Experi-ment 3). In line with the earlier findings of Ford (1995), the syllogistic strat-egies appear to be verbal-propositional versus spatial in nature. However, unlike Ford, we found few performance differences as a function of strategy. Experiment 2 confirmed this strategy distinction by showing that the two strategy groups draw differentially on the verbal and spatial components of working memory. Experiment 3 showed that the usage of these strategies is closely associated with those identified for transitive relational inference, which themselves appear to have abstract/syntactic/low spatial versus concrete/semantic/high spatial components.

Overall, our findings suggest that individual differences in reasoning strat-egies cannot be wholly accounted for by any one class of deductive theory. For syllogisms, both strategy groups perform best, and equally well, on same-form problems, but for different reasons. For spatial strategy users, these problems require the construction of just one model (as per mental models theory, Johnson-Laird & Byrne, 1991). For verbal strategy users, the quantifier for the correct conclusion is named in one or both of the premises.

Different-form syllogisms are harder to solve for both strategies. For spatial strategy users, these often require the consideration of multiple diagrams (mental models theory likewise predicts errors on these problems because of failure to search for counter-examples which may refute putative conclusions). In our experience, unlike Ford, few spatial reasoners consider the possibility of alternatives. They constructed Euler circle type representations, but without constructing all possible states of the premises. Nor did they construct separate diagrams for each premise and then combine them, as traditional Euler circle theory would suggest (Erickson, 1978). Although the failure to search for counter-examples may partly explain spatial performance on different-form problems, mental models theory does not seem to account for the verbal strategy users' approach. For these people, different-form syllogisms are particularly difficult because the correct conclusion quantifier is not contained in either premise.

Unlike the verbal strategies described by Ford, users of these in our studies seem to apply the same naive propositional rules to every syllogism, irrespective of its logical form. There is no evidence that they applied the more sophisticated processes which Ford describes. Our verbal reasoners relied very literally on premise form, which leads to erroneous conclusions, especially for different-form syllogisms. In this respect, their conclusions give the appearance of those predicted by the matching strategy of Wetherick and Gilhooly (1990): Where possible, verbal strategy users choose the *All* premise in order to obtain a value for the B term, even when this quantifier is presented in the second premise, because it gives the most informative description of any of the individuals (in matching theory terms, this premise is the least conservative). The remaining premise (the most conservative) is the one which is in effect 'matched'. Wetherick and Gilhooly (1995) highlight that such a strategy will work for 14 of the 27 valid syllogisms (the same-form problems) but not for the other 13 (different-form). But, as Wetherick and Gilhooly concede, some reasoners do get different-form syllogisms right. They state: 'Subjects who give correct conclusions to syllogisms in these moods cannot be matching, and it seems reasonable to suppose that their correct responses to other moods may not have been obtained by matching either' (1995, pp. 172–3). The fact that some verbal reasoners are able to generate correct conclusions to different-form syllogisms suggests that they are not relying wholly on naive heuristic processes either.

Chater and Oaksford's (1999) probability heuristics model of reasoning also predicts that conclusion mood will be the same as that for the least informative premise, but the matching heuristics are based upon probabilistic interpretations of syllogistic quantifiers. If all subjects in the present study were reasoning in this way, this might account for the fact that both verbal and spatial reasoners performed similarly across different forms of syllogism. However, the fact that those subjects who produced only written protocols showed strikingly similar individual differences to those who provided a verbal protocol too appears to refute Chater and Oaksford's suggestion that the verbal–spatial distinction is nothing more than a methodological artefact arising from the use of verbal protocol. This in turn calls into question the claim that their model provides an accurate fit for experimental data without the need to account for such differences. The converging evidence from the questionnaire, and from Experiments 2 and 3, further suggest that the strategies are not epiphenomenal.

Unfortunately, neither verbal nor written protocols make explicit the exact inference processes of spatial strategy users. In other words, are conclusions based on a literal interpretation of diagram structure, on manipulation of mental models whose structure precisely matches that specified by Johnson-Laird and Byrne (1991) or, indeed, on the application of some as yet unknown additional inference rules? The precise nature of the various verbal strategies has also been debated. Johnson-Laird and Bara (1984) and others have suggested that manipulation of models may underpin substitution behaviour. However, the present data suggest no evidence for this. Later work by Johnson-Laird (2001) has suggested that, over time, reasoners may learn to construct formal rules, and that this is an essential stage in the development of logic. Perhaps verbal reasoners have already learned pseudo-logical rules and applied them to this task. Certainly, there was no strong evidence for strategy discovery in our data, with reasoners tending to adopt a given approach at the outset of the task and stick with it throughout. The few that changed strategy did so during the practice phase (just two items) and then presented a consistent strategy during the experimental task itself.

Some authors (for instance, Johnson-Laird et al., 2000) have claimed that Euler circle type representations rely on vestigial memories of procedures learned in school. However, our questionnaire asked reasoners:

> Did you apply a rule or procedure which you already knew about from things you have done in the past, rather than develop a new rule/procedure for this task? If yes, please describe the rule/procedure and how you knew about it.

Of the 51 subjects in Experiment 1, only five answered in the affirmative, and three of these were verbal reasoners who described algebra and/or equations (Ford describes these as typical of verbal reasoners' methods). Of the other two, one mentioned 'spider diagrams' for summarising information and just one mentioned Venn diagrams learned in mathematics lessons at school. Although this indicates that the vestigial memories argument cannot be totally discounted, it does suggest that it applies only to a small minority of individuals and is not limited to spatial reasoners. We would suggest that such memories are selective and that the nature of recalled material is consistent with a tendency to reason in a verbal or spatial way. If so, we would expect strategy to be an inherent factor of the individual and hence robust across different tasks. Experiments 2 and 3 suggest this may indeed be the case.

In this chapter, we have demonstrated qualitative distinctions in the strategies that individuals use for reasoning, and have presented preliminary evidence that, although strategy preference did not reflect a difference in working memory capacity per se, verbal and spatial strategy users differ in how they draw on working memory resources. We have shown that not only are these differences apparent in syllogistic reasoning, but also that they are strongly associated with methods employed for transitive inference. Hence, we maintain that such individual differences do reflect a functional distinction in the way that people reason.

ACKNOWLEDGEMENTS

The experiments reported in this chapter were supported by funding from the Economic and Social Research Council (Award no. R42200034033) awarded to the first author.

REFERENCES

Bacon, A. M., Handley, S. J., & Newstead, S. E. (2003). Individual differences in strategies for syllogistic reasoning. *Thinking and Reasoning, 9*, 133–168.

Baddeley, A. D. (1986). *Working memory*. Oxford: Oxford University Press.

Baddeley, A. D., & Logie, R. H. (1999). Working memory: The multi-component model. In A. Miyake & P. Shah (Eds.), *Models of working memory: Mechanisms of active maintenance and executive control* (pp. 28–61). Cambridge: Cambridge University Press.

Braine, M. D. S., & O'Brien, D. P. (1998). *Mental logic*. Mahwah, NJ: Lawrence Erlbaum Associates, Inc.

Bucciarelli, M., & Johnson-Laird, P. N. (1999). Strategies in syllogistic reasoning. *Cognitive Science, 23*, 247–303.

Capon, A., Handley, S. J., & Dennis, I. (2003). Working memory and reasoning: An individual differences perspective. *Thinking and Reasoning, 9*, 203–244.

Chater, N., & Oaksford, M. R. (1999). The probability heuristics model of syllogistic reasoning. *Cognitive Psychology, 38*, 191–258.

Clark, H. H. (1969). Linguistic processes in deductive reasoning. *Psychological Review, 76*, 387–404.

Daneman, M., & Carpenter, P. A. (1980). Individual differences in working memory and reading. *Journal of Verbal Learning and Verbal Behaviour, 19*, 450–466.

De Soto, C. B., London, M., & Handel, S. (1965). Social reasoning and spatial paralogic. *Journal of Personality and Social Psychology, 2*, 513–521.

Egan, D. E., & Grimes-Farrow, D. D. (1982). Differences in mental representations spontaneously adopted for reasoning. *Memory and Cognition, 10*, 297–307.

Erickson, J. R. (1978). Research on syllogistic reasoning. In R. Revlin & R. E. Mayer (Eds.), *Human reasoning* (pp. 39–50). New York: Wiley.

Ericsson, E. A., & Simon, H. A. (1993). *Protocol analysis: Verbal reports as data*. Cambridge, MA: MIT Press.

Evans, J. St. B. T. (1982). *The psychology of deductive reasoning*. London: Routledge.

Evans, J. St. B. T. (2000). What could and could not be a strategy in reasoning. In W. Schaeken, G. De Vooght, A. Vandierendonck, & G. d'Ydewalle. (Eds.), *Deductive reasoning and strategies* (pp. 1–22). Mahwah, NJ: Lawrence Erlbaum Associates, Inc.

Evans, J. St. B. T., Newstead, S. E., & Byrne, R. M. J. (1993). *Human reasoning: The psychology of deduction*. Hove, UK: Lawrence Erlbaum Associates, Ltd.

Ford, M. (1995). Two modes of mental representation and problem solution in syllogistic reasoning. *Cognition, 54*, 1–71.

Garnham, A., & Oakhill, J. (1994). *Thinking and reasoning*. Oxford: Blackwell.

Gilhooly, K. J. (1998). Working memory and reasoning. In R. H. Logie & K. J. Gilhooly (Eds.), *Working memory and thinking* (pp. 7–22). Hove, UK: Psychology Press.

Gilhooly, K. J., Logie, R. H., Wetherick, N. E., & Wynn, V. (1993). Working memory and strategies in syllogistic reasoning tasks. *Memory and Cognition, 21*, 115–124.

Gilhooly, K. J., Logie, R. H., & Wynn, V. (2002). Syllogistic reasoning tasks and working memory: Evidence from sequential presentation of premises. *Current Psychology, 21*, 111–120.

Handley, S. J., Capon, A., Copp, C., & Harper, C. (2002). Conditional reasoning and the Tower of Hanoi: The role of spatial and verbal working memory. *British Journal of Psychology, 93*, 501–518.

Johnson-Laird, P. N. (2001). Mental models and deduction. *Trends in Cognitive Sciences, 5*, 434–442.

Johnson-Laird, P. N., & Bara, B. G. (1984). Syllogistic inference. *Cognition, 16*, 1–61.

Johnson-Laird, P. N., & Byrne, R. M. J. (1991). *Deduction*. Hove, UK: Lawrence Erlbaum Associates, Ltd.

Johnson-Laird, P. N., Savary, F., & Bucciarelli, M. (2000). Strategies and tactics in reasoning. In W. Schaeken, G. De Vooght, A. Vandierendonck, & G. d'Ydewalle. (Eds.), *Deductive reasoning and strategies* (pp. 209–240). Mahwah, NJ: Lawrence Erlbaum Associates, Inc.

Manktelow, K. (1999). *Reasoning & thinking*. Hove, UK: Psychology Press.

Polk, T. A., & Newell, A. (1995). Deduction as verbal reasoning. *Psychological Review, 102*, 533–566.

Rips, L. J. (1986). Mental muddles. In M. Brand & R. Harnish (Eds.), *The representation of knowledge and belief* (pp. 258–286). Tucson: University of Arizona Press.

Rips, L. J. (1994). *The psychology of proof*. Cambridge, MA: MIT Press.

Roberts, M. J. (1993). Human reasoning: Deduction rules or mental models, or both? *Quarterly Journal of Experimental Psychology, 46A*, 569–589.

Roberts, M. J. (2000). Individual differences in reasoning strategies: A problem to solve or an opportunity to seize? In W. Schaeken, G. De Vooght, A. Vandierendonck, & G. d'Ydewalle. (Eds.), *Deductive reasoning and strategies* (pp. 23–48). Mahwah, NJ: Lawrence Erlbaum Associates, Inc.

Shah, P., & Miyake, A. (1996). The separability of working memory resources for spatial thinking and language processing: An individual differences approach. *Journal of Experimental Psychology: General, 125*, 4–27.

Sternberg, R. J. (1982). Reasoning, problem solving and intelligence. In R. J. Sternberg (Ed.), *Handbook of human intelligence* (pp. 225–307). Cambridge: Cambridge University Press.

Vandierendonck, A., & De Vooght, G. (1997). Working memory constraints on linear reasoning with spatial and temporal contents. *Quarterly Journal of Experimental Psychology, 50A*, 803–820.

Wetherick, N. E., & Gilhooly, K. J. (1990). Syllogistic reasoning: Effects of premise order. In K. J. Gilhooly, M. T. Keane, R. H. Logie, & G. Erdos (Eds.), *Lines of thinking: Reflections on the psychology of thought* (Vol. 1, pp. 99–108). Chichester: Wiley.

Wetherick, N. E., & Gilhooly, K. J. (1995). 'Atmosphere', matching and logic in syllogistic reasoning. *Current Psychology*, *14*, 169–178.

CHAPTER FIVE

Adaptive strategy application in linear reasoning

Vicky Dierckx and André Vandierendonck
Department of Experimental Psychology, Ghent University, Belgium

One of the most fascinating aspects of our cognitive system is its adaptivity. In a wide variety of domains, such as mathematics, memory, spelling, decision making and question answering, it has been shown that people select their strategies in response to task instructions (e.g., Gardner & Rogoff, 1990; Reder, 1987), problem features (e.g., Lemaire & Siegler, 1995; McDougall & Velmans, 1993; Rittle-Johnson & Siegler, 1999), and the success rate of the strategies in the past (e.g., Lemaire & Reder, 1999; Reder, 1987). In doing so, people tend to solve problems by using the most efficient strategies available. To explain why people's strategy choices are adaptive, it is often suggested that all relevant features of the problem situation are taken into account. Recent strategy selection models, such as ASCM (Siegler & Lemaire, 1997; Siegler & Shipley, 1995), SCADS (Shrager & Siegler, 1998) and ACT-R (Lovett & Anderson, 1996), assume that this process consists of a weighting of the benefits (accuracy, speed) and the costs (processing resources) of the strategies, as experienced through their previous application. Depending on the instructions, either stressing accuracy and/or speed, or on the features of the problems, different strategies may be the most beneficial and/or the least costly, and thus the most adapted to a situation.

Although many studies testify to the claim that adaptivity is a general feature of people's strategy selection (e.g., Kerkman & Siegler, 1993; Siegler & Lemaire, 1997), recently a hypothesis has been put forward that individuals may differ in how adaptive their selections are (Schunn, Lovett, & Reder, 2001; Schunn & Reder, 2001). Schunn and Reder (2001) investigated

107

individual differences in adaptivity to changes in the *success rate of the strategies*. In their study, participants had to solve the *Kanfer-Ackerman Air Traffic Control Task* – a complex task that simulates aspects of the dynamics of real air traffic control. Participants have to control the movement of planes in the air, guiding them through the landing process onto one of two types of runway: long or short. All planes may use the long runway, but under certain circumstances the short runway should also be used so as to maximise the total number of planes landed. In order to land these, people must monitor information about the type of plane, the amount of fuel remaining, wind speed, the condition of the runways, etc. One important measure of performance is the ratio of *successful landings on the short runway* to *attempted landings on the short runway*. Schunn and Reder were also interested in the proportion of times participants attempted to land a plane on the short runway, out of all the times that an attempt was made to land a plane. In general, this proportion was higher the more successful landings on the short runway participants had previously experienced. People were hence found to be generally adaptive to the success rate of landing a plane on the short runway. However, they differed in their sensitivity to the success rate in terms of how much they adapted to this, and how quickly this occurred. These differences in adaptivity were found to be correlated with measures of inductive reasoning ability and working memory capacity.

Similar individual differences in adaptivity have been found using a simpler *Building Sticks Task* in which participants had to create a stick of a certain length by adding or subtracting shorter or larger sticks (Schunn et al., 2001). Participants could either start a problem with a shorter stick (the undershoot strategy) or a larger stick (the overshoot strategy) and they differed in the extent to which strategy selection was determined by the *past success rates* of these strategies. However, unlike Schunn and Reder (2001), Schunn et al. (2001) did not find a relationship between individual differences in the adaptivity of strategy selection and working memory capacity. Possibly, this difference between studies was due to the simplicity of the Building Sticks Task. This was far less demanding on working memory resources than the Kanfer-Ackerman Air Traffic Control Task.

In what follows, we give an overview of a series of experiments exploring whether people are sensitive to *current problem features* versus *past success rates* when selecting strategies, and also investigate individual differences in adaptivity of strategy selection. Given the conflicting findings concerning the importance of working memory capacity for adaptivity, we first investigated the relationship between working memory load – by manipulating task complexity – and the extent to which people chose strategies adaptively on the basis of problem features. In a second series of studies we induced a conflict, in which the most adaptive strategy to solve the current problems was the one with the *lowest* success rate in the past. We investigated whether people still managed to select their strategies adaptively on the basis of problem features, which factors made this more or less likely, and whether there were individual differences in adaptivity. These questions were investigated using linear reasoning tasks, which require inferences to be made about one-dimensional relationships between premise terms (e.g., 'Nowitzki is taller than Jordan', 'Jordan is taller than Iverson', 'Is Iverson taller than Nowitzki?').

STRATEGIES IN REASONING

Until recently (e.g., Schaeken, De Vooght, Vandierendonck, & d'Ydewalle, 2000; Schaeken, Vandierendonck, Schroyens, & d'Ydewalle, in press), little research has been devoted to the study of strategy choice in reasoning, let alone strategy adaptivity. This is the consequence of the fact that, for a long time, many studies have aimed to identify the nature of a unitary fundamental reasoning mechanism underlying all types of deductive reasoning (e.g., Johnson-Laird, Byrne, & Schaeken, 1992, 1994; Rips, 1989; Vandierendonck & De Vooght, 1996). More specifically, the controversy has concerned the issue of whether reasoning involves the application of mental deduction rules (e.g., O'Brien, Braine, & Yang, 1994; Rips, 1989) or the construction and manipulation of mental models (e.g., Johnson-Laird & Byrne, 1991). Although the majority of the findings favour the mental models view, the best way to resolve this controversy is to assume that different types of mechanisms may be at work depending upon the reasoner's ability and/or the task at hand (Roberts, 1993, 2000, see also Morris & Schunn, chapter 2 this volume).

In the present study, we devised linear reasoning problems in such a way that they were likely to be solved on the basis of mental models (as opposed to deduction rules), and so that it would be difficult for participants to develop shortcut heuristics while solving them (see Roberts, 1993, 2000). This was achieved by presenting problems that consisted of at least four premises, and then a conclusion, whose truth had to be evaluated in the light of the premises. This conclusion could relate any pair of terms from the premises. The premises were presented first, during 6 seconds, and the conclusion appeared only after they were removed. During premise encoding, participants did not know which pair of terms would be contained in the conclusion, and were thus forced to represent the entire order of premise terms. Typically (e.g., Evans, Newstead, & Byrne, 1993), this order is represented in a mental array (i.e., mental model) that is used to infer or validate a conclusion (e.g., Johnson-Laird & Byrne, 1991). To investigate strategy adaptivity, we focused upon different strategies for encoding the information in the premises and constructing a mental model equivalent representation. In order to allow a reliable detection of the strategies used to construct each model, we taught participants two verbal encoding strategies that both can be applied aloud: the *rehearsal strategy* and the *acronym strategy*. Table 5.1

TABLE 5.1

An illustration of the different types of problems encoded with rehearsal and with acronym strategies

Problems (all 'simple' in structure)		
Unbiased	Biased towards acronyms	Biased towards rehearsal
Fig before Olive	Cucumber before Eggplant	Lip before Ear
Olive before Melon	Eggplant before Beansprout	Ear before Toe
Melon before Pear	Beansprout before Tomato	Toe before Tooth
Pear before Apple	Tomato before Asparagus	Tooth before Eye
Apple before Date	Asparagus before Radish	Eye before Nose
Correct or incorrect?	Correct or incorrect?	Correct or incorrect?
Apple before Olive	Beansprout before Asparagus	Ear before Eye
Rehearsal strategy 'fig-olive-melon-pear-apple-date'	Rehearsal strategy 'cucumber-eggplant-beansprout-tomato-asparagus-radish'	Rehearsal strategy 'lip-ear-toe-tooth-eye-nose'
Acronym strategy 'f-o-m-p-a-d'	Acronym strategy 'c-e-b-t-a-r'	Acronym strategy 'l-e-t-t-e-n'

(left panel) shows an example of the application of these strategies to *unbiased problems* that can easily be encoded with either one. The rehearsal strategy consists of encoding the entire set of premise terms into a single string such that their order reflects that specified by the premises. To prevent this representation from decaying in working memory, participants are also told to rehearse the terms in the order in which they are placed in the string. The acronym strategy, on the other hand, is a variant of the rehearsal strategy, in which only the first letter of each premise term has to be encoded, and only this pseudo-word is rehearsed.

ADAPTIVITY AND TASK COMPLEXITY

In a first series of experiments we investigated the relationship between task complexity and adaptivity of strategy selection. We were particularly interested in whether the acronym and the rehearsal strategies are selected according to the features of the problems, whether individuals differ in how adaptive their strategy choices are to these features, and whether these differences are related to task complexity. The problem features manipulated were (1) the lengths of the premise terms and (2) whether some of the terms started with identical letters. Two types of problem sets were created: one set *biased towards the acronym strategy* and another set *biased towards the rehearsal strategy*. The problems *biased towards acronyms* consisted of six long premise terms, all starting with different letters (see Table 5.1, middle panel). For these, use of the acronym strategy is definitely the most adaptive choice since more resources are required to maintain a string of long words than a string of only six letters in working memory (the *word length effect*; e.g., Baddeley, Thomson, & Buchanan, 1975). The problems *biased towards rehearsal* consisted of short premise terms, some of which started with the same letter (see Table 5.1, right panel). Encoding only these starting letters will lead to an ambiguous representation, in which it is impossible to distinguish between identically lettered terms. Hence, for these problems, rehearsal is the most adaptive strategy. *Unbiased* problems were also used, in which premise terms were short, and all starting letters differed (see Table 5.1, left panel). However, for these the acronym strategy is also the less demanding to apply, and hence has a slight advantage.

Given that, for complex tasks, differences in working memory capacity are related to differences in adaptivity (Schunn & Reder, 2001), it is possible that the more complex, and hence the more resource-demanding the reasoning task, the less adaptivity overall, and the more differences in adaptivity will be found. To examine this issue, we will compare the results of three experiments in which the complexity of the representation construction process varied. For Experiment 1, representation construction was relatively easy. The relationships between the premise terms were described using the same relational term ('before') in each premise. Furthermore, the premise terms were presented in a continuous order between premises, meaning that the second term of each premise always reoccurred as the first term in the subsequent premise (AB, BC, CD, DE; see Tables 5.1 and 5.3). Using this format, participants do not have to attend to the relational term. Once the first premise is represented, each new premise term can be added to the same end of the representation. Given the easiness of representation construction, we expected almost all participants to apply either the acronym, or the rehearsal strategy, adaptively on the basis of the problem features.

In order to investigate the participants' strategy choice in Experiment 1, we used a reversed choice/no-choice paradigm (Siegler & Lemaire, 1997). First, participants had to apply the acronym strategy aloud, and then the rehearsal strategy (or vice versa), each to a set of unbiased problems (the no-choice phase, see Table 5.1). They were then asked to make an estimation of the number of problems they thought they had solved correctly in the no-choice phase. Finally, they were allowed to choose freely among the two strategies to solve a new set of problems as accurately as possible (the choice-phase). This set consisted of (1) problems biased towards acronyms; (2) problems biased towards rehearsal; (3) unbiased problems, all randomly intermingled. Participants continued to apply the strategies aloud, so that the strategy selected for each individual problem could be identified.

Our rationale for running the no-choice phase before the choice phase was as follows. First, participants were fully familiarised and practised with both strategies before being asked to choose between them. In addition, for the second series of experiments (see later), we needed a procedure in which it would also be possible to manipulate the past success rate of the strategies in order to detect the effect of this on people's strategy choices. This is impossible when a choice phase precedes a no-choice phase. A possible critique on the reversed choice/no-choice phase is that the order in which the strategies have been applied in the no-choice phase might affect people's strategy selection in the choice phase. However, this was not the case in our experiments.

For the choice phase of Experiment 1, the percentage acronym application over all participants for the three types of problems presented was calculated and analysed by means of logistic regression analyses using the GEE-approach, that takes into account the within-subject dependencies in the data (e.g., Diggle, Kung-Yee, & Zeger, 1994). The results confirmed our expectations: The acronym strategy was more frequently applied to the problems biased towards acronyms ($M = 86\%$) than to the problems biased towards rehearsal ($M = 10\%$), $\chi^2(1) = 18.41$, $p < .01$ (see Table 5.2). Only one participant out of 20 consistently applied the rehearsal strategy to all types of problem. All others tended to apply the strategies in an adaptive way. Finally, the unbiased problems were most frequently encoded with the acronym strategy ($M = 83\%$). Although these problems were not our principle focus, the latter finding also testifies to the adaptiveness of the participants' strategy application: With the acronym strategy, only a string of six letters, instead of six complete words – albeit short ones – have to be maintained in working memory. The adaptive edge of the acronym strategy when applied to the unbiased problems was confirmed by looking at data from the no-choice

TABLE 5.2
Structure of the problems and percentage acronym selection in the choice phase of
Experiments 1 to 3 by problem type

No-choice phase		Choice phase	
Problem type (no. of trials)	Instructed strategy	Problem type (no. of trials)	Acronym selection %
Experiment 1: Simple problems (N = 20)			
Unbiased (5)	Acronym	Unbiased (10)	83
Unbiased (5)	Rehearsal	Biased acronyms (10)	86
		Biased rehearsal (10)	10
Experiment 2: Intermediate problems (N = 24)			
Unbiased (10)	Acronym	Unbiased (10)	52
Unbiased (10)	Rehearsal	Biased acronyms (10)	74
		Biased rehearsal (10)	14
Experiment 3: Complex problems (N = 14)			
Unbiased (10)	Acronym	Unbiased (10)	39
Unbiased (10)	Rehearsal	Biased acronyms (10)	54
		Biased rehearsal (10)	4

phase. These types of problem were solved only slightly more accurately, but significantly faster when they were encoded with the acronym strategy ($M = 92\%$, $M = 2.8$ s) rather than with the rehearsal strategy ($M = 88\%$, $M = 3.7$ s), $F(1, 18) < 1$, $p > .05$, and $F(1, 18) = 7.55$, $p < .05$ respectively (for a more thorough discussion, see Dierckx, Vandierendonck, & Pandelaere, 2003).

In Experiment 2, we increased the complexity of representation construction by using 'before' as well as 'after' to describe the temporal order of the premise terms. In addition, instead of using a continuous presentation order of the premise terms, these were now presented in a semi-continuous order (e.g., Mynatt & Smith, 1977; Potts, 1972). Hence, a premise did not always contain a term from an immediately preceding premise, and each new premise term had to be attached to *either* the beginning *or* the end of the representation (see Table 5.3). In all other respects, the procedure was identical to Experiment 1 (see Table 5.2). As for Experiment 1, strategy application was adaptively determined by the problem features. The percentage of acronym application to the problems biased towards acronyms ($M = 74\%$) was higher than to the problems biased towards rehearsal ($M = 14\%$), $\chi^2(1) = 17.82$, $p < .01$. However, in line with the hypothesis that increasing the complexity of the task might reveal individual differences in adaptivity, the percentage acronym application to the problems biased towards acronyms was significantly lower than the corresponding percentage in the previous experiment ($M = 86\%$), $\chi^2(1) = 8.88$, $p < .01$. Closer inspection of the data revealed that 6 out of 24 participants consistently applied the same strategy to all problems (four of them the rehearsal strategy). When these participants were removed from the data, as well as the single non-adaptive participant in the previous experiment, the difference in acronym application for the problems biased towards acronyms was no longer significant ($M = 86\%$ for Experiment 1, $M = 90\%$ for Experiment 2), $\chi^2(1) = 1.50$, $p = .221$. The lower percentage of acronym application in Experiment 2 thus seems to be due to some participants preferring to apply one strategy, often rehearsal, consistently to all problems. Presenting problems that have a more complex representation construction process thus seems to reveal individual differences in the adaptivity of people's strategy choices.

In Experiment 3, representation construction was rendered even more difficult by presenting indeterminate linear reasoning problems. The relationship described by each set of premises was consistent with two different orders of the terms, necessitating the construction of two different representations (*two-model problems*, see Table 5.3 for an example). Since the premises and the conclusion are not presented together, it is not possible to apply the usual procedure of first evaluating a conclusion with respect to an initial representation, and then reinspecting the premises to construct the other possibility and confirm the validity of the conclusion (e.g., Johnson-Laird & Byrne, 1991). Consequently, participants have to represent (Schaeken, Van der

Henst, & Schroyens, in press), or at least mark (Vandierendonck, Dierckx, & De Vooght, 2004), the indeterminacy of the problems, thereby increasing working memory demands further. The percentage acronym application to the problems biased towards acronyms ($M = 54\%$) was still significantly higher than to the problems biased towards rehearsal ($M = 4\%$), $\chi^2(1) = 8.62$, $p < .01$. However, compared with the other two experiments (see Table 5.2) the percentage acronym application to the problems biased towards acronyms was relatively low ($M = 54\%$ for Experiment 3 versus 84% for Experiment 1 and 74% for Experiment 2), $\chi^2(1) = 31.05$, $p < .01$ and $\chi^2(1) = 11.67$, $p < .01$ respectively. To check whether this lower percentage was due to individual differences in adaptivity, we reconducted the analyses while again excluding those participants who consistently applied the rehearsal strategy (3/14) or the acronym strategy (1/14) to all problems. Even without these participants, the difference in acronym selection between Experiment 3 ($M = 73\%$) and Experiment 1 ($M = 90\%$) as well as Experiment 2 ($M = 86\%$), remained significant, $\chi^2(1) = 9.36$, $p < .01$ and $\chi^2(1) = 4.46$, $p < .01$ respectively. This suggests that by increasing the complexity of a task, not only *inter-individual* differences but also *intra-individual* differences in adaptivity might emerge. For the latter, although the remaining ten participants varied strategies on an item-by-item basis, five were less adaptive than the others. These people were less likely to be sensitive to problem features when

TABLE 5.3

An example of the problems used in the no-choice phase of Experiments 1 to 3 illustrating the differences in complexity between the problems

Problems (all unbiased with respect to strategies)

Simple (Exp. 1)	*Intermediate (Exp. 2)*	*Complex (Exp. 3)*
Sole before Crab	Ink before Fax	Bank before Abbey
Crab before Ray	Pen after Fax	Abbey before Villa
Ray before Eel	Glue before Ink	Villa before Igloo
Eel before Perch	Glue after Stamp	Villa before Tower
Perch before Trout		
Correct or incorrect?	Correct or incorrect?	Correct or incorrect ?
Perch before Crab	Fax before Ink	Igloo before Tower
Rehearsal strategy	Rehearsal strategy	Rehearsal strategy
'sole-crab-ray-eel-perch-trout'	'stamp-glue-ink-fax-pen'	'bank-abbey-villa-igloo-tower'
		'bank-abbey-villa-tower-igloo'
Acronym strategy	Acronym strategy	Acronym strategy
's-c-r-e-p-t'	's-g-i-f-p'	'b-a-v-t-i'
		'b-a-v-i-t'

selecting a strategy, thus sometimes choosing one that was the less efficient for a particular item.

In the present experiment, lack of adaptivity mostly manifested itself in the more frequent application of the rehearsal strategy: The percentage acronym application to the unbiased problems was only 39%. This was detectable even for the problems biased towards rehearsal, where the percentage acronym application was significantly lower in Experiment 3 ($M = 4\%$) than in the previous two ($M = 10\%$ for Experiment 1 and 14% for Experiment 2), $\chi^2(1) = 3.78$, $p = .052$ and $\chi^2(1) = 9.01$, $p < .01$ respectively.

Taken together, these results support Schunn et al.'s (2001; Schunn & Reder, 2001) hypothesis that people vary in the adaptiveness of their strategy selection, and further extend these findings by showing that these individual differences occur not only in the extent to which people are sensitive to the past success rate of the strategies, but also in the extent to which they are sensitive to the *current problem features*. In our experiments, these variations particularly manifested themselves when the task became more complex. This is in agreement with the recent findings of De Rammelaere, Duverne, Lemaire, and Vandierendonck (2003): They only detected impairments in the adaptiveness of people's strategy choices to problem features when complex arithmetic problems had to be solved. In addition, our results suggest that, depending upon the level of complexity of the problems, there may also be intra-individual differences in adaptivity. Speculatively, this might indicate that although some individuals may be highly adaptive for low complexity problems, these same people may become less sensitive to problem features, and hence less adaptive, when given high complexity problems. This finding suggests that a categorisation of individuals into 'adaptive' and 'non-adaptive' cannot be made easily without taking into account the complexity of the task at hand. Hence, in our view adaptivity does not seem to be a differential ability that individuals possess in a smaller or a larger degree (cf. Schunn & Reder, 2001), but rather is a generally possessed ability that, under certain circumstances, is not, or cannot be, relied upon by certain people.

We hypothesised that the decrease in inter- and intra-individual adaptivity may be due to an overtaxing of working memory. This is plausible assuming that during the strategy selection process the weighting of the benefits and the costs of the available strategies will also require a certain amount of working memory resources. Moreover, if problem features vary on an item-by-item basis, still further resources will be required because these features have to be identified and processed for every trial. Any increase in the complexity of representation construction may therefore force individuals to trade off resources between encoding and strategy selection processes. Given that the instructions were to solve the problems as accurately as possible, it may be expected that more resources will be allocated to the encoding of the problems, rather than to the trial-by-trial selection of the most appropriate encoding strategy. This may result in a less detailed evaluation of the item characteristics in relation to the strategies available, or even in skipping the strategy selection process altogether (see also Payne, Bettman, & Johnson, 1993). Given that there are individual differences in working memory capacity and processing resources, the appearance of individual differences in strategy adaptivity is therefore to be expected.

An important finding in this respect is that rigidity in strategy selection manifested itself as an application of the rehearsal strategy to most if not all problems. This is a relatively safe option since no information is discarded and, in principle, all problems – even those having long premise terms – can be encoded accurately (see Dierckx et al., 2003). Conversely, with the acronym strategy, wherever starting letters are identical it is impossible to encode accurately the order of premise terms. This suggests that when problem solving requires a relatively high level of resources and processing time, people may prefer a sufficiently efficient strategy to solve a particular type of problem rather than the strategy that is the most adapted to it.

CONFLICTS IN ADAPTIVITY

Most studies investigating the adaptivity of strategy selection focus upon this either with respect to problem features (e.g., McDougall & Vellmans, 1993; Siegler & Lemaire, 1997), or with respect to the past success rate of strategies (Schunn et al., 2001; Schunn & Reder, 2001). In those few studies that consider both types of adaptivity (Lemaire & Reder, 1999; Reder, 1987), these are rarely set up in opposition to each other. One exception, however, is Lovett and Anderson (1996). For the Building Sticks Task, they created problems for which the most adaptive strategy was no longer the one that had been successfully applied to previous problems. The results showed that both (1) the past success rate of the strategies and (2) current problem features influenced strategy choice independently from one another. In the course of the experiments, participants changed from being sensitive to past success rates to being sensitive to the problem features, or vice versa, depending on the study. However, for all experiments, problems could only be solved by one of the two strategies, either one that was adaptive on the basis of the problem features, or one that was adaptive on the basis of its past success rate. Consequently, participants had no option but to change strategies if they wanted to solve the task.

In the following series of experiments we explored people's strategy choice in a similar conflicting situation, but, unlike Lovett and Anderson (1996), we used problems that *could* be solved accurately with all strategies available. This procedure allowed us to investigate whether people's strategy choices are still adaptive to current problem features, as established in our previous series of experiments, or whether the past success rate of the strategies might play a more important role.

For Experiment 4, in order to create a conflict between both potential sources of adaptivity, we manipulated the success rate of the acronym and the rehearsal strategy in the no-choice phase (see Table 5.4). All trials for the second series of experiments were simple problems, having the same structure as those of Experiment 1 (see Tables 5.1 and 5.3). Participants were instructed to apply the *acronym strategy* to problems which were *biased against this*, hence resulting in a low success rate. However, they were instructed to apply *rehearsal* to *unbiased* problems – that could be easily encoded in this way – thus resulting in a high success rate for this strategy. In the choice phase, unbiased problems were presented. These can be solved accurately by either strategy, although the acronym strategy is most appropriate choice since fewer resources are required when encoding only the first letters of the premise terms. Participants normally prefer to apply the acronym strategy to unbiased problems (see Experiments 1 to 3; also Dierckx, 2001).

In Experiment 4, a comparison of the accuracy of the acronym and the rehearsal strategy in the *no-choice* phase, and of the rated accuracy of the strategies, as expressed by the participants, revealed that our manipulation had worked. Fewer problems were solved correctly with the acronym ($M = 61\%$) than with the rehearsal strategy ($M = 77\%$) and this difference was also reflected in the participants' estimations of accuracy (respectively $M = 43\%$ vs. $M = 69\%$). The past success rate of the strategies in the no-choice phase influenced strategy application in the choice phase for 14 out of 15 participants. Averaged over them, only 9% of these unbiased problems, which could be encoded most efficiently with the acronym strategy, were actually solved in this way. Almost all participants thus seemed to have selected their strategies on the basis of past success rates rather than on the basis of the current problem features.

This result suggests that the past success rate of strategies is a very influential factor in their selection, potentially even more influential than the current problem features (to which participants were found to be highly sensitive in Experiments 1 to 3). Anecdotal evidence revealed that, in this experiment, participants did not seem to be aware of the fact that the problems in the choice phase had premise terms each with different starting letters, making them suited for encoding with the acronym strategy. Hence, they often reported rejecting the acronym strategy because they (incorrectly) believed that all items had ambiguous premise term first letters. Strategy selection mechanisms in this experiment thus seem to be less thorough than implied previously, only taking into account the past success rate of the strategies, while ignoring relevant problem features.

In Experiment 5, we prompted participants not only to consider the past success rate of the strategies but also the current problem features in their selection process, by making the latter features more salient. To this end, starting from the fourth problem in the choice phase, the first letters of the premise terms were printed in colour (see Table 5.4). This procedure allowed us to detect which strategy participants preferred initially – the one adaptive to the past success rate or the one adaptive to the current problem features – and which one they preferred after the relevant problem feature had been accentuated.

Colouring the first letters indeed influenced strategy selection. Across all participants in the choice phase, the percentage of acronym application to the uncoloured problems amounted to 30%, whereas for the coloured problems this increased to 64%, $\chi^2(1) = 9.92$, $p < .01$. However, there were important individual differences in adaptivity. About one-third of the participants (8/26) consistently applied the rehearsal strategy to the uncoloured as well as to the coloured problems. These participants thus always based their strategy use on their past success rates. Another third of the participants (8/26) consistently applied the acronym strategy to all problems, hence immediately adapting their strategy use to the current problem features, even when the first letters were not coloured. The remaining ten participants switched from the rehearsal to the acronym strategy after first receiving the coloured letters. Hence they changed from being adaptive to the past success rate of the strategies to being adaptive to the current problem features. In this group also individual differences emerged, but now in the speed with which participants adapted to the problem features. Some immediately did so whereas others only did so after two or even three coloured problems had been presented.

Besides colour, strategy choice was related to the relative success rate of the strategies in the no-choice phase. Hence, this was predicted by the difference in accuracy between the acronym versus the rehearsal strategy (Acronyms minus Rehearsal): using logistic regression, $\chi^2(1) = 5.67$, $p < .05$.[1] Closer inspection of the data suggests that this relative success rate may be an important cause of individual differences in adaptivity. The participants who applied the rehearsal strategy consistently in the choice phase were the ones for which the rehearsal strategy had the greatest accuracy advantage over the acronym strategy previously ($M = 54\%$ for the acronym strategy versus $M = 79\%$ for the rehearsal strategy, a difference of 25%). For these people, the rehearsal strategy had indisputably been the most successful. This difference in performance between the acronym and the rehearsal strategy was significantly larger than for people who immediately applied the acronym strategy in the choice phase ($M = 61\%$ for the acronym strategy versus $M = 64\%$ for the rehearsal strategy, a difference of only 3%), $F (1, 23) = 6.62$, $p < .05$. Hence, for the acronym-throughout participants, the small difference in past success rates clearly did not bias their future strategy selection.

---

[1] The difference in the rated accuracy of the acronym strategy versus the rehearsal strategy was also a significant predictor, but somewhat less influential than the difference in the actual accuracy scores, $\beta = .44$, $\chi^2(1) = 3.91$, $p < .05$.

For the people who switched strategies during the choice phase, the difference in accuracy for the previous no-choice phase lay in between the other two groups (M = 57% for the acronym strategy versus M = 68% for the rehearsal strategy, a difference of 11%), but did not differ significantly from either of them, $F (1, 23)$ = 2.85, p = .105 and $F (1, 23)$ = 1.05, p = .32. Although the participants who changed strategy preferred rehearsal at first, the relative success rate of the strategies in the past was not so extreme that they could not be 'convinced' to adapt their strategy use to the current problem features. However, it seems that one precondition has to be met to bring about this change: The appearance of the colour must be immediately useful. If this is not the case, as in Experiment 6, participants are less likely to switch strategies. For Experiment 6, the first two coloured-first-letter items (trials 4 and 5) were composed of premise terms containing identical starting letters, and hence these were biased against the acronym strategy (see Table 5.4). The third, fourth, and fifth coloured items were unbiased (trials 6, 7, 8). In this experiment, the coloured first letters *did not* influence subsequent strategy selection, even though considering this feature from the third coloured trial (trial 6, an unbiased item) would have led to the selection of the more efficient strategy. Only 4 out of 27 participants began using

TABLE 5.4

Structure of the problems and percentage acronym selection in the choice phase of Experiments 4 to 7 by problem type

No-choice phase		Choice phase	
Problem type (no of trials)	Strategy	Problem type (no of trials or trial numbers)	Acronym selection %
Experiment 4 (N = 15)			
Biased rehearsal (10)	Acronym	Unbiased (10)	9
Unbiased (10)	Rehearsal		
Experiment 5 (N = 26)			
Biased rehearsal (10)	Acronym	Unbiased uncoloured (1 to 3)	30
Unbiased (10)	Rehearsal	Unbiased coloured (4 to 10)	64
Experiment 6 (N = 27)			
Biased rehearsal (10)	Acronym	Unbiased uncoloured (1 to 3)	25
Unbiased (10)	Rehearsal	Biased rehearsal coloured (7)[a]	7
		Unbiased coloured (7)[a]	29
Experiment 7 (N = 21)			
Biased rehearsal (10)	Acronym	Unbiased (10)	55
Unbiased (10)	Rehearsal	Biased acronyms (10)	73
		Biased rehearsal (10)	3

[a] These trials were intermixed, but biased rehearsal coloured items were always shown for Trials 4 and 5, Unbiased for Trials 6, 7, 8.

the acronym strategy as soon as they encountered an unbiased coloured trial (see Dierckx, 2001). Many of the participants (12/27) never applied the acronym strategy (or applied it only once, to the first coloured problem), preferring rehearsal, i.e., the strategy with the highest success rate during the previous no-choice sessions. The remaining participants either immediately adapted their strategy choice to the problem features, having already applied the acronym strategy to the uncoloured problems (6/27), or only began using the acronym strategy having encountered several unbiased coloured trials (5/27). Hence, for the strategy selection process, if it is not immediately useful to take account of the highlighting of the starting letters of the premise terms, most of the participants seem to ignore this feature subsequently.

Given the substantial role of past success rates of strategies, in Experiment 7 we attempted to replicate the findings of Lovett & Anderson (1996) in the context of reasoning. Hence, if we were to have a choice phase in which problem features are heavily biased against the use of the previously most-successful strategy, would participants during the choice phase nonetheless select the strategy which previously had the highest success rate during the no-choice phase, or use the strategy that is the most adapted to current problem features? Experiment 7 combined the procedures of the two series of experiments discussed thus far (see Table 5.4). We were especially interested in the participants' strategy application to the problems biased towards acronyms, i.e., problems with long premise terms. These problems can be solved much more efficiently with the acronym strategy than with the rehearsal strategy, but the acronym strategy was associated with the lower past success rate in the no-choice phase.

Figure 5.1 displays the proportion of participants applying the acronym strategy to biased and unbiased problems as a function of their order of occurrence. As can be seen, the more problems solved that were biased towards acronyms, the more adapted strategy application to this type of problem became, $F(1, 19) = 12.42$, $p < .01$. From the third problem on, the proportion of acronym strategy application was almost as high as on the tenth problem, $F(1, 19) = 2.11$, $p = .163$. This change, from being adaptive to the past success rate of the strategies to being adaptive to the current problem features, thus occurred soon in the course of the choice phase. Two 'failures' with the preferred rehearsal strategy were sufficient to sensitise people to problem features in their subsequent strategy selections. Interestingly, for the unbiased problems, to which the rehearsal strategy can be applied accurately but the acronym strategy is the better option, strategy use also became somewhat more adapted to the problem features the more problems encountered, but not as adapted as for the problems biased towards acronyms. By the third occurrence of these problems, 60% of the participants selected the acronym strategy. Only 3 of the 21 participants consistently applied the rehearsal

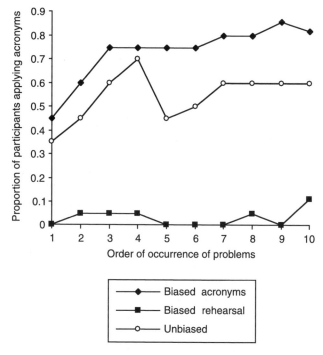

Figure 5.1 Proportion of participants applying the acronym strategy to the problems biased towards acronyms, the problems biased towards rehearsal and the unbiased problems, in the order of occurrence of the problems.

strategy to all problems. The results for Experiment 7 thus suggest that, although individual differences in adaptivity still exist, most of the participants are able to adapt their strategy use to the current problem features, regardless of the success rate of the strategies in the past. However, this comes with the proviso that being adaptive to the features must genuinely help them to perform better, for example, the items should have a definite best strategy that can be applied to them.

DISCUSSION

The experiments presented in this chapter demonstrate that people's strategy application in linear reasoning is generally highly adaptive. As for other domains, such as mathematics (e.g., Siegler & Lemaire, 1997) and memory (e.g., McDougall & Velmans, 1993), people tended to encode premises using the strategy that was the most adapted for solving individual problems (Experiment 1). However, under certain circumstances, a decrease in adaptivity was established. One of the factors that made strategy application less adaptive was the complexity of the reasoning problems (Experiments 2 and 3; see also De Rammelaere et al., 2003). With more complex problems, fewer individuals adapted their strategy use to problem features on an item-by-item basis, even though this reduced their level of performance. Interestingly, increased rigidity in strategy selection manifested itself as a more frequent application of the rehearsal strategy, with which all problems can be encoded accurately, even though when the premise terms are long, this requires a larger investment of processing resources. For the indeterminate reasoning problems (Experiment 3), the most complex problems in this study, this decrease in adaptivity also occurred within individuals: Many people varied strategy usage on a trial-by-trial basis, but several of them were less able to select the most efficient strategy to encode each and every problem.

Another factor that influenced the adaptivity of people's strategy choice was the success of the strategies in the past. The importance of this factor as a determinant of strategy selection has already been indicated in several other studies (e.g., Lemaire & Reder, 1999; Lovett & Anderson, 1996; Reder, 1987). However, in our experiments, selecting the strategy that was most effective in the past led to the use of a strategy that was less adaptive to the current problem features. Despite this, most of our participants preferred to apply the strategy that was previously the most successful over the one that was the most suited to the features of the current problems (Experiments 4 and 6). Only those participants for whom the difference in success rates of the strategies were small or moderate during the no-choice phase, and hence were not particularly biased by their previous experience, took account of current problem features during the choice phase (Experiment 5) and used the acronym strategy. However, those with moderate differences between the two strategies also did so after the relevant problem features were made more salient. It is not clear why the acronym-throughout users in the choice phase of Experiment 5 had managed to apply the two strategies equally accurately during the no-choice phase. One possible explanation could be that they may have implicitly modified the acronym strategy, allowing them to construct more distinguishable acronyms where premise terms started with the same letter (e.g., by also encoding the second letter in silence or by adding meaning to the letters). However, it is not clear why these participants in particular modified the acronym strategy. The accuracy data in the no-choice phase shows that these participants applied the acronym strategy more accurately than the others ($M = 61\%$ versus $M = 54\%$ for people who applied only the rehearsal strategy during the choice phase, and $M = 57\%$ for people who changed strategies). However, these people performed *less well* when using the rehearsal strategy during the no-choice phase ($M = 64\%$ versus $M = 79\%$ for people who applied only the rehearsal strategy during the choice phase, and $M = 68\%$ for people who changed strategies) which cannot be explained.

An exception to the preference for relying on the past success rates of strategies was found when items were strongly biased against the use of previously successful strategies (Experiment 7). After experiencing only a few failures with the preferred, previously successful – but now inappropriate strategy – choices became highly adaptive to the current problem features.

One important question that may be raised is, on what grounds are participants able to select the most accurate strategy when no explicit feedback on their past performance is given? The answer to this question seems to be twofold. First of all, participants are not necessarily novices in using encoding strategies such as rehearsal or acronyms. They possess a lot of knowledge about the performance of these strategies, accumulated through their previous applications in similar or different domains (e.g., Siegler & Lemaire, 1997). This prior knowledge is certainly relied upon during strategy selection. Participants in our study often expressed their preference for the faster and less resource-demanding acronym strategy over the rehearsal strategy, before they had even applied the former. Furthermore, in the course of the experiment, participants also receive implicit feedback about their performance with each strategy. This feedback is mostly based on the ease with which they can construct a representation within time limits, and the ease and certainty with which they can derive a conclusion based on this representation. If a representation is low quality because it is unstable, incomplete, or ambiguous, participants will have the impression that the strategy they used to construct it is not particularly suited to the task. There is a high correlation between the actual accuracy scores and the estimated accuracy by the participants which shows that their impression indeed has a basis in reality. Hence strategy accuracy, which is a consequence of ease of representation construction and representation quality, can determine strategy selection.

The most noticeable observation in all our experiments is that people often seem to prefer a satisfactory strategy to the optimal strategy. This is a very reasonable way of behaving, given the limitations of human information processing, and has been termed, variously, Bounded Rationality (e.g., Gigerenzer & Todd, 1999; Simon, 1956) or Rationality$_1$ (e.g., Evans, 2000; Evans & Over, 1997). The idea behind these terms is that people often settle for a solution that satisfies their goals instead of a solution that reaches a level of performance which may be expected according to a normative theory (e.g., Anderson, 1999; Evans, 2000; Evans & Over, 1997). Selecting a strategy that worked well before, or else consistently applying a strategy which yields a sufficiently accurate answer, are indeed reasonable procedures. By choosing according to these criteria, strategy selection is reduced to a very basic process requiring only a minimal amount of resources. The fact that strategy selection procedures themselves may require a certain amount of resources is often neglected by recent models (e.g., Lovett & Anderson, 1996; Shrager & Siegler, 1998; Siegler & Lemaire, 1997). In order to be able to weight the benefits and costs of all the strategies available, while taking into account all relevant problem features and instructions, there is a risk that unlimited time and resources may be required. This is, of course, an untenable assumption.

An interesting possibility that bypasses the cognitive demands of the strategy selection procedure is that people may perform a rough cost-benefit analysis before the actual strategy selection procedures are carried out. The outcome of this determines how detailed the strategy selection process will be. We are not proposing that people actually weigh the full costs and benefits of carrying out a detailed selection process, because that too would require a certain amount of resources, and leads to a potential infinite regress. Instead, we believe that people tend to apply only a basic low-cost strategy selection procedure, and that they will only change to a more detailed and ongoing procedure if there is a good reason. One possible good reason is that taking into account problem features on an item-by-item basis is required in order to perform acceptably accurately (see Experiment 7), an alternative good reason is that doing so considerably reduces the effort in solving the problems.

The potential to improve performance considerably, and/or reduce costs of execution may, for example, explain why, when multiplying two-digit numbers, participants change from using a calculator to mental calculation when the multiplicand is ten (e.g., Siegler & Lemaire, 1997). Solving such problems only requires the application of a simple rule, for which the amount of resources to be invested is a lot smaller than using a calculator. Additionally, numbers ending in 0 are very salient, like the coloured letters in our Experiments 5 and 6, making the identification and processing of this problem feature relatively easy. The small amount of extra cost associated with processing this feature may be worth investing, provided that it results in the selection of a more appropriate strategy, as it does for this type of multiplication problem, and in Experiment 5. However, when there are no immediate benefits associated with this more thorough strategy selection procedure (Experiment 6), it is a better option to stick with a very basic strategy selection procedure.

What about individual differences in adaptivity? In line with our cost-benefit approach to the strategy selection process itself, individual differences in working memory capacity and processing resources may influence the extent of the strategy selection process, and consequently the adaptiveness of people's strategy choices. Under certain circumstances, some people may not have enough resources, or have to invest too many of them, to accomplish adequately both a detailed strategy selection process and solve the task. In such a situation, they may choose to apply one single strategy to all problems, ignoring relevant features, even though this strategy might not be well suited to certain problems (see also De Rammelaere et al., 2003). So, in line with Schunn and Reder (2001), we expect individual differences in ability, as measured by psychometric tests, also to be related to sensitivity to the problem features when selecting strategies.

As a final remark, we would like to urge reasoning researchers to pay more attention to the strategies that people use when solving reasoning problems; this aspect is overlooked much too often in this domain. Based on our findings, showing that even in a very restricted environment, people's strategy choices are extremely flexible and rational, one might wonder about the richness and sophistication of strategy application in a context in which people are free to solve complex reasoning problems in any way they like.

ACKNOWLEDGEMENTS

This chapter presents research results of the Belgian programme on Interuniversity Poles of Attraction initiated by the Belgian State, Prime Minister's Office, Science Policy programming, Grants no. P3/31 and no. P4/19 from the Department of Science Policy to the second author. The scientific responsibility is assumed by its authors.

REFERENCES

Anderson, J. R. (1999). *The adaptive character of thought*. Hillsdale, NJ; Lawrence Erlbaum Associates, Inc.

Baddeley, A. D., Thomson, N., & Buchanan, M. (1975). Word length and the structure of short-term memory. *Journal of Verbal Learning and Verbal Behavior, 14*, 575–589.

De Rammelaere, S., Duverne, S., Lemaire, P., & Vandierendonck, A. (2003). *Working memory load changes strategy adaptivity only when the task is hard*. Unpublished manuscript.

Dierckx, V. (2001). *Strategies and representation in temporal reasoning*. Unpublished doctoral dissertation, Ghent University, Ghent.

Dierckx, V., Vandierendonck, A., & Pandelaere, M. (2003). Is model construction open to strategic decisions? An exploration in the field of linear reasoning. *Thinking and Reasoning, 9*, 97–131.

Diggle, P. J., Kung-Yee, L., & Zeger, L. S. (1994). *Analysis of longitudinal data*. New York: Oxford University Press.

Evans, J. St. B. T. (2000). What could and could not be a strategy in reasoning. In W. Schaeken, G. De Vooght, A. Vandierendonck, & G. d'Ydewalle (Eds.), *Deductive reasoning and strategies* (pp. 1–20). New York: Lawrence Erlbaum Associates, Inc.

Evans, J. St. B. T., & Over, D. E. (1997). Rationality in reasoning: The problem of deductive competence. *Current Psychology of Cognition, 16*, 3–38.

Evans, J. St. B. T., Newstead, S. E., & Byrne, R. M. J. (1993). *Human reasoning: The psychology of deduction*. Hove, UK: Psychology Press.

Gardner, W. P., & Rogoff, B. (1990). Children's deliberateness of planning according to task circumstances. *Developmental Psychology, 26*, 480–487.

Gigerenzer, G., & Todd, P. M. (1999). Fast and frugal heuristics: The adaptive toolbox. In G. Gigerenzer & P. M. Todd (Eds.), *Simple heuristics that make us smart* (pp. 3–34). New York: Oxford University Press.

Johnson-Laird, P. N., & Byrne, R. M. J. (1991). *Deduction*. Hove, UK: Psychology Press.

Johnson-Laird, P. N., Byrne, R. M. J., & Schaeken, W. (1992). Propositional reasoning by model. *Psychological Review, 99*, 418–439.

Johnson-Laird, P. N., Byrne, R. M. J., & Schaeken, W. (1994). Why models rather than rules give a better account of propositional reasoning: A reply to Bonatti and to O'Brien, Braine, and Yang. *Psychological Review, 101*, 734–739.

Kerkman, D. D., & Siegler, R. S. (1993). Individual differences and adaptive flexibility in lower-income children's strategy choices. *Learning and Individual Differences, 5*, 113–136.

Lemaire, P., & Reder, L. M. (1999). What affects strategy selection in arithmetic? The example of parity and five effects on product verification. *Memory and Cognition, 27*, 364–382.

Lemaire, P., & Siegler, R. S. (1995). Four aspects of strategic change: Contributions to children's learning of multiplication. *Journal of Experimental Psychology: General, 124*, 83–97.

Lovett, M. C., & Anderson, J. R. (1996). History of successes and current context in problem solving: Combined influences on operator selection. *Cognitive Psychology, 31*, 168–217.

McDougall, S., & Velmans, M. (1993). Encoding strategy dynamics: When relationships between words determine strategy use. *British Journal of Psychology, 84*, 227–248.

Mynatt, B. T., & Smith, K. H. (1977). Constructive processes in linear ordering problems revealed by sentence study times. *Journal of Experimental Psychology: Human Learning and Memory, 3*, 357–374.

O'Brien, D. P., Braine, M. D. S., & Yang, Y. (1994). Propositional reasoning by mental models? Simple to refute in principle and in practice. *Psychological Review, 101*, 711–724.

Payne, J. W., Bettman, J. R., & Johnson, E. J. (1993). *The adaptive decision maker.* Cambridge: Cambridge University Press.

Potts, G. R. (1972). Information processing strategies used in the encoding of linear orderings. *Journal of Verbal Learning and Verbal Behavior, 11*, 727–740.

Reder, L. (1987). Strategy selection in question answering. *Cognitive Psychology, 19*, 90–137.

Rips, L. J. (1989). The psychology of knights and knaves. *Cognition, 31*, 85–116.

Rittle-Johnson, B., & Siegler, R. S. (1999). Learning to spell: Variability, choice and change in children's strategy use. *Child Development, 70*, 322–348.

Roberts, M. J. (1993). Human reasoning. Deduction rules or mental models, or both? *Quarterly Journal of Experimental Psychology, 46A*, 569–589.

Roberts, M. J. (2000). Individual differences in reasoning strategies: A problem to solve or an opportunity to seize? In W. Schaeken, G. De Vooght, A. Vandierendonck, & G. d'Ydewalle (Eds.), *Deductive reasoning and strategies* (pp. 23–48). New York: Lawrence Erlbaum Associates, Inc.

Schaeken, W., Van der Henst, J.-B., & Schroyens, W. (in press). The mental models theory of relational reasoning: Premises' relevance, conclusions' phrasing, and cognitive economy. In W. Schaeken, A. Vandierendonck, W. Schroyens, & G. d'Ydewalle (Eds.), *The mental models theory of reasoning: Refinements and extensions.* Mahwah, NJ: Lawrence Erlbaum Associates, Inc.

Schaeken, W., De Vooght, G., Vandierendonck, A., & d'Ydewalle, G. (Eds.). (2000). *Deductive reasoning and strategies.* New York: Lawrence Erlbaum Associates, Inc.

Schaeken, W., Vandierendonck, A., Schroyens, W., & d'Ydewalle, G. (Eds.). (in press) *The mental models theory of reasoning: Refinements and extensions.* Mahwah, NJ: Lawrence Erlbaum Associates, Inc.

Schunn, D. D., & Reder, L. M. (2001). Another source of individual differences: Strategy adaptivity to changing rates of success. *Journal of Experimental Psychology: General, 130*, 59–76.

Schunn, D. D., Lovett, M. C., & Reder, L. M. (2001). Awareness and working memory in strategy adaptivity. *Memory and Cognition, 29*, 254–266.

Shrager, J., & Siegler, R. S. (1998). A model of children's strategy choices and strategy discoveries. *Psychological Science, 9*, 405–410.

Siegler, R. S., & Lemaire, P. (1997). Older and younger adults' strategy choices in multiplication: Testing predictions of ASCM using the choice/no-choice paradigm. *Journal of Experimental Psychology: General, 126*, 71–92.

Siegler, R. S., & Shipley, C. (1995). Variation, selection, and cognitive chance. In T. Simon & G. Halford (Eds.), *Developing cognitive competence: New approaches to process modeling* (pp. 31–76). Hillsdale, NJ: Lawrence Erlbaum Associates, Inc.

Simon, H. A. (1956). Rational choice and the structure of the environment. *Psychological Review, 63*, 129–138.

Vandierendonck, A., & De Vooght, G. (1996). Evidence for mental-model-based reasoning: A comparison of reasoning with time and space concepts. *Thinking and Reasoning, 2*, 249–272.

Vandierendonck, A., Dierckx, V., & De Vooght, G. (2004). Mental model construction in linear reasoning: Evidence for the construction of initial annotated models. *Quarterly Journal of Experimental Psychology, 57A*, 1369–1391.

CHAPTER SIX

Strategy usage in a simple reasoning task: Overview and implications

Maxwell J. Roberts
Department of Psychology, University of Essex, UK

Elizabeth J. Newton
Department of Human Communication Science, University College London, UK

What is 5 + 2?

This is a relatively easy question, and most people can recall its answer, having memorised it as a result of past experience. However, if the answer is not known, there are many strategies that could be applied to find it, and some are more effective than others. One strategy, often used by children, is to count out two raised fingers on one hand, and then five raised fingers on the other, and then count the total number of raised fingers (the *sum strategy*). However, a more effective method is to count up from the larger addend. For example, starting at 5 and counting two upwards: '5, 6, 7'. Not only does this *min strategy* require fewer operations (hence saving time and improving accuracy), but it can also be used for *impasse problems* – such as *what is 11 + 2?* – which defeat the sum strategy. Of course, to recall a correct solution is the most effective strategy of all, but this requires appropriate past experience. In order to acquire sufficient experience at solving a wide range of problems, the min strategy is therefore an important component of children's strategy repertoires. However, there are quite substantial individual differences in how quickly this is developed. It appears that the children who are the most adept at the less effective strategies, such as the sum strategy, are those who are more likely to discover the min strategy (e.g., Siegler, 1996).

If some of the artists are not beekeepers
and if some of the chefs are beekeepers
then we can conclude that:
a)   *all of the chefs are artists*
b)   *none of the chefs are artists*
c)   *some of the chefs are artists*
d)   *some of the chefs are not artists*
e)   *no valid conclusion linking chefs in terms of artists*

Identifying conclusions to categorical premise pairs is a much harder task, with as many as two-thirds of students giving incorrect answers for the example (e.g., Dickstein, 1978). However, it is far easier to solve if the strategy of applying the *two-somes* rule is used: If the quantifier *some* appears in each of the two premises, then there is never a valid conclusion. Again, the people who are best at identifying conclusions *without using* the rule are those who are more likely to discover it (Galotti, Baron, & Sabini, 1986).

Given that:

> *John is taller than Paul*
> *Dave is taller than Paul*
> *Tom is taller than Dave*
> *Ian is taller than Tom*
> *Dave is taller than John*

Who is taller, John or Ian?

Most people appear to solve *linear reasoning problems* by mentally constructing a *spatial array* (at least to begin with); something along the lines of:

> *Ian*
>   *Tom*
>   *Dave*
>   *John*
>   *Paul*

However, if all of the premises are presented simultaneously (parallel presentation), this problem can also be solved by scanning the two sides of the display: John and Ian both appear on the left, but only John appears on the right, and so Ian must be the taller. This is a far speedier and more accurate procedure. Wood (e.g., 1978) found that those who were best at solving items by using spatial arrays initially were the people who were most likely to discover short-cuts such as scanning strategies.

Where would a person end up, relative to the starting point after taking:

> *one step north*
> *one step east*
> *one step south*
> *one step west*
> *one step south*
> *one step west*
> *one step north*
> *one step north*

There are two strategies for solving *compass point directions task* problems. The most frequently used is the *spatial strategy*. For this, an attempt is made to trace the path, mentally if no external means of representation are available. A generally faster, more accurate, and less stressful approach is to use *cancellation*: Opposite directions cancel, and those that remain constitute the correct answer. Those people who are best at reasoning spatially tend to be those who avoid the spatial strategy altogether, and use cancellation instead (see Roberts, Gilmore, & Wood, 1997; Wood, 1978).

More recently, Siegler and Svetina (2002) have investigated children solving matrix problems. For these, three pictures along with an empty cell were given in a 2 × 2 grid. The task was to identify the rules that linked the pictures (e.g., animals in the left cells face left, animals in the right cells face right; shapes in the upper cells are red, shapes in the lower cells are green) in order to identify the contents of the empty cell. Two groups of children were identified who initially performed poorly: *learners* and *nonlearners*. In the first block of trials, both groups on average solved fewer than 20% of items correctly. They tended to apply a *matching strategy* in which their chosen answers merely matched one of the pictures shown in the other cells. Despite numerous trials, nonlearners continued with this strategy, and their performance never improved. In comparison, the learners improved rapidly. They first learnt a strategy in which a subset of rules was identified and applied, followed by the correct strategy of identifying and applying all rules in order to generate the correct answer. Interestingly, the learners' performance was initially slightly better (approx. 17% correct versus 9%) and they also performed better at the structurally similar Raven's Coloured Progressive Matrices (Raven, Raven, & Court, 1993), on average scoring at the 56th percentile, versus the 36th for the nonlearners.

What do these tasks have in common? They all show that the best strategies are not necessarily available to everyone. On first encountering a task, few people may be in possession of the better strategies, and so less effective methods will have to be used initially. However, with experience improvements become available, but only to certain people: those who were best at executing the more demanding and/or less effective initial strategies. How are new strategies discovered, and why mainly by the best performers, who in theory need such improvements the least?

Before commencing, we should note that we will be using a *broad definition* of the term *strategy*: Hence, Siegler and Jenkins (1989) suggest that a strategy is 'any procedure that is non-obligatory and goal directed' (p. 11). A strategy is therefore any self-contained set of cognitive processes which, in theory, could be modified or dispensed with. *Narrow definitions* add additional criteria to this, but Roberts and Newton (2003) argue that these additions are at best unnecessary, and at worse may actually damage progress in the field.

The question *what determines strategy availability?* is important for *all* researchers into strategy usage. For those who study mechanisms of *strategy selection*, it is essential to know the contents of people's strategy repertoires.[1] People can only choose between strategies that are either (1) present in their strategy repertoires on commencement of a task, having been added as a result of instruction, or past experience with the same or related tasks; or (2) added to their strategy repertoires as a result of experience with the current task. For particular tasks and populations, people's strategy repertoires may be relatively homogeneous and unchanging. However, where people's repertoires differ and/or expand at different rates, this can complicate studies. One solution is for researchers to inform subjects of all possible strategies (e.g., Lemaire & Lecacheur, 2001; Lovett & Schunn, 1999, Exp. 1), perhaps then asking them to practise with these, before giving them a free choice between the options (e.g., see Dierckx & Vandierendonck, chapter 5 this volume; Newton & Roberts, 2000).

Findings from various studies of *strategy selection* suggest that this tends to be rational: People choose the strategies that result in the most effective performance, even varying usage on a trial by trial basis if necessary (e.g., Lemaire, Lecacheur, & Farioli, 2000; Lemaire & Siegler, 1995; Siegler & Lemaire, 1997). However, researchers disagree as to the exact mechanism for this. Some emphasise the importance of people's knowledge of strategy properties, such as past success, both overall and in relation to particular features of target problems (e.g., Shrager & Siegler, 1998; Siegler, 1996, 1999). Others suggest that the problem features by themselves are more important (e.g., Reder & Schunn, 1996; Schunn, Reder, Nhouyvanisvong, Richards, & Stroffolino, 1997). Even so, strategy selection will only be optimal if the correct cues for usage are salient and have been represented (Lovett &

---

[1] It is important to note that researchers use the term *strategy repertoire* in different ways. Here, use of this term refers to the strategies that an *individual* is aware of for performing a particular task. Hence, individuals' strategy repertoires may differ, with the consequence that different people will have different options to choose between during the strategy selection process. Strategy repertoire has also been used to denote all possible strategies for a task, irrespective of whether all people are aware of them, or are prepared to use them (e.g., see Lemaire & Fabre, chapter 1 this volume).

Schunn, 1999) and there may well be developmental (e.g., Lemaire & Siegler, 1995) and individual differences (e.g., Dierckx & Vandierendonck, chapter 5 this volume; Schunn & Reder, 2001) in strategy adaptivity, so that some people are better able to identify more appropriate methods than others.

Strategy selection is not entirely rational in terms of the definition above: Biases have been detected which can result in suboptimal choices. For example, Siegler & Lemaire (1997) found that both younger and older adults underused a calculator in situations where this had an advantage over mental arithmetic. Such biases may reflect long-term success at using inefficient strategies – mental arithmetic in this case – coupled with comparative inexperience with new, more effective strategies – using a calculator – (see also Dierckx and Vandierendonck, chapter 5 this volume). In addition, Rittle-Johnson and Siegler (1999) found that children often resorted to inherently slow and inaccurate strategies when attempting to spell (e.g., sounding out a word). This increased effort, compared with attempts simply to recall the spelling, and did little or nothing to improve their performance. This probably reflects children's lack of confidence when attempting to recall spellings, even though the recall strategy was never the least effective. Hence, both sets of results can be accommodated in the models of strategy selection proposed so far. In contrast, selection mechanisms based entirely or largely on the preferences of people to encode information in different ways (so-called cognitive style accounts, e.g., Riding & Rayner, 1998; Sternberg, 1997) can generally be ruled out (e.g., Roberts & Newton, 2001).

Individuals' strategy repertoires are unlikely to be entirely static, even for adults, and it is highly unlikely that people acquire strategies only as a result of instruction. It cannot be disputed that strategy discovery also takes place spontaneously, as demonstrated by numerous studies into mathematical, inductive, and deductive reasoning. Hence, sooner or later, the issue of how people discover new strategies for themselves will have to be addressed. The acquisition of a new strategy, whether by adult or child, is primarily a developmental question: How do people's cognitive processes change as a result of experience? What do people learn while they are reasoning, and why do people differ in what they learn? Evidence from both adults and children is equally relevant to this question, especially as researchers such as Siegler and colleagues (e.g., Siegler, 1996) suggest that no strategy acquisition processes are unique to any particular age group, and that all developmental changes can be understood in terms of the accumulation and modification of individual strategies with experience. Assuming that this is correct, the task for people researching strategy discovery is greatly simplified. Unfortunately, the strategy discovery processes themselves are difficult to study, which perhaps explains the comparative rarity of such work compared with strategy selection studies. Such events tend to be rapid and fleeting. They may occur at any point during a long sequence of trials, or not at all for certain people.

A researcher may attempt to target people who will be particularly likely to make such discoveries, and alter items and their presentation formats so as to make them maximally conducive to this. However, ultimately strategy discovery is more or less under the 'control' of the subject.

Despite difficulties in studying strategy discovery, a consistent picture is emerging. The five tasks described earlier have all supplied data which suggests that strategy discovery is success-based. In situations where identical strategies are used, the more successful problem solvers must be those who encode, represent, and process information the most successfully. In other words, successful performance equals consistent performance, so that the best performers are better able to detect regularities, identify and remove redundant procedures, and create less cumbersome, more elegant strategies. Given this, while unsuccessful performance may lead to an awareness of the need for new strategies, this will also prevent their discovery. The 'noisy' encoding, representation, and processing which led to poorer performance also mean that regularities are less detectable. Overall, the best get better, and the less successful are left behind.

Failure-based theories of strategy discovery have also been proposed (e.g., VanLehn, 1988), but are currently less favoured. For these, strategy discovery takes place as a result of the failure of a current strategy to generate a satisfactory answer when solving a problem, i.e., an *impasse*. When encountering an impasse, problem solving focuses on overcoming this, and the new strategies that are discovered as a result are added to an individual's repertoire. However, when investigating children's addition strategies, Siegler and Jenkins (1989) found that impasse problems could trigger the adoption of new strategies, but *only* if they had been discovered on previous trials. No trace of impasse-related behaviour (e.g., many errors) could be identified just before the point where new strategies were *really* discovered.

STRATEGY USAGE AND THE COMPASS POINT DIRECTIONS TASK

The purpose of the current chapter is to take an in-depth look at data from the *compass point directions task*. With its two distinct strategies, and apparent clear differences in their effectiveness, this task is one of several that are well suited to answering the question: Who discovers new strategies, and why? When this task is formatted so that all steps are presented at once on a single screen (parallel presentation), and there is no opportunity to use external means such as pencil and paper, typically, one-third to one-half of adults in a sample will adopt cancellation. Hence, it is immediately apparent that this strategy is neither self-evident nor trivial to discover.

The key findings that led to a success-based account of strategy discovery for this task are as follows. Roberts et al. (1997) found that spatial ability predicted strategy selection, such that people with high spatial ability were more likely to use cancellation than people with low ability (an inverted aptitude–strategy relationship). Spatial ability has always emerged as the best predictor of strategy usage for this task when compared directly with other dimensions. These include personality scales and a measure of self-rated imagery (Roberts, 1991), verbal ability (Roberts et al., 1997; Roberts & Roberson, 2001), and intelligence (Roberts et al., 1997). These findings led to the suggestion that people who are better able to execute the spatial strategy, as indicated by high spatial ability, are the most likely to discover cancellation. As an illustration, if a person finds that taking one step east, one step north, and one step west always results in a heading of due north, it is straightforward to infer that opposite steps are redundant, and may be cancelled no matter how many others intervene, so that the entire process of constructing the spatial representation is also redundant. Compare this with a person whose answers range from north-east to north-west for the same steps – these errors are not unknown even amongst university students. Here, a person will be aware that performance is inconsistent, but this inconsistency – which reveals a need to change strategies – conceals the strategy that could be discovered.

Corroborative evidence for high and low spatials differing in their accuracy at executing the spatial strategy was obtained from a subsequent task in which directions for two people were given, one at a time (i.e., serial presentation), and the position of one relative to the other was the required answer (Roberts et al., 1997, Exp. 1). Very few subjects were able to identify a cancellation strategy for this task, but those who had used cancellation for the one-person version previously were the better group by far at solving the two-person task by using a spatial strategy. Those who had used the spatial strategy previously for the one-person task were the worst group by far at the two-person version.

Thus far, success has been proposed as a limiting factor in *strategy discovery*. However, Roberts et al. (1997) suggested that people may also need to *evaluate* the validity of newly discovered strategies before they can be available for use. This came from the observation that many subjects reported identifying cancellation while solving the directions task, experimenting with this – with a corresponding increase in solution times – but eventually rejecting the strategy as invalid. A newly discovered strategy, whose validity is uncertain, may therefore potentially not be available, despite being present in an individual's strategy repertoire. Incorrect evaluation may thus act as a barrier to adoption for some, even when the new strategy is very effective. The requirement for evaluation is again more likely to present a difficulty to people less able to execute the original strategy successfully. This is because, where necessary, the only means of evaluation is to compare the output of the new strategy with one that is known to be valid – the one from which it was derived. Even if the answers generated by the new strategy are the more accurate, the people who are unable to execute the original strategy successfully will find a persistent disagreement in answers. This must inevitably lead to the rejection of the new strategy. Newton and Roberts (2000) corroborated this suggestion by manipulating levels of feedback. Partial feedback (correct/incorrect) led to no more adoption of cancellation than no feedback at all, while full feedback (the correct answer if an error was made) led to significantly more people adopting cancellation. It was argued that full feedback was unlikely to be increasing the likelihood that cancellation was discovered. Instead, for those who discovered this strategy, full feedback was facilitating its evaluation by providing a benchmark answer against which its accuracy could be compared. Partial feedback is unlikely to assist to the same extent: Knowing that an answer is incorrect need not mean that a conflicting answer found by using a different strategy must be correct.

To date, several experiments using the directions task have been conducted by Roberts and colleagues (Newton, 2001; Newton & Roberts, 2000; Roberts, 1991; Roberts et al., 1997; Roberts & Roberson, 2001) and from these, a total of 686 subjects have completed a straightforward version of the task *and* have been pre-tested for spatial ability. With such a number, various combined analyses not envisaged in the original studies are possible. These provide a number of important insights, corroborate many of the suggestions made above, and also point towards some issues to resolve in the future. Although the studies differed in their fine details, they share numerous common features, and an overview is given in the methods section in conjunction with Table 6.1 (individual papers should be consulted for precise details).

METHODS

Subjects

Of the 686 subjects whose data are analysed here, 558 were university students pre-tested with the Saville and Holdsworth Spatial Reasoning test (ST7) (Saville and Holdsworth Ltd, 1979). This was used both as a predictor of strategy usage (e.g., Roberts et al., 1997) and as a means of matching subjects between experimental groups (e.g., Newton & Roberts, 2000). The exceptions are Roberts and Roberson (2001, Exp. 2) who tested 64 adolescents aged 12 to 16 years, and Roberts et al. (1997, Exp. 3) who tested 64 elderly people aged from 60 to 71 years. The elderly subjects received the ASE (NFER-Nelson) General Ability Test *Spatial Test* (Smith and Whetton, 1988), not the ST7.

Materials and apparatus

Most people received the same set of 'standard trials'. These consisted of one practice trial and 36 experimental trials (divided into two blocks of 18). Each block consisted of six each of six-, seven- and eight-step items. They were devised with two criteria: (1) no two adjacent steps should be opposites (i.e., east would never follow west, etc.); (2) the path had to end on one of the 16 compass points, and would never end back at the start. Some studies varied the number of trials and/or trial length and structure. These exceptions are shown on Table 6.1. Where even numbers of steps are used, only the simple compass points (N, S, E, W, NE, NW, SE, SW) are possible as answers. For one study (Newton, Exp. 5), *trial structure* was varied, and this will be described later. Stimuli were either presented on individual cards, or by computer. Computer presentation utilised either MacLab (Costin, 1988) or PsyScope (Cohen, MacWhinney, Flatt, & Provost, 1993).

Procedure

All subjects were pre-tested for spatial ability before performing the directions task. For all studies, on commencement, subjects were shown a diagram of the compass points required as answers, followed by a compass point naming task. These familiarised subjects with the answers that would be required subsequently. For the directions task, written instructions were followed by a practice trial, and then a diagram showing its path and answer (irrespective of whether the subject's answer was correct). The directions task trials were then shown, always using parallel presentation of the steps. Subjects spoke their answers, and were timed either by the experimenter stopping a timer, or by the subjects pressing a button on commencement of speaking. Where trials were divided into blocks, subjects were given the opportunity to rest between these. For certain studies, subjects were given the option to use pencil and paper while solving items; for others, subjects were instructed to use cancellation to solve sets of items.

Depending on the strategy used and its speed of execution, 36 trials would typically take between 10 and 30 minutes to complete. After completion of all tasks, subjects were asked to describe in writing the strategies that they had used for the directions task, including any shifts or mixing of strategies that they had been aware of. They were asked to indicate point(s) of strategy change if they claimed a clean break, or indicate relative proportions if strategies were claimed to be mixed throughout. All were able to do so without difficulty, though some also gave verbal descriptions to help clarify matters.

Design and analyses

For the analyses to be performed below, subjects' strategies form a classification variable, with error rates and mean solution times being the dependent variables. The availability of spatial ability test scores and large numbers of subjects means that Analysis of Covariance can be used in order to remove

TABLE 6.1
Studies and experimental conditions used for the current analyses

Row	Study	Exp.	N	Steps	Sample	Block 1 Trials	Block 1 Task	Block 2 Trials	Block 2 Task
1	Roberts et al. (1997)	1	40	6/7/8	students	18	standard	18	standard
2		2	40	6/7/8	students	18	p&p[a]	18	p&p[a]
3	Roberts (1991)	3	64	5/6	elderly	16	standard	16	standard
4	Roberts & Roberson (2001)	5	24	6/7/8	students	18	instructed[b]	18	instructed[b]
5		1	40	6/7/8	students	18	standard	18	standard
6		2	64	6	adolescents	24	standard	–	–
7	Newton & Roberts (2000)	1	20	6/7/8	students	18	standard	18	standard
8			20	6/7/8	students	18	p&p[a]	18	standard
9			20	6/7/8	students	18	instructed[b]	18	standard
10			20	6/7/8	students	18	dax/med[c]	18	standard
11		2	20	6/7/8	students	18	p&p[a]	18	p&p[a]
12			20	6/7/8	students	18	instructed[b]	18	p&p[a]
13		3	72	6/7/8	students	18	standard[d]	18	standard[d]
14	Newton (2001)	5	111	7/8[e]	students	16	standard	16	standard
15		6	111	[f]	students	16	standard	16	standard

Notes:

[a] Where pencil and paper (p&p) were offered, it was stressed that this was optional, and that subjects should only use it if it was felt that this would improve their performance.

[b] Cancellation was described and subjects were instructed to use this for all trials. It was emphasised that all temptation to visualise the paths should be avoided. For Block 2, depending on the experiment, either the requirement to use cancellation continued, or subjects were given a free choice of strategy (with the option to use pencil and paper for one study). Where a free choice was given, few subjects exercised this option, and continued to use cancellation.

[c] The dax/med task was an analogous task which required the cancellation of nonsense words equivalent to north, south, east, or west. The rules for this task were taught by example. Despite learning to use cancellation for this task, few subjects transferred this strategy to the directions task.

[d] Subjects were given varying degrees of feedback after responses to each trial. Trials remained on display after feedback. Full feedback (confirmation of correct answer, or correction of incorrect answer) boosted the development of cancellation, whereas partial feedback (whether the answer was correct or incorrect) did not. It was suggested that full feedback assisted subjects who were able to discover cancellation, but were unable to evaluate its validity.

[e] Step ordering was varied between groups: One group received standard trials, another received trials in which opposite steps were adjacent wherever possible (i.e., east/west and north/south). The final group received trials in which same-direction steps were always adjacent.

[f] Trial length was varied between groups: 5/6 step, 7/8 step, and 9/10 step trials.

the effects of spatial ability when comparing performance between strategies. In conjunction with this, means reported are *least square means* (*LSM*). In other words, levels of performance are corrected for spatial ability. In addition, strategy usage as a function of spatial ability test score will also be investigated.

RESULTS AND DISCUSSION

Error rates are based upon whether or not answers were exactly correct. Permutation slips were permitted, for example, an answer of ENN where the correct answer was NNE. In order to have sufficient data points to calculate accurate means, solution times were included for answers that were no more than one compass point out (e.g., NNE for N, but not NE). Subjects were classified into strategy groups in two ways on the basis of their written retrospective reports. The *dominant strategy* was the strategy reported as being used for the majority of trials. This was used when analysing performance, which must reflect best the strategy used most often. To investigate strategy selection, reports were also classified by *final choice of strategy*. This distinction is necessary since, for example, some subjects only selected cancellation towards the end of the trials, and thus the spatial strategy would dominate performance. Subjects were generally able to report their strategies with little difficulty. Where two strategies were described, most reported changing with a clean break. For consistency, those who claimed to have used both strategies for an equal number of trials were classified as spatial strategy dominant. Typically, fewer than 5% of subjects were difficult to assign to a particular group, reporting using a mixture throughout the trials. For example, a subject might report using the spatial strategy for the majority of trials, but occasionally using cancellation to double check. Here, the majority strategy was taken to be both dominant and the final choice.

The majority of subjects in the various experiments were university students who received an identical set of 36 trials. By combining these, larger scale comparisons of performance as a function of dominant strategy are possible. Hence, on Table 6.1, combining the data from rows 1, 2, 4, 5, 7, 9, 11, 12, 13, we have: (1) subjects who were instructed to use cancellation, and reported continuing to use if they were subsequently given a choice of strategies ($N = 60$); (2) subjects who spontaneously reported using cancellation for the majority of the trials ($N = 63$); (3) subjects who reported using the spatial strategy for the majority of trials ($N = 119$); (4) subjects who used the spatial strategy assisted by pencil and paper for the majority of trials ($N = 51$). The three remaining subjects used cancellation assisted with pencil and paper. This combined group of subjects will be named the *main data set*.

(1) People instructed to use cancellation perform very similarly to people who report adopting cancellation spontaneously

In all studies reported, strategies were identified by the use of retrospective verbal reports. While this technique is non-invasive, doubts have been expressed in the past concerning its accuracy. It is highly unlikely that these reports are worthless. Indeed, where subjects have the opportunity to use pencil and paper, the correspondence between their use of this and their retrospective reports is almost perfect, despite not having their drawings available when reporting. In spite of this, two recent studies imply a need for some caution. Siegler and Stern (1998) gave children simple arithmetic problems (e.g., $18 + 5 - 5$) and found that subjects' performance implied that they were skipping the redundant steps for several trials before their verbal reports admitted to this. In addition, Alibali (1999) found that for problems such as $4 + 3 + 5 = ??? + 5$, children's gestures gave a richer picture of strategy use than their verbalisations. Hence, are the reports for the directions task concealing a very high level of strategy variability, such that the performance differences between strategy groups are really due to, say, the spatial ability differences of subjects rather than supposed strategy selection differences?

The performance of people instructed to use cancellation is interesting from this point of view. One useful rule of thumb is that if subjects who are instructed to use a strategy perform similarly to subjects who report using the strategy spontaneously, then this suggests that the reports of the latter are a good reflection of reality. For the directions task, if non-instructed subjects' verbal reports suggest that they are cancellation dominant, but in reality the spatial strategy was used for almost as many trials, we would expect considerably slower performance, and many more errors, compared with instructed subjects.

A total of 64 subjects in the main data set have been instructed to use cancellation (see Table 6.1), but in two of the studies the requirement to use cancellation ceased after the first block of 18 trials. Most of these subjects nonetheless remained with cancellation for Block 2. Hence a total of 60 subjects have been instructed to use cancellation, and have verbal reports indicating that they were dominant for this strategy. These were compared with the 63 subjects in the main data set who received no strategy instructions, and who spontaneously reported using cancellation for the majority of trials (without using pencil and paper where this option was available). Analysis of Covariance was used to investigate performance.

For error rates, with spatial ability test raw score as the covariate, and *instruction* (*cancellation* versus *no strategy instructions*) as the factor, the covariate × factor interaction was non-significant, $F(1, 119) = 0.12, p > .05$. On deleting the interaction from the model, the covariate was significant,

$F(1, 120) = 38.9$, $p < .01$ ($r^2 = 24\%$), but there was no significant effect of instruction, $F(1, 120) = 0.73$, $p > .05$. For instructed subjects, the least square mean was 25% errors (*SD* 16) versus 22% for the non-instructed subjects (*SD* 16).

For solution times, the covariate × factor interaction was also non-significant, $F(1, 119) = 0.01$, $p > .05$. On deleting the interaction from the model, the covariate was significant, $F(1, 120) = 36.7$, $p < .01$ ($r^2 = 23\%$), and there was also a significant effect of instruction, $F(1, 120) = 6.46$, $p < .05$. For instructed subjects, the least square mean was 7.1 seconds (*SD* 2.8) versus 8.4 seconds for the non-instructed subjects (*SD* 2.8).

Overall, there was only a significant difference in solution times, with the instructed subjects being slightly faster than the non-instructed subjects. Not only was the difference in error rates non-significant, but the non-instructed subjects were the better performers at this measure. As will be seen later, the groups are performing far more similarly to each other than to the other strategy groups. Later, it will also be argued that error rates are a far more interesting measure of performance than solution times. Hence, it seems safe to conclude that instructed versus spontaneous cancellation strategy users are virtually identical in terms of the solution processes that they apply.

(2) Cancellation strategy users perform best irrespective of task and ability

One difficulty when determining strategy effectiveness in general is that different strategies may be used for different items and/or by people with different levels of ability (e.g., see Siegler & Lemaire, 1997; Lemaire & Fabre, chapter 1 this volume). When conducting directions task studies in the past, it has been assumed (1) that the retrospective verbal reports are usefully accurate; (2) that cancellation is the best strategy for all subjects irrespective of ability and task. It is worth pausing here to seek evidence that confirms the plausibility of both of these assumptions.

Although people who report using cancellation are generally faster and more accurate than people who report using the spatial strategy, cancellation users also have higher spatial ability on average. One suggestion, occasionally made by strategy report sceptics, is that everyone really used identical processes. If high spatials merely had different phenomenological experiences compared with low spatials, then this would yield different reports. The apparent difference in performance between strategy groups may therefore simply reflect the ability of high spatials to execute these identical processes more effectively than low spatials. If this were genuinely the case, then once spatial ability score is removed as a covariate, we would expect no difference between strategy report groups.

An important finding from the previous analysis is that spatial ability predicts a substantial proportion of the variance in performance when using cancellation: Low spatials find cancellation harder to apply than high spatials. It is therefore also important to confirm the assumption that cancellation is always the best strategy to adopt: If low spatials find even cancellation difficult to apply, there may be little or no advantage in their changing to this from the spatial strategy. This would therefore provide an alternative explanation for the avoidance of cancellation by low spatials.

Table 6.2 shows a comparison of performance between cancellation and spatial strategies for the main dataset. For this, instructed and spontaneous cancellation groups have been combined. Two other datasets also enable separate straightforward analyses of this type (Roberts et al., 1997, Exp. 3; Roberts & Roberson, 2001, Exp. 2), and have also been included on Table 6.2. Even after correcting the means for spatial ability, cancellation yields a striking improvement in accuracy compared with the spatial strategy, and a consistent improvement in speed (albeit non-significant for Roberts & Roberson, 2001). The lack of any covariate × factor interactions shows that the advantage is, on average, identical right across the spatial ability range.

Two experiments from Newton (2001) enable further interesting analyses to be performed. For these studies, trial type was varied. *Trial structure* was manipulated in Experiment 5. All trials were seven or eight steps in length, but for one group of subjects, opposite steps (e.g., one step north, one step south) were adjacent wherever possible. For another group, steps in the same direction were always grouped together (e.g., one step north, one step north) and opposites were never adjacent. The final group received standard-structured trials. *Trial length* was manipulated in Experiment 6. All subjects received standard-structured trials, but for one group, these were five or six steps long, seven or eight steps long for another group, and eight or nine steps long for the final group. We can therefore see not only whether cancellation strategy users are better than spatial strategy users across the ability range, but also whether trial type has any influence on the relative size of the advantage.

Four Analyses of Covariance were used to analyse the data. These all had one covariate (spatial ability test raw score) and two factors (*trial type*; three levels for each analysis, and *strategy*; spatial versus cancellation). For each ANCOVA, there are three interactions which include the covariate. None of these approached significance: the greatest/most significant F ratio was for the trial type × covariate interaction for the solution time analysis of the trial length experiment, $F(2, 99) = 1.88$, $p > .05$. The lack of significant interactions again shows that the factor effects are identical irrespective of ability level, and all covariate interactions were deleted from all models. Least square means, i.e., controlling for spatial ability, were calculated and are given where relevant.

First, considering solution times for the trial length study, after deleting the covariate × factor interactions from the model, there was a significant

TABLE 6.2

Comparison of performance for spatial and cancellation strategy users, controlling for spatial ability

Study		Analysis of covariance				Least square means		
		Interaction	Factor	Covariate		N	M	SD
Comparisons of error rates between strategies								
Main data set	F	2.84	180**	52.4**	Spat	119	53%	16%
	df	1, 238	1, 239	1, 239	Canc	123	25%	16%
Roberts & Roberson (2001) (Exp. 2)	F	0.66	13.0**	0.17	Spat	53	44%	20%
	df	1, 60	1, 61	1, 61	Canc	11	20%	18%
Roberts et al. (1997) (Exp. 3)	F	1.10	7.74**	11.1**	Spat	55	55%	19%
	df	1, 60	1, 61	1, 61	Canc	9	34%	20%
Comparisons of mean solution times between strategies								
Main data set	F	1.53	91.1**	9.02**	Spat	119	14.2s	4.9s
	df	1, 238	1, 239	1, 239	Canc	123	8.0s	4.9s
Roberts & Roberson (2001) (Exp. 2)	F	0.00	1.28	0.65	Spat	53	13.3s	5.5s
	df	1, 60	1, 61	1, 61	Canc	11	11.0s	6.0s
Roberts et al. (1997) (Exp. 3)	F	0.32	4.94*	3.58*	Spat	55	15.8s	5.8s
	df	1, 60	1, 61	1, 61	Canc	9	10.9s	6.1s

Notes: F ratios for the factors and covariates are given after the covariate × factor interactions have been removed from the models. **: $p < .01$; *: $p < .05$.

effect of strategy, $F(1,104) = 17.1, p < .01$, and a significant effect of trial type, $F(2,104) = 13.4, p < .01$. The interaction between the two factors was not significant, $F(2,104) = 0.27, p > .05$. The covariate was not a significant predictor of performance, $F(1,104) = 1.80, p > .05$ ($r^2 = 2\%$). Hence, controlling for ability and irrespective of trial length, cancellation strategy users (*LSM* 8.5 seconds, *SD* 4.7) enjoyed a time advantage of approximately 3.9 seconds per trial compared with spatial strategy users (*LSM* 12.4 seconds, *SD* 4.5).

Second, considering error rates for the trial length study, there was a significant effect of strategy, $F(1,104) = 57.6, p < .01$, and a significant effect of trial type, $F(2,104) = 5.18, p < .01$. The interaction between the two factors was not significant, $F(2,104) = 1.06, p > .05$. The covariate was a significant predictor of performance, $F(1,104) = 8.94, p < .01$ ($r^2 = 8\%$). Hence, controlling for ability and irrespective of trial length, cancellation strategy users (*LSM* 28%, *SD* 17) on average made 26% fewer errors compared with spatial strategy users (*LSM* 54%, *SD* 16). Irrespective of strategy used, high spatial ability was associated with fewer errors than low spatial ability.

Third, considering solution times for the trial structure study, there was a significant effect of strategy, $F(1,104) = 27.3, p < .01$, and a significant effect of trial type, $F(2,104) = 3.21, p < .05$. The interaction between the two factors was not significant, $F(2,104) = 1.54, p > .05$. The covariate was not a significant predictor of performance, $F(1,104) = 2.84, p > .05$ ($r^2 = 3\%$). Hence, controlling for ability and irrespective of trial structure, cancellation strategy users (*LSM* 6.9 seconds, *SD* 4.4) enjoyed a time advantage of approximately 4.9 seconds per trial compared with spatial strategy users (*LSM* 11.8 seconds, *SD* 4.2).

Fourth, considering error rates for the trial structure study, there was a significant effect of strategy, $F(1,104) = 67.2, p < .01$, and a significant effect of trial type, $F(2,104) = 4.36, p < .05$. The interaction between the two factors was significant, $F(2,104) = 4.95, p < .01$. The covariate was a significant predictor of performance, $F(1,104) = 7.50, p < .01$ ($r^2 = 7\%$). Despite the interaction, post hoc *t*-tests showed that differences between cancellation and spatial strategy users were significant for each of the three trial types (smallest $t = 2.85, p < .01$). Hence, controlling for ability, cancellation strategy users on average made fewer errors compared with spatial strategy users, but the advantage was distinctly smaller for opposites-adjacent trials (cancellation *LSM* 20%, *SD* 16, spatial *LSM* 36%, *SD* 16) compared with standard trials (cancellation *LSM* 21%, *SD* 17 spatial *LSM* 56%, *SD* 17) and sames-adjacent trials (cancellation *LSM* 19%, *SD* 17 spatial *LSM* 61%, *SD* 17). Irrespective of strategy used, high spatial ability was associated with fewer errors than low spatial ability.

Overall, using Analysis of Covariance to control for spatial ability provides a very clear picture on the relative effectiveness of the spatial and cancellation strategies. This gives further evidence validating the use of retrospective verbal reports for this task: Even after controlling for spatial ability, there are large differences in strategy performance in line with subjects' reports. In terms of the relative effectiveness of the strategies, irrespective of ability and item type, using cancellation will result in a massive increase in accuracy, and a substantial reduction in solution time. The failure of the majority of even university students to use cancellation becomes even more interesting in the light of this.

(3) Pencil and paper improves execution of the spatial strategy, but performance is still related to ability

A success-based theory of strategy discovery implies that any manipulation which increases success should increase the discovery of cancellation. However, studies by Roberts et al. (1997) and Newton and Roberts (2000) have shown that this is not necessarily the case: The option to use pencil and paper suppresses cancellation markedly, but when people are instructed first to use cancellation, a subsequent offer of pencil and paper (in conjunction with a free choice of strategy) does not suppress the use of cancellation. Hence, Roberts and colleagues suggest that pencil and paper suppresses cancellation *discovery*, rather than suppressing the use of a strategy already present in an individual's repertoire.

Of course, the original failed prediction – that increasing success will increase strategy discovery – hinges on the assumption that externalising the spatial strategy via pencil and paper genuinely boosts success. On the other hand, if pencil and paper were to boost success to the extent that performance is as good as for cancellation, then it should come as no surprise if the use of cancellation were to be suppressed.

From the major dataset, there are 51 subjects who solved the majority of trials by externalising the spatial strategy via pencil and paper. These can be compared with the 119 subjects who were spatial strategy dominant (no externalisation) and the 123 subjects who were cancellation dominant. Analysis of Covariance with one covariate (spatial ability raw score) and one three-level factor (dominant strategy) was used to investigate performance.

For solution times, the covariate $\times$ factor interaction was not significant, $F(2, 287) = 1.71, p > .05$, and was deleted from the model. Subsequently, there was a significant effect of strategy, $F(2, 289) = 51.3, p < .01$, and the covariate also significantly predicted performance, $F(2, 289) = 17.2, p < .01$ ($r^2 = 6\%$). Post hoc t-tests comparing least square means showed that both spatial ($LSM = 14.1$ seconds, SD 4.8) and pencil and paper spatial groups (LSM 13.2 seconds, SD 4.7) significantly exceeded the solution time of the cancellation group (LSM 8.1 seconds, SD 4.8), $t = 9.64$ and 6.56 respectively, $p < .01$. However, the two spatial groups did not differ from each other, $t = 1.11, p > .05$.

Hence, using pencil and paper confers little or no time advantage for the spatial strategy, and with or without pencil and paper, using the spatial strategy results in a considerable time disadvantage over cancellation.

For error rates, the covariate × factor interaction was not significant, F (2, 287) = 1.42, p > .05, and was deleted from the model. Subsequently, there was a significant effect of strategy, F (2, 289) = 91.9, p < .01, and the covariate also significantly predicted performance, F (2, 289) = 67.3, p < .01 (r^2 = 19%). Post hoc t-tests showed that both spatial (LSM = 53%, SD 16) and pencil and paper spatial groups (LSM 36%, SD 16) significantly exceeded the errors of the cancellation group (LSM 25%, SD 16), t = 13.5 and 4.12 respectively, p < .01. In addition the two spatial groups did differ from each other, t = 6.56, p < .01. Hence, although pencil and paper does confer additional accuracy for spatial strategy users, the accuracy of cancellation is still not achieved.

Overall, these findings suggest that any purely success-based theory of strategy discovery cannot tell the whole story. Pencil and paper clearly increases success when measured by accuracy, which later will be argued to be the crucial measure of success in terms of determining strategy discovery – but clearly does not improve speed – which at first sight is a more tangible measure of success from the point of view of the subject. Hence, the continuing slow task should give the necessary impetus to seek improved methods, while the improved quality of representation, and hence accuracy, should give the means necessary to discover them. However, strategy discovery is instead suppressed.

One explanation of this is simply that the task is now 'too easy'. The working memory load is much reduced by pencil and paper, and subjects are not inclined to try to perform as quickly and as accurately as possible, despite instructions to the contrary. This explanation goes against the *metacognitive intervention* account of strategy discovery put forward by Crowley, Shrager, and Siegler (1997) and Shrager and Siegler (1998). This suggests that the freeing of metacognitive resources – albeit as a result of practice at a task in their account – enables these to be devoted to identifying and deleting redundant procedures so as to discover new strategies. Financial or other incentives might encourage subjects to reflect more, but if self-perceived levels of performance are high, subjects may discount even the possibility that performance could be improved still further. How might subjects know whether their performance is satisfactory? Time taken per item is reasonably salient, but irrelevant in this particular case because pencil and paper does not improve the speed of execution of the spatial strategy. However, estimates of accuracy are also possible: Fundamentally, accurate performance at this task equals consistent performance. If executing identical sequences of steps results in the same outcome time and time again, then it can be inferred that overall performance is accurate.

Overall, it is not clear what aspect of using pencil and paper is suppressing strategy discovery: (1) the reduction in cognitive load leading to laziness, or (2) the improvement in consistency yielding a false sense of security regarding the need for new methods. Either way the finding that making a task easier suppresses strategy discovery is important, and its generality needs to be assessed.

Before moving on, there is one final aspect of pencil and paper usage that is of interest. Recall that the covariate × factor interactions were not significant. For error rates, this is telling us that spatial ability predicts performance at the pencil and paper spatial strategy as well as it does for the spatial strategy by itself, and also cancellation ($r^2 = 19\%$). This is surprising, and is confirmed by calculating the correlation coefficient between spatial ability scores and error rates for just the pencil and paper users ($r = -.48$, $r^2 = 23\%$). In other words, people who are disadvantaged due to low spatial ability, when using either cancellation or the spatial strategy, are equally disadvantaged when given the option to use pencil and paper. Hence, people who are bad at internalising are also bad at externalising. Although surprising, this finding is not unprecedented (e.g., see Schaeken, Van der Henst, & Schroyens, in press) and suggests that certain people may have a general deficit in constructing any representations at all, anywhere. This is perhaps in addition to any difficulty in retaining and manipulating them in working memory.

(4) Within strategy groups, spatial ability predicts accuracy better than it predicts solution time

Table 6.3 summarises the proportion of variance accounted for by spatial ability test score, when predicting performance, within strategy groups, for the five datasets analysed in (2) earlier. It should be noted that other than for the main data set, the analyses are restricted in the range of spatial ability, either due to a lack of high spatials amongst the elderly and adolescents

TABLE 6.3

Comparison of proportions of variance accounted for by spatial ability test raw score when predicting error rates versus predicting solution times within strategy groups

	Major data set Not p&p	Roberts et al. (1997) E3	Roberts & Roberson (2001) E2	Newton (2001) E5	Newton (2001) E6
N	242	64	64	111	111
Accuracy	18%**	15%**	0%	8%**	7%**
Speed	2%**	6%*	1%	2%	3%

Notes: **: $p < .01$; *: $p < .05$.
These values are calculated on the basis of the ANCOVA results reported earlier. Because the covariate (spatial ability) did not interact with any of the factors, this indicates that spatial ability is equally good (or bad) at predicting performance for *either* spatial *or* cancellation strategy users.

(Roberts et al., 1997, Exp. 3; Roberts & Roberson, Exp. 2 respectively) or due to the deliberate exclusion of subjects with very low spatial ability (Newton, 2001, Exps. 5 and 6). Even so, there is a recurring pattern to these results: Where spatial ability predicts any performance at all within strategy groups, it is a better predictor of accuracy than it is of speed. Hence, spatial ability test score appears to be more indicative of how *accurately* a representation can be created, updated, and interpreted, rather than how *rapidly* these processes can be carried out. The reason why this is interesting will be discussed in the next section.

(5) Spatial ability predicts strategy selection

The key finding of Roberts et al. (1997) was that spatial ability predicted strategy selection, such that people with high spatial ability were more likely to use cancellation than people with low spatial ability. The original study was an extreme-groups design, intended explicitly to test for the presence of this relationship. However, Table 6.4 shows that it is present in every study

TABLE 6.4
Proportion of variance accounted for when using spatial ability test raw score to predict final choice of strategy

Row of Table 6.1	Study	Exp.	Canc	Spat	r^2	Notes
1	Roberts et al. (1997)	1	21	19	31%**	Extreme groups design: no mid-spatials.
3		3	17	47	11%**	Few high spatials in sample.
1, 5	Roberts & Roberson (2001)	1	33	47	16%**	40 mid-spatials added to Roberts et al. (1997).
6		2	11	53	22%**	Few high spatials in sample.
7, 8, 10	Newton & Roberts (2000)	1	22	38	10%*	Instructed cancellation group excluded.
13		3	23	49	11%**	Cancellation usage increased by feedback.
14	Newton (2001)	5	34	77	14%**	Very low spatials excluded.
15		6	35	76	7%**	Very low spatials excluded.
	All data		175	387	12%**	

Note: **: $p < .01$; *: $p < .05$.

which could reasonably be expected to show it. (Studies where such a relationship would not be expected are those with the option to use pencil and paper for all trials – where discovery of cancellation is suppressed – and those where subjects are initially instructed to use cancellation.) The robustness of the relationship is particularly impressive when it is considered that several studies have a restricted range of spatial ability, and/or have included subjects with moderate ability levels.

Recall also that spatial ability predicts *accuracy* at the directions task within strategy groups better than it predicts *speed*. This finding complements well the fact that spatial ability predicts strategy discovery. It corroborates the original suggestion that high spatial ability is a marker of a person's ability to generate and update a stable *accurate* representation of space, and *accurately* identify conclusions from this. Hence, spatial ability predicts accuracy for spatial strategy users, and a person who is more accurate is better able to discover new strategies. In contrast, the less successful prediction of solution time by spatial ability indicates that those factors which influence the speed of representation construction for spatial strategy users have little bearing on strategy discovery.

Figure 6.1 illustrates the relationship between individual differences in task proficiency and strategy discovery. Set out in this way, the further prediction entailed by any success-based theory of strategy discovery is highlighted: *Any factors which influence task accuracy should influence strategy discovery just as much as individual differences in ability to execute a task do so.* Hence, success-based strategy discovery implies a simple progressive model: If we make tasks easier, then strategy discovery will increase, and if tasks are made harder, then strategy discovery will decrease. Unfortunately, as was shown earlier, pencil and paper yields an improvement in accuracy for the spatial strategy, but simultaneously suppresses the discovery of cancellation.

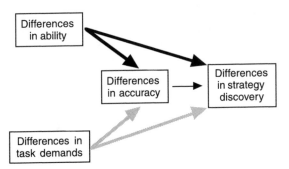

Figure 6.1 Pathways illustrating the factors that influence strategy discovery. Bold lines illustrate empirically demonstrated findings; the light line indicates a plausible inference. Grey lines indicate predictions which need to be tested in order to corroborate success-based theories of strategy discovery.

Newton and Roberts (2000) therefore conclude that making people more successful at a task will not necessarily lead to better methods if this removes the need to identify them (see also Newton & Roberts, Chapter 7 this volume).

(6) The relationship between ability and strategy selection is 'stepped'

As spatial ability increases, what happens to the likelihood that cancellation will be adopted? Depending on the exact relationship, this may tell us more about strategy discovery processes. Roberts (1991) suggested that strategy discovery and strategy evaluation are separate procedures, so that a new strategy might be discovered, but nonetheless rejected if it were subsequently to fail an evaluation. Given that this is an important procedure, it is likely that evaluation will be more demanding than the process of strategy discovery: If this were not the case, failures to adopt newly discovered strategies would never be reported by subjects, and would be impossible to detect by any other means. Roberts (1991) therefore speculated that this might manifest itself as separate thresholds and plateaux on a frequency histogram. In other words, a certain level of spatial ability is required in order to execute the directions task sufficiently accurately so as to identify cancellation as a possible candidate strategy. However, a greater level of ability is required in order to execute the spatial strategy sufficiently accurately in order for it to provide a benchmark against which answers found by using cancellation may be compared (good agreement being required in order for cancellation to be accepted).

A fine-grained analysis of cancellation usage as a function of spatial ability would require data from many hundreds of subjects. However, with the data analysed in (5) above (562 subjects), a tentative investigation may be attempted. The main difficulty is that there is currently a shortage of high spatial subjects. In addition, subjects differed in age, and received different numbers of differently lengthed and structured trials. Some subjects also received feedback. A relatively informal analysis therefore follows. However, it should be noted that there are no important confounds between the precise task details and the parts of the range of spatial distribution sampled.

Even with 562 subjects, some aggregation is required. Subjects were grouped into ten bands on the basis of percentiles determined from published test norms (Saville & Holdsworth Ltd, 1979; Smith & Whetton, 1988). The proportion of people adopting cancellation as the final choice of strategy within each band is shown on Figure 6.2.

Figure 6.2 shows some very interesting patterns of results. First, up to and including the 9th percentile, cancellation is very rare indeed, with just 6% of subjects adopting this. At such low levels of ability, subjects are likely to have difficulty in representing and/or even understanding the task. This is in line

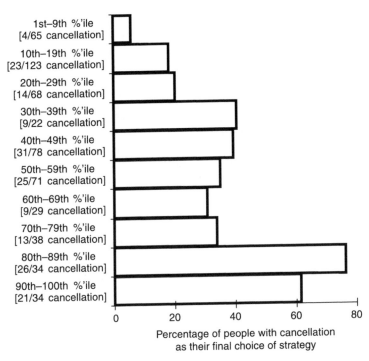

Figure 6.2 Proportions of people adopting cancellation as their final choice of strategy when banded into spatial ability groups.

with the suggestion by Gohm, Humphreys, and Yao (1997) that very low spatial ability may indicate qualitative differences in the ability to construct spatial representations, compared with higher levels. After this band, there is a jump in the adoption of cancellation, which remains at roughly 19% from the 10th to the 19th percentile of ability. Here, it is plausible that although subjects can understand the task, their poor performance with the spatial strategy prevents the discovery of any alternatives. Beyond this point, we reach another jump in adoption, followed by another plateau. Here, we can speculate that cancellation is often discovered, but frequent evaluation failures result in adoption by only 37% of subjects. It is also worth noting the downward trend in adoption from the 30th to the 79th percentile. One tentative possibility is that although strategy evaluation is difficult for everyone in this ability range, as ability increases, success at executing the spatial strategy increases, with the consequence that the need to identify alternatives slightly decreases. Finally, on reaching the 80th percentile, there is another jump, now to 69% of people using cancellation. Perhaps it is only at this level of ability that cancellation may both be discovered and evaluated with relative ease. Again, it is interesting to speculate on the apparent downward trend from here onwards. Perhaps, for many people with particularly high spatial ability, the execution of the spatial strategy is so effortless that the need for alternatives simply is not contemplated.

CONCLUSIONS AND IMPLICATIONS

The analyses in this chapter present a very consistent picture. For the directions task with parallel presentation, cancellation is the most effective strategy by far. (It is almost always the preferred strategy for people who are genuinely aware that both may be used; Newton & Roberts, 2000.) Spatial ability predicts accuracy within strategy groups, and also predicts the likelihood that cancellation will be used. Spatial ability is less effective at predicting speed within strategy groups. Overall, the success-based model of strategy discovery is corroborated. The distribution of frequency of cancellation usage as a function of spatial ability appears to show thresholds and plateaux, suggesting that minimal levels of spatial ability are required in order (1) to discover cancellation and in turn (2) to determine whether this is a valid strategy. This corroborates that strategy discovery and evaluation are separate procedures.

Implications for other strategy usage researchers

In line with other strategy discovery studies, the results highlight the importance of understanding how strategies enter an individual's repertoire: People cannot choose strategies whose existence they are not aware of. In addition, as a further example of success-based strategy discovery, these results add further support to this category of theory as a whole. However, other results do not necessarily fit in with findings from other strategy discovery studies.

Trial-by-trial variability for the directions task

Low trial-by-trial variability is typically reported by subjects: The spatial strategy is the sole choice unless cancellation is discovered. Once evaluated, this is generally rapidly selected in preference. In contrast, other strategy researchers suggest that high trial by trial variability is an important and recurring feature of human cognition (e.g., Alibali, 1999; Lemaire & Siegler, 1995; Rittle-Johnson & Siegler, 1999; Schunn & Reder, 2001; Shrager & Siegler, 1998; Siegler 1996, 1999). Furthermore, where superior strategies are discovered, these are generally held to propagate slowly, taking time to dominate to the exclusion of others. Hence, this leads to Siegler's (e.g., 1996) *wave model* of strategy development. One explanation for the differences between tasks is the relatively great advantage that cancellation has over the spatial strategy. Were the advantage to be less, or confined to certain types of trial, it is likely that the use of cancellation would ebb and flow in much the same way as is observed for other tasks (Newton & Roberts, 2000). Siegler and Svetina's (2002) study is another example where strategy adoption is relatively abrupt, and they also attributed this to the massive difference in accuracy between strategies, coupled with trial-by-trial feedback (see also Newton & Roberts, 2000). It should also be noted that in arithmetic, the min strategy generalises relatively rapidly once trials are encountered in which it has a definite accuracy advantage over the sum strategy (Siegler & Jenkins, 1989). However, Alibali (1999) also suggests that relative strategy accuracy may be related to abruptness of strategy adoption, but her data only offered weak support for this.

An alternative explanation of low trial-by-trial variability for the directions task concerns the means of strategy identification. Many researchers advocate the use of the *microgenetic method* (subjects are videotaped and describe the strategies that they apply after each and every trial; see Kuhn, 1995; Siegler & Crowley, 1991). For the directions task studies described here, a single retrospective report was taken. It may therefore be the case that this simpler means of response is concealing a more complicated picture of strategy usage. However, it should be noted that there is always the risk that a microgenetic study will alert subjects to its purpose, leading to more experimentation than is usual, especially for adults. In addition, the analyses described earlier show that there are substantial differences between strategy groups, which is not really compatible with more varied usage of directions task strategies than hitherto suspected. Concealed variability also goes against the finding of extremely similar performance for instructed versus spontaneous cancellation users.

Whatever the reason for the differences between studies and tasks, it is clearly important to identify the circumstances in which strategy usage is highly varied or relatively homogeneous, and also the circumstances in which new strategies are generalised more or less rapidly.

The curious pencil and paper findings

The finding that pencil and paper improves *accuracy* but not speed at the spatial *strategy*, and yet *suppresses* rather than *promotes* strategy discovery, must be puzzling to any advocate of success-based strategy discovery. For any account that proposes that the freeing of metacognitive resources leads to strategy discovery (e.g., Crowley et al., 1997), the execution of the spatial strategy via pencil and paper provides exactly the right environment for the discovery of cancellation. Such accounts therefore need to be reconsidered in the light of the strategy discovery suppression finding. Of course, this finding may be unique to the directions task, but the alternative is that strategy discovery occurs most often not only when accuracy permits, but also when there is sufficient incentive to identify new methods.

The need for strategy evaluation

Strategy evaluation may be an important stage of strategy development in its own right, subsequent to strategy discovery. Siegler and colleagues suggest that strategy discovery is constrained by the *goal sketch* (e.g., Siegler, 1996, 1999; Siegler & Crowley, 1994). This is a representation of all of the subgoals that must be satisfied in order to solve a problem. When this is coupled with the requirement that all new strategies must satisfy these subgoals, then as long as the goal sketch represents valid goals, only valid strategies are discovered. The presence of the goal sketch was suggested as the reason why children competent at addition were never observed to use pathological strategies (Siegler & Jenkins, 1989). Also relevant is children's ability to evaluate the elegance not just of strategies that they discover by themselves (e.g., Siegler & Jenkins, 1989) but also strategies that are described to them but are too cognitively demanding for them to use (e.g., Siegler & Crowley, 1994). If we assume that the goals of the directions task are well understood and represented on a goal sketch, then this should likewise constrain the discovery of new strategies. Why then might some students be unaware of, or have difficulty in evaluating, the validity of cancellation? It is possible that although strategy discovery may be constrained, people are not necessarily aware that this is the case. We therefore need to identify when strategy evaluation is likely to be an important determinant of availability.

Implications for other reasoning researchers

The directions task is a deduction task, and as such the findings also have implications for researchers into reasoning. Most importantly, as yet another demonstration that people need not use any particular strategy or means of representing information in order to draw conclusions, this task, along with many others, highlights the difficulties faced by researchers who wish to assert that people only reason by using one category of process, or represent information in only one way (see Roberts, 1993, 1997, 2000; see also Morris & Schunn chapter 2 this volume). Some more specific implications are as follows.

What aspects of deduction should be explained?

Strategy usage need not be stable over time. Most deduction tasks contain regularities that can be exploited in order to boost success, and their discovery need not be confined to reasoning researchers. For example, what can be concluded from the following *conditional reasoning problem*:

Given it is true that:
> *if Walter is in Leuven, then Simon is in Plymouth*
and we know that:
> *Simon is not in Plymouth*
Then we can conclude that:
- (*a*)   *Walter is in Leuven*
- (*b*)   *Walter is not in Leuven*
- (*c*)   *no further conclusions are possible*

The correct answer to this example is (b) and the name of this inference is *modus tollens*. Both deduction rule (e.g., Rips, 1994) and mental model theories of deduction (e.g., Johnson-Laird & Byrne, 1991) predict that this is a hard inference to make because it requires numerous solution steps. However, spotting the repeating pattern: *If P then Q, not-Q, therefore: not-P* is not difficult, and should scarcely be beyond the capabilities of many subjects. What then is the appropriate behaviour to study: Deduction with just a few items (before anyone has a chance to identify strategy improvements) or deduction after many items, so that as many people as possible have made discoveries, and behaviour has stabilised? Data from either method would be an oversimplification: We need to know how people approach novel tasks, and how procedures are modified with practice. Put another way, how can we understand human reasoning without understanding how people learn to improve their reasoning?

Who should be the subjects for deductive reasoning experiments?

People discover new strategies at different speeds: instantaneously at one extreme, not at all at the other. Care needs to be taken that the types of subjects who are most freely available to researchers (their students) are not different in their adeptness at identifying improved strategies, compared with non-students. In general, researchers assume that although university students may differ in speed and accuracy from other people, they do not differ by process. However, if there are differences in rates of strategy discovery, then a series of items presented to university students may evoke different patterns of performance compared with people who are less accurate (and who therefore will be less able to discover alternatives). If people do not differ in their ability to discover new strategies, then this difficulty can be ignored, but people *do* differ. One solution is to design items so as to minimise strategy discovery. For example, from the analyses above, we can predict that any manipulation that reduces accuracy should reduce new discoveries. However, without taking account of individual differences in strategy discovery, how certain can researchers really be that they are assembling a comprehensive overview of human reasoning. We need to know how task and individual difference variables influence strategy development.

Do we need to know about the directions task?

Of course, the directions task was not chosen by accident to investigate strategy discovery. Of the various deduction tasks available, this one is a particularly well-suited tool (although when formatted appropriately, linear reasoning tasks are also well suited). The task is novel, yet its requirements are easy to understand. The strategies appear to be highly available to conscious recall, even retrospectively. There is a very close relationship between reported strategy and performance. The availability of relatively accurate retrospective reports means that hypotheses can be tested without the need for an intrusive lengthy microgenetic study. Unlike the tasks studied by other researchers, the majority of people do not report mixing strategies on a trial-by-trial basis. Thus, categorising people by dominant and final choice of strategy is relatively easy. Finally, there are very many potential task variations and manipulations, enabling a variety of hypotheses concerning strategy discovery and selection to be tested.

However, the advantages of the directions task also mean that it is possible to argue that its findings are unique and unrepresentative, and that this task is therefore not an appropriate one for the study of strategy use. In response to this, it should first be noted that the directions task is not unique. It has yielded many results which are in line with findings from other tasks, for example, success-based strategy discovery. As another example, Siegler and colleagues found that discovery of the min strategy is often preceded by a extended trial solution time, and this has also been observed with the directions task for cancellation. Rather than contradicting previous findings, several insights (e.g., the need for evaluation of newly discovered strategies) were previously unsuspected. Where there appear to be contradictions, these should be taken to indicate the potential for advancement of knowledge, rather than a meaningless assertion of priority. For example, cancellation, once discovered (and evaluated), has been shown to generalise quickly, as opposed to slower generalisation found for the min strategy. However, the two tasks are similar in that a new strategy is discovered and generalised, albeit on a different time scale. One explanation that resolves this difference is that strategy generalisation may depend upon the relative advantage afforded by the new strategy.

Overall, the evidence is strong to suggest that the directions task is certainly not less suitable for studying strategy development than any other task used previously. In any case, a genuinely wide-ranging account of strategy usage would have to be able to explain this task as well as all others. Of prime importance is to seek and understand differences in patterns of results between tasks, as well as their similarities.

REFERENCES

Alibali, M. W. (1999). How children change their minds: Strategy changes can be gradual or abrupt. *Developmental Psychology, 35*, 127–145.

Cohen, J. D., MacWhinney, B., Flatt, M., & Provost, J. (1993). PsyScope – an interactive graphic system for designing and controlling experiments in the psychology laboratory using Macintosh computers. *Behavior Research Methods, Instruments, and Computers, 25*, 257–271.

Costin, D. (1988). MacLab: A Macintosh system for psychology labs. *Behavior Research Methods, Instruments and Computers, 20*, 197–200.

Crowley, K., Shrager, J., & Siegler, R. S. (1997). Strategy discovery as a competitive negotiation between metacognitive and associative mechanisms. *Developmental Review, 17*, 462–489.

Dickstein, L. (1978). The effect of figure on syllogistic reasoning. *Memory and Cognition, 6*, 76–83.

Galotti, K. M., Baron, J., & Sabini, J. P. (1986). Individual differences in syllogistic reasoning: Deduction rules or mental models? *Journal of Experimental Psychology: General, 115*, 16–25.

Gohm, C. L., Humphreys, L. G., & Yao, G. (1997). Characteristics of 12th-grade students seriously deficient in spatial ability. *Intelligence, 25*, 161–178.

Johnson-Laird, P. N., & Byrne, R. M. J. (1991). *Deduction.* Hove, UK: Psychology Press.

Kuhn, D. (1995). Microgenetic study of change: What has it told us? *Psychological Science, 6*, 133–139.

Lemaire, P., & Lecacheur, M. (2001). Older and younger adults' strategy use and execution in currency conversion tasks: Insights from French franc to euro and euro to French franc conversions. *Journal of Experimental Psychology: Applied, 7*, 195–206.

Lemaire, P., Lecacheur, M., & Farioli, F. (2000). Children's strategy use in computational estimation. *Canadian Journal of Experimental Psychology, 54*, 141–148.

Lemaire, P., & Siegler, R. S. (1995). Four aspects of strategic change: Contributions to children's learning of multiplication. *Journal of Experimental Psychology: General, 124*, 83–97.

Lovett, M. C. & Schunn, C. D. (1999). Task representations, strategy variability, and base-rate neglect. *Journal of Experimental Psychology: General, 128*, 107–130.

Newton, E. J. (2001). *Individual differences in strategy development.* Unpublished doctoral dissertation, University of Essex.

Newton, E. J., & Roberts, M. J. (2000). An experimental study of strategy development. *Memory and Cognition, 28*, 565–573.

Raven, J., Raven, J. C., & Court, J. H. (1993). *Manual for Raven's Progressive Matrices and Mill Hill Vocabulary Scales: Section 1.* Oxford: Oxford Psychologists Press.

Reder, L. M., & Schunn, C. D. (1996). Metacognition does not imply awareness: Strategy choice is governed by implicit learning and memory. In L. M. Reder (Ed.), *Implicit memory and metacognition* (pp. 45–77). Mahwah, NJ: Lawrence Erlbaum Associates, Inc.

Riding, R. J., & Rayner, S. (1998). *Cognitive styles and learning strategies.* London: David Fulton.

Rips, L. J. (1994). *The psychology of proof.* Cambridge, MA: MIT Press.

Rittle-Johnson, B., & Siegler, R. S. (1999). Learning to spell: Variability, choice, and change in children's strategy use. *Child Development, 70*, 332–348.

Roberts, M. J. (1991). *Individual differences and strategy selection in reasoning.* Unpublished doctoral dissertation, University of Nottingham.

Roberts, M. J. (1993). Human reasoning: Deduction rules or mental models, or both? *Quarterly Journal of Experimental Psychology, 46A*, 569–589.

Roberts, M. J. (1997). On dichotomies and deductive reasoning research. *Cahiers de Psychologie Cognitive/Current Psychology of Cognition, 16*, 196–204.

Roberts, M. J. (2000). Individual differences in reasoning strategies: A problem to solve or an opportunity to seize? In W. Schaeken, G. De Vooght, A. Vandierendonck, & G. d'Ydewalle (Eds.), *Deductive reasoning and strategies* (pp. 23–48). Mahwah, NJ: Lawrence Erlbaum Associates, Inc.

Roberts, M. J., Gilmore, D. J., & Wood, D. J. (1997). Individual differences and strategy selection in reasoning. *British Journal of Psychology*, *88*, 473–492.

Roberts, M. J., & Newton, E. J. (2001). Understanding strategy selection. *International Journal of Human-Computer Studies*, *54*, 137–154.

Roberts, M. J., & Newton, E. J. (2003). Individual differences in the development of reasoning strategies. In D. Hardman & L. Macci (Eds.), *The international handbook of reasoning and decision making*. Chichester: Wiley.

Roberts, M. J., & Roberson, D. (2001). Predicting strategy usage for the compass point directions task: Spatial ability versus verbal ability across the lifespan. *Cahiers de Psychologie Cognitive/ Current Psychology of Cognition*, *20*, 3–18.

Saville & Holdsworth Ltd. (1979). *Advanced test battery: Manual and user's guide*. Thames Ditton: Saville & Holdsworth Ltd.

Schaeken, W., Van der Henst, J-B., & Schroyens, W. (2003). The mental models theory of relational reasoning: Premises', relevance, conclusions' phrasing, and cognitive economy. In W. Schaeken, A. Vandierendonck, W. Schroyens, & G. d'Ydewalle (Eds.), *The mental models theory of reasoning: Refinements and extensions*. Mahwah, NJ: Lawrence Erlbaum Associates, Inc.

Schunn, C. D., & Reder, L. M. (2001). Another source of individual differences: Strategy adaptivity to changing rates of success. *Journal of Experimental Psychology: General*, *130*, 59–76.

Schunn, C. D., Reder, L. M., Nhouyvanisvong, A., Richards, D. R., & Stroffolino, P. J. (1997). To calculate or not to calculate: A source activation confusion model of problem familiarity's role in strategy selection. *Journal of Experimental Psychology: Learning, Memory, and Cognition*, *23*, 3–29.

Shrager, J., & Siegler, R. S. (1998). SCADS: A model of children's strategy choices and strategy discoveries. *Psychological Science*, *9*, 405–410.

Siegler, R. S. (1996). *Emerging minds: The process of change in children's thinking*. New York: Oxford University Press.

Siegler, R. S. (1999). Strategic development. *Trends in Cognitive Sciences*, *3*, 430–435.

Siegler, R. S., & Crowley, K. (1991). The microgenetic method: A direct means for studying cognitive development. *American Psychologist*, *46*, 606–620.

Siegler, R. S., & Crowley, K. (1994). Constraints of learning on non-privileged domains. *Cognitive Psychology*, *27*, 194–226.

Siegler, R. S., & Jenkins, E. A. (1989). *How children discover new strategies*. Hillsdale, NJ: Lawrence Erlbaum Associates, Inc.

Siegler, R. S., & Lemaire, P. (1997). Older and younger adults' strategy choices in multiplication: Testing predictions of ASCM using the choice/no-choice method. *Journal of Experimental Psychology: General*, *126*, 71–92.

Siegler, R. S., & Stern, E. (1998). Conscious and unconscious strategy discoveries: A microgenetic analysis. *Journal of Experimental Psychology: General*, *127*, 377–397.

Siegler, R. S., & Svetina, M. (2002). A microgenetic/cross-sectional study of matrix completion: Comparing short-term and long-term change. *Child Development*, *73*, 793–809.

Smith, P. and Whetton, C. (1988). *General Ability Tests User's Guide*. Windsor: NFER-Nelson.

Sternberg, R. J. (1997). *Thinking styles*. Cambridge: Cambridge University Press.

VanLehn, K. (1988). Towards a theory of impasse driven learning. In H. Mandl & A. Lesgold (Eds.), *Learning issues for intelligent tutoring systems* (pp. 19–41). New York: Springer-Verlag.

Wood, D. J. (1978). Problem solving – the nature and development of strategies. In G. Underwood (Ed.), *Strategies in information processing* (pp. 329–356). London: Academic Press.

CHAPTER SEVEN

The window of opportunity: A model for strategy discovery

Elizabeth J. Newton
Department of Human Communication Science,
University College London, UK

Maxwell J. Roberts
Department of Psychology, University of Essex, UK

Imagine someone about to embark on a substantial written project, for example, writing a thesis using a word-processing package. The person has to make a decision about whether to start to write immediately and go back later on to ensure that titles, headings, figures and tables are formatted appropriately, and then to extract that information to construct a table of contents. An alternative strategy is to begin the piece of work by setting up appropriate *style sheets*. This latter method allows the writer to change his or her formatting easily, but requires effort to be expended at the beginning, rather than getting on with the actual writing. These are two clearly distinct strategies which can both lead to the same end result: a thesis. Why do individuals use different strategies?

It is important to define what we mean by a 'strategy'. There is some disagreement, but the preferred definition here is that of Siegler and Jenkins (1989, p. 11): a strategy is 'any procedure that is non-obligatory and goal directed'. Although a procedure may be obligatory (e.g., opening a book before reading it), the term *non-obligatory* is used to emphasise that, for a variety of tasks, there may be nothing inherent in the human cognitive architecture that compels a particular solution procedure. This definition also makes no assumption about whether strategies are consciously created or consciously chosen, and thus avoids recent phenomenological controversies. For example, Reder and Schunn (1996) argue that metacognitive procedures (e.g., choosing between strategies) need not require awareness, whereas Evans (2000) defines a strategy as 'thought processes that are elaborated in time, systematic, goal-directed, and under explicit conscious control' (p. 2). If strategies are defined according to their phenomenological status, there is a risk that researchers may place more effort in debating what is and what is not a strategy, rather than understanding the use of the strategies themselves. Furthermore, Evans argues that certain processes are fundamental (and hence not strategic) and that *strategies* may supplement them. A contrary view is Siegler's, who argues that strategies are merely non-obligatory. Thus, it is important to understand each researcher's work within the context of his or her own definitions.

People adopt a wide range of strategies even for simple reasoning tasks (Roberts, 1993, 2000). Important questions concern why not all strategies are *available* to all people. Hence, why are some people better at discovering new, more effective strategies than others. To date, the evidence suggests that the more successful performers are most likely to go on to discover and adopt improved methods (e.g., Galotti, Baron, & Sabini, 1986 with *categorical syllogisms*; Wood, 1978, with *linear syllogisms*). However, the most comprehensive studies of strategy development to date are by Siegler and colleagues, primarily in the domain of children's arithmetic (e.g., Crowley, Shrager, & Siegler, 1997; Siegler, 1996). Here, the successful execution of basic arithmetic strategies is most likely to lead to the discovery of improved procedures.

This chapter is relevant to questions of strategy discovery, although it takes its evidence from the *directions task* alone. The one-person directions task (see Wood, 1978) requires the subject to determine the compass point at which a person would end up in respect to the starting point if a series of same-size steps in the given directions are taken (see Figure 7.1). An item can be solved by using either a spatial strategy (generating a spatial representation of each step, one at a time, and identifying the final bearing in relation to the starting point) or a cancellation strategy (cancelling out opposite directions, e.g., north/south, and naming the final position from the steps remaining). The two strategies are very different in their demands and effectiveness, and cancellation is more efficient, both in terms of response times and error rates (Roberts & Newton, chapter 6 this volume).

Roberts, Gilmore, and Wood (1997) used the directions task as described above with subjects pretested for verbal and spatial ability. They found an *inverted aptitude – strategy relationship*: Low spatials tended to use the spatial strategy and high spatials were more likely to use cancellation. Verbal ability was not related to strategy usage (see also Roberts & Roberson, 2001). The spatial ability relationship was explained in terms of a *success-based* model. Given that subjects with high spatial ability are better able to construct accurate, stable spatial representations, this enables them to execute the spatial strategy more successfully. Simultaneously, such subjects are better able to identify that opposite steps are redundant no matter how many intervene, and hence that the entire process of constructing the spatial representation is also redundant. Furthermore, greater success with the spatial strategy enables the newly discovered cancellation strategy to be evaluated more effectively if necessary: If its validity is uncertain, this can be evaluated by comparing its answers with the spatial strategy (which is known to be valid). Only if the answers are identical can the new strategy be accepted, and only high spatial ability subjects are likely to be capable of identifying identical correct answers by using *both* strategies (see Newton & Roberts, 2000; Roberts et al., 1997; Roberts & Newton, chapter 6 this volume).

If we assume that success at a task depends not just on the level of ability necessary for its execution, *but also* the difficulty of the task, then a success-based account of strategy discovery *must* at the very least lead to a *progressive relationship* between ability and task difficulty. The easier that tasks are, the more strategy discovery will occur; the harder tasks are, the less strategy discovery will take place. Hence, for the directions task, easier versions will lead to more successful execution of the spatial strategy, and in turn more frequent discovery of cancellation along with more effective evaluation, if necessary (see Table 7.1). This therefore implies a simple means of dramatically raising the performance of people with low ability: By making tasks easier, there should always be an increase in the discovery of improved strategies. However, there is at least one important proviso to this: Past research with the directions task has investigated one means of increasing success by reducing task difficulty. Subjects were given the option to use pencil and paper in order to assist their performance (Newton & Roberts, 2000; Roberts et al., 1997; Roberts & Newton, chapter 6 this volume). The expectation was that, if poor performers at the spatial strategy made use of pencil and paper, this would improve their performance sufficiently for cancellation to be discovered. Instead, the opposite was found: The option to use pencil and paper suppressed cancellation markedly due to a reduction in the *need to discover new strategies*. Models may therefore be required to take account of this when considering task difficulty and its relationship to strategy discovery.

Combining the *need for discovery* with the progressive model suggests that there is a *window of opportunity* for strategy discovery. Returning to the example at the beginning of this chapter, if a writer is performing well using a word-processing package, he or she may feel that it is unnecessary to learn about style sheets (perhaps missing the opportunity to improve performance still further). Alternatively, a person who is struggling with the basics of word processing may be unable to learn to use style sheets at all. Thus, the person most likely to adopt style sheets is the one who is able to use the word-processing package reasonably well, but feels that there is scope for making the task easier.

TABLE 7.1

A progressive model of strategy usage (upper) and a window of opportunity model of strategy usage (lower) as applied to cancellation discovery for the directions task

Spatial ability	Task difficulty		
	Easy	Moderate	Hard
High	High cancellation	High cancellation	High cancellation
Medium	High cancellation	High cancellation	Low cancellation
Low	High cancellation	Low cancellation	Low cancellation

Spatial ability	Task difficulty		
	Easy	Moderate	Hard
High	Too easy to need cancellation		High cancellation
Medium	Too easy to need cancellation	High cancellation	Too hard to develop cancellation
Low	High cancellation	Too hard to develop cancellation	

INVESTIGATING THE WINDOW OF OPPORTUNITY MODEL

Returning to the directions task, the window of opportunity model predicts that high spatial subjects would be most likely to discover and use cancellation for harder trials. Easy and medium difficulty trials would be relatively easy for this group to solve using a spatial strategy, and therefore there would be less need to discover cancellation. For mid spatial ability subjects, cancellation would only be discovered for medium difficulty trials. Easy trials would yield little need for cancellation, while hard trials would render the spatial strategy difficult to use accurately, and thus inhibit the discovery and/or the evaluation of improvements. In comparison, easy trials would be hard enough for those with low spatial ability to need to discover cancellation, while it still being possible for this group to execute the spatial strategy sufficiently accurately to discover alternatives. For low spatial subjects, medium and hard trials would simply be too difficult for cancellation to be discovered (see Table 7.1).

For the directions task, there are numerous manipulations that potentially could influence task difficulty when executing the spatial strategy. It is therefore necessary to consider what makes a task difficult, and which measures of performance this will influence. For example, if a task is changed so that more errors are made, will this necessarily also lead to increased solution time? In fact, these two measures need not be directly linked, given findings showing: (1) that within strategy groups, spatial ability predicts accuracy, but not solution time for the directions task; (2) that for spatial strategy users, the use of pencil and paper can improve accuracy with no effect on solution time (Roberts & Newton, chapter 6 this volume). Considering the window of opportunity model, changes in task difficulty (and hence success) may therefore manifest themselves either as changes in solution times or error rates (or both). What, therefore, are the key manipulations for influencing strategy discovery? These are the issues to be addressed in this chapter.

In fact, response time can probably be dismissed as an interesting measure of performance in this respect. Roberts and Newton (chapter 6 this volume) have shown that (1) within strategy groups, high spatial ability is associated with greater accuracy far more than it is linked to rapid solution times; (2) high spatial ability is linked to the use of cancellation. Hence, an accurate person is better able to discover and evaluate cancellation than someone who is inaccurate, irrespective of speed of solution. Therefore it is probable that manipulations which particularly influence success as measured by accuracy are those that are most likely to influence strategy usage. Also important is the finding by Newton and Roberts (2000) that feedback increased the use of cancellation, but only if the correct answer was given to subjects (i.e., full feedback, as opposed to partial feedback, merely telling the subject that an error had been made). This finding was explained by feedback assisting the evaluation of cancellation for those who had already discovered it, but were not sure about its validity. This is clearly an instance in which the availability of *accurate answers* raises the usage of cancellation, again for success-based reasons.

Why might a person make an error when solving a directions task item? For the spatial strategy (which must be executed accurately for cancellation to be discovered), *procedural errors* may occur at any individual step for at least four reasons: (1) step sizes are not represented as identical lengths; (2) angles between steps are not represented as 90°. In addition to these *calibration errors*: (3) a step can be represented in the opposite direction to the one specified; (4) there can be a memory trace decay, leading to uncertainty about the location of the starting point. What manipulations could be attempted in order to influence these sources of error? Task difficulty can be varied at three different levels: *micro*, *macro*, and *global*.

In terms of the directions task, manipulations at the *micro* level would alter the structure of the trials, whilst keeping the overall demands the same. Hence, having the same number of steps throughout, but varying the order of the steps within each trial would be a manipulation at the micro level. This may influence the probability that an error will be made when representing an individual step. To manipulate the directions task at the *macro* level alone would involve altering overall task demands, but without influencing the difficulty of performing individual steps: for example, altering the trial length while keeping the structural qualities the same throughout. A further example would be manipulating presentation: parallel presentation of the steps (all on view simultaneously) versus serial presentation (each step presented one and a time, then removed, in sequence); individual steps would remain the same, thus keeping difficulty at the micro level constant. Manipulating difficulty at the macro level will not influence the probability that an error will be made for any individual step, but nonetheless will influence the likelihood that a representation will contain one or more errors. Finally, the *global* level refers to the way a task can change as it proceeds. This can occur as a result of either a micro or macro manipulation, or both. For example, a task can be changed in both trial structure, and trial length during a session. Manipulations at the global level should not influence the accuracy of individual trials, and therefore will not be considered further here (but see Newton, 2001, Exp. 4).

In order to test the window of opportunity model, Newton, 2001 (Exps. 5 and 6) investigated the strategy usage of groups of high, low and mid spatial ability subjects, and also their performance, on different directions task trial types. These will henceforth be referred to as the *trial type experiments*. Experiment 5 manipulated *trial structure*, and hence difficulty solely at the micro-level. Experiment 6 manipulated *trial length*, and hence difficulty solely at the macro-level. University students were pre-tested with the Saville and Holdsworth Advanced Test Battery *Spatial Reasoning* test (Saville & Holdsworth Ltd., 1979) and were allocated to spatial ability bands identified in past research (Roberts et al., 1997). A score of 22 or more reflected high spatial ability, and a score of 16 or less reflected low spatial ability. People with very low spatial ability (scores of 10 or below) were excluded: Cancellation is extremely rare at this level of ability (see Roberts & Newton, chapter 6 this volume) and it was felt that it would not be possible to raise success sufficiently for such people to be able to discover cancellation.

The trial structure experiment

For the directions task, incorrectly represented steps lead to inaccuracy for the spatial strategy. Hence, arranging an item so that it is more difficult to represent any individual step should increase task difficulty (therefore reducing success), which in turn should reduce the usage of cancellation. There were three different trial types: *standard, opposites-adjacent*, and *samesadjacent*. The opposites-adjacent trials were formed by taking 7- and 8-step trials, and ordering the steps so that opposite compass points were together wherever possible. The sames-adjacent trials had 7- and 8-step trials ordered so that same-direction steps were always adjacent. The standard trials had some unavoidable minimal sames-adjacent grouping but never opposites-adjacent steps. These were thus similar to previous directions task studies, and served as the baseline.

The opposites-adjacent trials should be easier to solve compared with the other trial types for people using a spatial strategy: Procedural errors should be less likely when representing: (1) step size (adjacent directly opposite steps can easily be represented as the same length); (2) direction (it does not matter if, say, one step east is misrepresented as west, as long as the immediately following step west is represented as the opposite direction); (3) angles (directly opposite steps do not require the accurate representation of a right-angle between them). Thus accuracy (and hence success) should be increased compared with other trial structures. In addition, if redundancy is detected, fewer errors at the spatial strategy will render the evaluation of cancellation more effective. In terms of the window of opportunity model, it is expected that for low ability subjects, opposites-adjacent trials will lead to an increase in cancellation compared with the standard trials. For high ability subjects the reduction in difficulty will reduce the need to discover cancellation. It is therefore likely that the normal ability–strategy use relationship, in which spatial ability predicts strategy usage such that high spatials tend to use cancellation, and low spatials tend to use the spatial strategy (see Roberts & Newton, chapter 6 this volume) will be absent for this trial type. It is less clear how mid spatial subjects will be influenced by these trials. One possibility is that these will likewise be too easy for them to need to discover cancellation, hence leading to reduced usage. If this is not the case, then as for the low spatials, there should be increased use of cancellation compared with the standard trials.

The sames-adjacent trials should be hardest to solve using a spatial strategy: These trials should be the most difficult to form an accurate spatial representation for, particularly when attempting to calibrate equal step sizes. For example, three steps north could be represented as the same distance as two subsequent steps south.[1] This would also prevent accurate evaluation of cancellation if this were discovered. For low spatial subjects, where cancellation is difficult to discover even for standard trials, the expected increase in difficulty for sames-adjacent trials will probably not result in a detectable reduction in its use. However, for mid spatial subjects, it is predicted that there will be less cancellation for these trials when compared with the standard trials. Subjects with high spatial ability will have strategy discovery least disrupted by this trial type, and cancellation will continue to be most frequently used by them compared with other ability levels. Hence, for this trial type, it is likely that the normal ability–strategy use relationship will be observed (likewise for the standard trials).

In terms of a progressive model of strategy discovery, it would be predicted that the most cancellation will occur for the opposites-adjacent trials, since high, mid and low spatials will discover and use the strategy for

---

[1] Observations of subjects when solving directions task problems using pencil and paper indicate that such errors are by no means uncommon.

these. For the standard trials, those with low spatial ability will not discover cancellation, therefore only mid and high spatials will use the strategy. Finally, the sames-adjacent trials, which are predicted to be the most difficult to solve spatially, would result in only the high spatial ability group using cancellation.

The trial length experiment

In the trial structure experiment, difficulty was manipulated by altering the structure of the item, keeping the actual number of steps constant. The trial length experiment varied the numbers of steps in the items, keeping the structure of all trials the same (matching the standard trials in the trial structure experiment). There were three different lengths: 5- and 6-step, 7- and 8-step, 9- and 10-step trials. The 7- and 8-step trials were identical to the standard trials in the previous experiment, and again served as the baseline.

Increasing the number of steps increases difficulty (and reduces success) by raising the quantity of information to be processed. This is likely to increase solution time, but should also reduce accuracy: Given a finite probability of making a procedural error for any individual step, then more steps should raise the probability that at least one error will be made for any given trial. Just one misrepresentation will result in an incorrect response (although additional representation errors could result in the right answer for the wrong reasons). Therefore, as trial length increases, so should overall error rate. However, the probability of procedural errors for individual steps should be identical between different trial lengths. Hence, the manipulation in this experiment varies the likelihood that the overall correct answer will be available to the subject. The ease with which redundancy can be detected via the construction of the representation itself should not be influenced. This is important because Newton and Roberts (2000) argued that while the availability of the correct answer should make cancellation easier to evaluate, this should not make the strategy easier to discover. Manipulating trial length is therefore predicted to influence the usage of cancellation, but effects may well be smaller compared with the trial structure experiment, where *both* the ease of representing individual steps accurately, *and also* (in consequence) the likelihood that the overall correct answer would be available for each trial, were manipulated.

Although it is reasonable to assume that as trial length increases, so will mean solution time, this is unlikely to be directly related to strategy discovery.[2] Speed is only likely to influence accuracy if a person is slapdash,

---

[2] Speed might be indirectly related to strategy discovery by providing a tangible means of self-evaluation of performance. However, even if trials are being solved particularly slowly, prompting a need to search for alternatives, an inaccurate representation will nonetheless prevent these from being discovered (see also Siegler & Jenkins, 1989).

which would result in a speed–accuracy trade-off. If a person is accurate in his or her spatial representation, then it would be irrelevant how long is taken to solve the trial. A correct response would still be given, and new strategies would be likely to be discovered and/or evaluated accurately. Conversely, a poor representation will result in an incorrect response, and simultaneously make cancellation harder to discover and/or evaluate no matter how long is spent constructing the representation.

Overall, given that trial length is related to task difficulty, and assuming that the causes of difficulty are related to strategy discovery, then the window of opportunity model would predict that with 5- and 6-step trials, those with low spatial ability – who have difficulty in executing the spatial strategy accurately – are most likely to be able to discover and evaluate cancellation. However, the model would also predict that 5- and 6-step trials will be very easy for those with high spatial ability to solve using a spatial strategy. This is likely to suppress the need to discover cancellation, and hence its use, compared with 7- and 8-step trials.

In terms of task difficulty, the 9- and 10-step trials will require the most processing, and thus the probability of making errors will be greatest for everyone compared with the shorter trials. However, for those with high spatial ability, the increase in the probability of error is least likely to become large enough to suppress the discovery of cancellation. For those with low or mid spatial ability, the 9- and 10-step trials are more likely to result in errors, thus preventing the discovery of cancellation compared with shorter trials.[3]

METHOD

Subjects

Two hundred and ninety-six students from the University of Essex participated. All were naive with respect to the tasks and received either a course credit or a cash payment. They were pre-tested with the Saville and Holdsworth Advanced Test Battery *Spatial Reasoning* test. From these, 222 subjects were selected on the basis of spatial ability (scoring 11 out of 40 or over). They were divided between the two experiments as follows:

---

[3] Crowley et al. (1997) suggest that as metacognitive load decreases, strategy discovery will increase. Newton and Roberts (2000, Exps. 1 and 2) showed that strategy discovery did not increase as result of giving the option to use pencil and paper. However, if pencil and paper is a special case, it is still plausible that reducing trial length will also reduce metacognitive load, and may increase the discovery of cancellation. Thus, it is expected that there will be more cancellation for shorter trial lengths, either due to decreased probability of error, or decreased metacognitive load, or both. Even so, it is not clear that metacognitive load need be considered separately to the cumulative probability of making procedural errors.

Trial structure experiment

Twenty-four subjects (12 male, 12 female) with high spatial ability (scoring 22 or over), 42 subjects (15 male, 27 female) with mid spatial ability (scoring between 17 and 21 inclusive) and 45 subjects (11 male, 34 female) with low spatial ability (scoring between 11 and 16 inclusive).

Trial length experiment

Twenty-four subjects (13 male, 11 female) with high spatial ability (scoring 22 or over), 42 subjects (16 male, 26 female) with mid spatial ability (scoring between 17 and 21 inclusive) and 45 subjects (11 male, 34 female) with low spatial ability (scoring between 11 and 16 inclusive).

To ensure that spatial ability was matched for equivalent ability bands for each of the three conditions in both experiments, the test scores were used to assign subjects to them. Each experimental condition had 8 high spatial subjects, 14 mid spatial subjects, and 15 low spatial subjects.

Apparatus

Stimuli were presented by an Apple Power Macintosh 7200/90 micro-computer running PsyScope (Cohen, MacWhinney, Flatt, & Provost, 1993).

Materials

For each of the groups, the directions task trials consisted of one practice and two blocks of experimental trials. The practice trial was a standard-structured 7-step problem, and was the same for each group. Block 1 contained 16 appropriately constructed experimental trials. For the 9- and 10-step problems of the trial length experiment, Blocks 1 and 2 contained 16 trials. For the other five conditions, Block 2 consisted of 16 experimental trials as appropriate and immediately following these were an additional four 9/10 step standard-structured trials (known as the *trigger trials*).[4] All steps for each trial were shown simultaneously on single screens (i.e., parallel presentation, see Figure 7.1).

---

[4] When the experiments were originally devised, it was not known whether any of the manipu-lations might reduce the advantage of cancellation over the spatial strategy to the extent that there was little incentive to adopt cancellation even if discovered. The trigger trials were therefore added with the intention of prompting the use of cancellation in this event (cf. the impasse problems used by Siegler and Jenkins, 1989). In actuality, none of the manipulations removed the advantage of cancellation, and every single subject who used cancellation for the trigger trials had also used this strategy for previous trials. The trigger trials will therefore not be analysed or discussed further.

Trial structure experiment

All standard trials were devised using the same criteria as previously: (1) no two adjacent steps should be opposites (i.e., east would never follow west, etc.); (2) the path had to end on one of the 16 compass points, and would never end back at the start. Occasional grouping of steps was unavoidable. The opposites-adjacent trials were devised such that opposite steps (north/south, east/west) followed each other wherever possible. The sames-adjacent trials were devised such that all steps in the same direction were adjacent to each other, and opposite directions were never adjacent. Figure 7.1 shows examples of each trial structure.

Trial length experiment

All trials had the same structure as the standard trials in the trial structure experiment. Occasional grouping of steps was unavoidable. Examples of each trial length are shown in Figure 7.1.

Standard	Opposites adjacent	Sames adjacent
One step West	One step South	One step North
One step North	One step North	One step North
One step West	One step West	One step West
One step North	One step East	One step West
One step West	One step North	One step West
One step South	One step West	One step South
One step East	One step West	One step East

6-step trial	8-step trial	10-step trial
		One step West
	One step North	One step North
One step East	One step East	One step East
One step North	One step North	One step North
One step West	One step West	One step West
One step North	One step North	One step North
One step East	One step East	One step East
One step East	One step East	One step East
	One step South	One step South
		One step East

Figure 7.1 Example items from the directions task for the trial structure experiments (upper) and trial length experiments (lower).

Design

Each experiment was primarily a between-subjects design in which the trial type was an independent variable. For the trial structure experiment, its levels were standard, opposites-adjacent, and sames-adjacent. For the trial length experiment, its levels were 5- and 6-step, 7- and 8-step, and 9- and 10-step. Spatial ability group was a classification variable; its levels were high, mid, and low ability in each experiment. The reported strategy choice was the dependent variable. In addition, the strategy described for the directions task was also used as a classification variable, with solution time and accuracy as the dependent variables used in order to investigate task performance.

Procedure

For all studies, on commencement, subjects were shown a diagram of the compass points required as answers, followed by a compass point naming task. These familiarised subjects with the answers that would be required subsequently. For the directions task, written instructions were followed by a practice trial, and then a diagram showing its path and answer (irrespective of whether the answer to the practice trial was correct). The experimental trials were then shown. All steps for each trial were shown simultaneously on single screens (i.e., parallel presentation). Subjects spoke their answers, and were timed by the experimenter on commencement of speaking. Subjects were given the opportunity to rest between blocks of trials. Within each block, the order of the 16 experimental trials was randomised. Order of block presentation was counterbalanced. At the end of the tasks, subjects were asked to describe in writing the strategies that they had used for the directions task, including any shifts or mixing of strategies that they had been aware of. All were able to do so without difficulty.

RESULTS

Error rates (the percentage of problems incorrect) are reported throughout. Permutation slips were permitted, for example, an answer of ENN where the correct answer was NNE. In order to have sufficient data points to calculate accurate means, solution times were included for answers that were no more than one compass point out (e.g., NNE for N, but not NE). Subjects were able to report their chosen strategies clearly, with little difficulty or uncertainty. Where two strategies were reported, most subjects reported a clean break between them. Using the verbal reports to categorise subjects, it was found that dominant strategy (i.e., that reported as being used for the majority of trials) and the final choice of strategy were identical for all individuals.

Performance of the strategy groups by trial type

For the analyses that follow, subjects' strategies form a classification variable, with error rates and mean solution times being the dependent variables. However, spatial ability is associated with strategy usage *and also* is associated with performance at the strategies. It is therefore necessary to perform Analysis of Covariance in order to remove the effects of spatial ability when comparing performance between trial types for the different strategies. In conjunction with this, means reported are *least square means*. In other words, overall levels of performance are corrected for spatial ability. For all analyses, performance data are shown in Table 7.2 and are plotted on Figure 7.2.

All analyses have the same design: one covariate (spatial ability test raw score) and two factors (*trial type*; three levels for each analysis, and *strategy*; spatial versus cancellation). For each ANCOVA, there are three interactions which include the covariate. None of these 12 effects approached significance: the greatest/most significant F ratio was for the trial type × covariate interaction for the solution time analysis of the trial length experiment, $F(2, 99) = 1.88, p > .05$. The lack of significant interactions shows that all of the effects of trial type and strategy were identical irrespective of ability level, and all covariate interactions were deleted from all models.

The trial structure experiment: error rates

On deleting the covariate × factor interactions from the model, the covariate was a significant predictor of performance, $F(1,104) = 7.5, p < .01$. With the effects of the covariate controlled for, there was a significant main effect of

TABLE 7.2

Least square means of solution times and error rates by strategy usage for the trial structure and trial length experiments (standard deviations in italics)

	Trial structure experiment			Trial length experiment		
	Standard	*Opposites adjacent*	*Sames adjacent*	*5- & 6- step*	*7- & 8- step*	*9- & 10- step*
	Percentage error					
Cancellation	21.2	20.3	18.6	19.0	34.1	30.5
	17.3	*16.5*	*16.8*	*16.5*	*16.2*	*16.2*
Spatial	55.8	36.5	60.7	48.2	54.0	61.2
	16.7	*16.5*	*16.6*	*16.3*	*16.2*	*16.2*
	Mean solution time (secs)					
Cancellation	7.8	7.8	5.1	4.8	9.4	11.2
	4.3	*4.1*	*4.2*	*4.5*	*4.4*	*4.4*
Spatial	13.9	10.5	11.0	9.6	12.7	14.8
	4.2	*4.1*	*4.1*	*4.4*	*4.4*	*4.4*

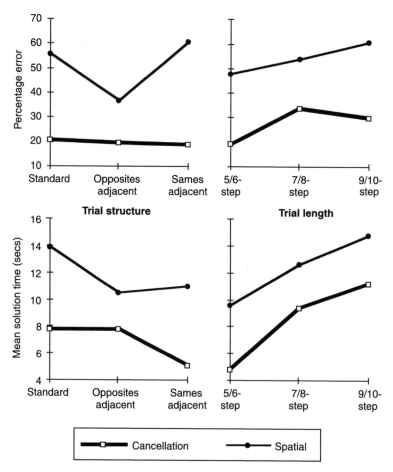

Figure 7.2   Least square means of solution times (upper panels) and error rates (lower panels) by strategy usage for the trial structure experiment (left panels) and trial length experiment (right panels).

strategy $F(1,104) = 67.2, p < .01$ and a significant main effect of trial structure $F(2,104) = 4.4, p < .05$. However, the interaction between the two factors was also significant $F(2,104) = 4.9, p < .01$.

Pairwise comparisons showed that spatial strategy users were significantly more accurate for opposites-adjacent trials when compared to both standard ($t = 4.2, p < .01$) and sames-adjacent trials ($t = 5.29, p < .01$). There was no significant difference in accuracy between standard and sames-adjacent trials for spatial strategy users ($t = 1.13, p > .05$). Cancellation strategy users' accuracy did not differ significantly, regardless of trial structure (greatest $t = 0.34, p > .05$). Looking at the differences in accuracy dependent upon strategy used, within each trial type, cancellation strategy users were always significantly more accurate than spatial strategy users regardless of task structure and ability (smallest $t = 2.85, p < .01$).

The trial structure experiment: solution times

On deleting the covariate × factor interactions from the model, the covariate did not significantly predict performance, $F(1,104) = 2.8, p > .05$. With the effects of the covariate controlled for, there was a significant main effect of strategy $F(1,104) = 27.3, p < .01$ and a significant main effect of trial structure $F(2,104) = 3.2, p < .05$. The interaction between the two factors was non-significant $F(2,104) = 1.5, p > .05$.

Thus, cancellation strategy users were always significantly faster than spatial strategy users, regardless of task structure and ability. Looking at the differences in mean solution time for each trial type irrespective of strategy, pairwise comparisons showed that standard trials took significantly longer than sames-adjacent trials ($t = 2.5, p < .05$). However, the differences in mean solution time were non-significant for both the standard trials versus opposites-adjacent trials ($t = 1.6, p > .05$) and the opposites-adjacent trials versus sames-adjacent trials ($t = 1.0, p > .05$). Thus, trial structure only made a significant difference in solution times for sames-adjacent versus standard trials.

The trial length experiment: error rates

On deleting the covariate × factor interactions from the model, the covariate was a significant predictor of performance, $F(1,104) = 8.9, p < .01$. With the effects of the covariate accounted for, there was a significant main effect of strategy $F(1,104) = 57.6, p < .01$ and a significant main effect of trial length $F(2,104) = 5.2, p < .01$. The interaction between the two factors was non-significant $F(2,104) = 1.1, p > .05$.

Thus, cancellation users were always significantly more accurate than spatial strategy users, regardless of trial length and ability. Looking at the differences in error rate for each trial length, irrespective of strategy, pairwise comparisons showed that 5- and 6-step trials produced fewer errors than either 7- and 8-step trials ($t = 2.7, p < .01$) or 9- and 10-step trials ($t = 2.9, p < .01$). There was no significant difference in the error rate between 7- and 8-step trials and 9- and 10-step trials ($t = 0.44, p > .05$).

The trial length experiment: solution times

On deleting the covariate × factor interactions from the model, the covariate did not significantly predict performance, $F(1,104) = 1.8, p > .05$. With the effects of the covariate controlled for, there was a significant main effect of strategy $F(1,104) = 17.1$, $p < .01$ and a significant main effect of trial length $F(2,104) = 13.4$, $p < .01$. The interaction between the two factors was non-significant $F(2,104) = 0.27$, $p > .05$.

Thus, cancellation users were always significantly faster than spatial strategy users, regardless of trial length and ability. Looking at the differences in mean solution time for each trial length, irrespective of strategy, pairwise comparisons showed that 5- and 6-step trials were solved significantly faster than either 7- and 8-step trials ($t = 3.6$, $p < .01$) or 9- and 10-step trials ($t = 5.0$, $p < .01$). There was no significant difference in the mean solution time between 7- and 8-step trials and 9- and 10-step trials ($t = 1.7$, $p > .05$).

Summary: The effects of trial type manipulation on performance

For both experiments, cancellation is always the most effective strategy. For the trial structure experiment, for spatial strategy users, opposites-adjacent trials were solved more accurately than either standard trials or sames-adjacent trials. Regardless of strategy used, sames-adjacent trials were solved faster than standard trials. For the trial length experiment, the 5- and 6-step trials were solved faster and more accurately than the either 7- and 8- or 9- and 10-step trials, the latter two did not differ by either measure.

Strategy usage by ability and trial type

The trial structure experiment

To determine whether trial structure and/or spatial ability group was related to strategy usage, Table 7.3 was compiled. Of the six χ^2 analyses of final choice of strategy, only three were significant. Trial structure was significantly associated with strategy usage for low spatial subjects: Cancellation was more frequent for opposites-adjacent trials than for either of the other trial types. Trial structure was not associated with strategy usage for the other two ability groups. In addition, ability level was associated with strategy usage for both standard and sames-adjacent trials: High spatials were more likely to use cancellation than the other ability levels. Ability level was not associated with strategy usage for the opposites-adjacent trials.

Overall, there is evidence that task structure as well as spatial ability can influence the use of cancellation. Looking at patterns of strategy usage, there was little evidence for any difference between the standard and sames-adjacent trials, and for all intents and purposes, these are identical in terms of strategy selection. For both low and mid spatial ability groups, there was an increase in use of cancellation for the opposites-adjacent trials compared with the other two types, and this difference was significant for low spatial

TABLE 7.3
Overall analysis of final choice of strategy for the trial structure experiment (all d.f. = 2)

	Standard	*Opposites adjacent*	*Sames adjacent*	
High spatial				
Cancellation	5 (62.5%)	3 (37.5%)	5 (62.5%)	$\chi^2 = 1.3$
Spatial	3 (37.5%)	5 (62.5%)	3 (37.5%)	$p > .05$
Mid spatial				
Cancellation	3 (21%)	7 (50%)	5 (36%)	$\chi^2 = 2.5$
Spatial	11 (79%)	7 (50%)	9 (64%)	$p > .05$
Low spatial				
Cancellation	1 (7%)	5 (33%)	0 (0%)	$\chi^2 = 8.1$
Spatial	14 (93%)	10 (67%)	15 (100%)	$p < .05$
	$\chi^2 = 8.9$	$\chi^2 = .87$	$\chi^2 = 11.2$	
	$p < .01$	$p > .05$	$p < .01$	

subjects. There also appears to be *less use* of cancellation for high spatial subjects for opposites-adjacent trials compared with the other trial types. Thus, for these, the spatial ability-strategy use relationship has been lost. Hence, there is evidence that these trials resulted in qualitatively different performance to the other two types.

When these factors are taken into account, a new collapsed table can be constructed (see Table 7.4). This distinguishes between the trial structures which have been shown to have a spatial ability–strategy use relationship (samples-adjacent and standard) versus those that do not (opposites-adjacent). There is also a distinction between the low/mid spatial ability groups, where the most use of cancellation occurred for the opposites-adjacent trials, versus the high ability group, who showed the least cancellation for these. It should be noted that this is not a planned comparison, but is a post-hoc attempt to provide a clear summary of the overall pattern of data. Thus, although

TABLE 7.4
Final choice of strategy for the task structure experiment, collapsed table (all d.f. = 1)

		Sames adjacent + standard	*Opposites adjacent*	
High spatial ability	Cancellation	10 (63%)	3 (37%)	$\chi^2 = 1.3$
	Spatial	6 (37%)	5 (63%)	$p > .05$
Mid + low spatial ability	Cancellation	9 (16%)	12 (41%)	$\chi^2 = 7.1$
	Spatial	49 (84%)	17 (59%)	$p < .01$
		$\chi^2 = 14.5$	$\chi^2 = .04$	
		$p < .01$	$p > .05$	

not entirely justified statistically, its purpose is to provide focus on future hypotheses to test.

Table 7.4 shows evidence in support of the window of opportunity model. For those with low/mid spatial ability, the use of cancellation increases for opposites-adjacent trials, compared with standard/sames-adjacent trials. For those with high spatial ability, for opposites-adjacent trials, use of cancellation does not go up, and may even decrease compared with the other trial types. With so few high spatial subjects it is not possible to confirm any apparent trends statistically. However, it appears reasonable to conclude that different trial structures influence strategy discovery in different ways dependent upon spatial ability group.

The trial length experiment

To determine whether trial length and/or spatial ability group had influenced strategy discovery, Table 7.5 was compiled. Of the six χ^2 analyses of final choice of strategy, only one was significant. Ability level was associated with strategy usage for 5- and 6-step trials: High spatials were more likely to use cancellation than the other groups.

Overall, these results suggest that trial length does not influence the use of cancellation as strongly as either spatial ability or trial structure has been shown to in other studies. With so few significant effects, it is only possible to speculate about apparent trends. The 7- and 8-step trials are problematic, and with fewer high spatials than mid spatials using cancellation, appear to go against the normal expected pattern of strategy usage. It was therefore decided to produce a table excluding these trials, and to collapse the low and mid spatial ability groups together, as was done for the trial structure experiment.

TABLE 7.5
Overall analysis of final choice of strategy for the trial length experiment (all d.f. = 2)

	5- & 6-step	7- & 8-step	9- & 10-step	
High spatial				
Cancellation	6 (75%)	3 (37.5%)	3 (37.5%)	$\chi^2 = 3.0$
Spatial	2 (25%)	5 (62.5%)	5 (62.5%)	$p > .05$
Mid spatial				
Cancellation	3 (21%)	7 (50%)	4 (29%)	$\chi^2 = 2.8$
Spatial	11 (79%)	7 (50%)	10 (71%)	$p > .05$
Low spatial				
Cancellation	3 (20%)	5 (33%)	1 (7%)	$\chi^2 = 3.3$
Spatial	12 (80%)	10 (67%)	14 (93%)	$p > .05$
	$\chi^2 = 8.1$	$\chi^2 = 1.9$	$\chi^2 = 4.2$	
	$p < .05$	$p > .05$	$p > .05$	

The removal of the 7- and 8-step trials is further justified as it was found that they did not produce significantly fewer errors than the 9- and 10-step trials, and the most worthwhile comparison is between the sets of trials that produced the biggest error difference. Even then, this difference (13% for spatial strategy users) is considerably smaller than the difference between opposites-adjacent and standard/sames-adjacent trials in the trial structure experiment (22%), and so a smaller influence of trial length on strategy usage is to be expected. Looking at strategy usage, there is a clear difference between the high spatial group versus the low/mid spatial groups, but only for the 5- and 6-step problems (see Table 7.6). Hence, there is a spatial ability–strategy use relationship for the 5- and 6-step trials, but not for the 9- and 10-step trials. There was also no effect of trial length for the low/mid spatial ability groups, and only a possible trend for the high spatial ability group.

DISCUSSION

The trial structure experiment

Looking first at the opposites-adjacent trials, for spatial strategy users, errors were reduced for this trial structure compared with the others. Simultaneously, compared with standard/sames-adjacent trials, the numbers of low/mid spatial subjects adopting cancellation was significantly raised. In the light of this, it is reasonable to conclude that enhanced accuracy and hence success when using the spatial strategy has increased the discovery of cancellation for these ability bands. Thus far, this implies a progressive model: By boosting accuracy, discovery and use of cancellation has also been boosted. However, there was no corresponding increase in cancellation for high spatials. If anything, there was suppression, although the small sample size prevented this from being detected statistically. The normal relationship between spatial ability and strategy use, which has previously been shown to be very robust, therefore disappeared for this trial type. Overall, there is good support for the window of opportunity model. These trials were difficult enough for

TABLE 7.6
Final choice of strategy for the task length experiment, collapsed table (all d.f. = 1)

		5- & 6-step	9- & 10-step	
High spatial ability	Cancellation	6 (75%)	3 (37.5%)	$\chi^2 = 2.3$
	Spatial	2 (25%)	5 (62.5%)	$p > .05$
Mid/low spatial ability	Cancellation	6 (21%)	5 (17%)	$\chi^2 = 0.1$
	Spatial	23 (79%)	24 (83%)	$p > .05$
		$\chi^2 = 8.4$	$\chi^2 = 1.5$	
		$p < .01$	$p > .05$	

low/mid spatials to need to discover cancellation, and easy enough to enable this to happen. The trials were too easy for high spatials to need to discover cancellation, and hence this was inhibited for them, although any conclusions can only be speculative. This finding also provides evidence against a progressive model, which predicts that if there is an increase in cancellation amongst a low ability group, then there should also be an increase, or at least no decrease, for other ability groups.

Looking at the sames-adjacent trials, those using the spatial strategy were faster compared with the standard trials, although the error rates were similar. The performance data shows that the original prediction, that sames-adjacent trials would be more difficult than standard trials, was wrong. In terms of strategy usage, the results for the sames-adjacent trials are indistinguishable to those for the standard trials and, unlike the opposites-adjacent trials, high spatial ability is still associated with the use of cancellation. Overall, these finding lend support to the suggestion that factors which influence speed are not necessarily the same as those which influence strategy discovery. Hence, for spatial strategy users: (1) trials which were more accurate but not faster compared with standard trials (opposites-adjacent) differed in strategy usage; (2) trials which were faster but not more accurate compared with standard trials (sames-adjacent) did not differ. Of additional interest, therefore, is the way in which the trial structure manipulation influenced the two possible measures of difficulty independently. Also important is that it is again apparent that factors which influence speed are less related to strategy discovery than factors which influence accuracy (see also Roberts & Newton, chapter 6 this volume).

One explanation for the lack of a difference in accuracy between sames-adjacent and standard trials, and hence strategy usage, could be that there are different sources of inaccuracy, but the net result is the same. For sames-adjacent trials, unless effort is made to differentiate adjacent steps in the same direction, a spatial representation effectively has at most only four 'lines'. This would yield a high potential for calibration errors of step size, but a relatively low potential for calibration errors of angle representation. Standard trials, in which no same directions are adjacent, have up to eight lines to represent. This might yield less potential for calibration errors of step size, but there are many more angles that need to be represented accurately. Hence, there is similar performance and strategy use for the two trial types.

Overall, the window of opportunity relationship is not contradicted by the results of this experiment, and is supported in preference to the progressive model. However, opposites-adjacent trials could lead to increased cancellation for reasons other than high accuracy: Perhaps this trial structure emphasised the redundancy of going back and forth, and thus prompted the discovery of cancellation. However, it is not clear why this did not assist the high spatial subjects.

The trial length experiment

First, it should be noted that the 7- and 8-step trials produced odd results. These trials were the same as the standard trials of the trial structure experiment, yet have not yielded the expected (and robust) relationship between ability and usage of cancellation. This cannot be explained, and can only add weight to the argument that large numbers of subjects are required in order to explore the window of opportunity model.

Looking at the 5- and 6-step trials, the window of opportunity model predicted that fewer high spatials would use cancellation for these, but that these would be the trials for which there would be the most cancellation for people with low spatial ability. This was not found: These trials resulted in significantly more cancellation for the high spatials versus the low/mid spatials. There were also no differences in strategy usage for the low/mid spatials between the 5- and 6- versus 9- and 10-step trials. One possible explanation of this is that even 5- and 6-step trials are not sufficiently easy for these subjects to discover cancellation: Compare 48% errors for 5- and 6-step trials using the spatial strategy with 37% errors for opposites-adjacent trials, a difference of over 10%. If this were so, then despite the short trial length, 48% errors may indicate the exceeding of a maximum difficulty level, beyond which cancellation will be rare for low/mid spatial subjects: They were therefore outside of the 'window of opportunity'. In other words, task difficulty was such that these subjects were unable to discover cancellation. This could be tested by having trials with 4- and 5-step problems: Shorter trials still may bring the lower spatial subjects into the window.

Turning to the 9- and 10-step trials, in addition to there being no difference in strategy usage for the low/mid spatial groups compared with 5- and 6-step trials, there was a suggestion of a decrease in the proportion of high spatials cancelling for this trial length, compared with 5- and 6-step trials, albeit non-significant. It is possible that the high spatial subjects were now 'out of the window' for these trials, so that the task was too difficult for them to discover cancellation. Thus, at the very least these results cannot be said to contradict the window of opportunity model, and suggest that with a larger design, positive evidence will be identified: With small numbers of high spatial subjects, it is difficult to draw firmer conclusions than this. Many more high spatial subjects need to be recruited, and a further trial type may be required: *very hard* (for example 12 and 13 steps). This would reduce accuracy and hence maximise the difficulty difference between trial lengths. However, it is important to note that overall, there is a larger change in accuracy from 5- and 6-step to 7- and 8-step trials than from 7- and 8-step to 9- and 10-step trials. This suggests that 5- and 6-step trials yield a low probability of cumulative procedural errors, such that accuracy is relatively high, but for 7- and 8-step trials, the probability of cumulative error is large enough to reach a threshold beyond which poorer performance still from longer trials is difficult to detect. Despite the difficulties in interpreting these findings so far, for a progressive model to hold, the use of cancellation for the 9- and 10-step trials should have been observed to drop for low/mid spatials compared with 5- and 6-step trials. This was barely the case, and therefore may be evidence against it.

For the trial length experiment, it was predicted that those with high spatial ability would not cancel for the 5- and 6-step problems because these would be easy enough to suppress the need to discover cancellation. However, this clearly did not occur. This finding should be compared with Roberts and Newton (chapter 6 this volume), who have shown that pencil and paper raises success in terms of how accurately people can perform. However, this increase *does* suppress strategy discovery (presumably due to reducing the need to discover new methods – see Newton and Roberts, 2000, Exp. 2; Roberts et al., 1997). This suggests that rendering a task easier through external means (pencil and paper) may influence strategy discovery in a different way to making a task easier by reducing the number of processing steps.

Comparing experiments

It is clear that increasing task length did not influence task difficulty to the same extent as manipulating task structure: For the trial length experiment, a much smaller difference in error rates was observed between the least and the most accurate trials (48% and 61% for spatial strategy users), when compared with the greatest difference in error rates for the trial structure experiment (37% and 61%). This may also explain the smaller differences in patterns of strategy usage for the trial length experiment. Hence, the results of these experiments suggest that when manipulating task difficulty, it is important not only to understand what factors actually make a task difficult, but also to maximise difficulty differences between conditions.

The difference in the error rate between the opposites-adjacent trials of the trial structure experiment, and the 5- and 6-step trials of the trial length experiment, suggest that each experiment possibly manipulated task difficulty in different ways. The error rate of spatial strategy users for the opposites-adjacent trials in the trial structure experiment was lower (37%) and yet these trials were slower (10.5 secs) than the 5- and 6-step trials in the trial length experiment (48% and 9.6 secs): More errors were made for 5- and 6-step trials despite fewer steps to be taken. In addition, the longer times for opposites-adjacent trials suggest that subjects were not simply increasing accuracy by skipping opposite steps.

Overall, the results of these experiments suggest that there may indeed be a window of opportunity for strategy usage, with strategy use related to task success and spatial ability score. A simple progressive model cannot easily account for the observed patterns of strategy discovery. It has been shown that success can be manipulated in a number of ways, and that these can have independent consequences in terms of the two possible measures of difficulty. There is also evidence that, for the directions task, it is the factors which influence success as measured by accuracy which particularly influence strategy use. Factors that influence success as measured by speed do not appear to be directly related to strategy use: The trial structure experiment showed that solution time is not related to strategy use to any extent, unlike accuracy. The results of these experiments combined also suggest that accuracy may need to be increased beyond a minimum range, and above a minimum level, before strategy use can be measurably influenced between trial types. It is clear that the window of opportunity model requires more investigation, with much larger sample sizes, before it can be accepted and its full implications can be understood. This model suggests that we may need to re-examine popular beliefs regarding learning. It may no longer be appropriate to say that we learn from our mistakes; we learn from our success.

REFERENCES

Cohen, J. D., MacWhinney, B., Flatt, M., & Provost, J. (1993). PsyScope – an interactive graphic system for designing and controlling experiments in the psychology laboratory using Macintosh computers. *Behavior Research Methods, Instruments, and Computers, 25*, 257–271.

Crowley, K., Shrager, J., & Siegler, R. S. (1997), Strategy discovery as a competitive negotiation between metacognitive and associative mechanisms. *Developmental Review, 17*, 462–489.

Evans, J. St. B. T. (2000). What could and could not be a strategy in reasoning? In W. Schaeken, G. De Vooght, A. Vandierendonck, & G. d'Ydewalle (Eds.), *Deductive reasoning and strategies* (pp. 1–22). Mahwah, NJ: Lawrence Erlbaum Associates, Inc.

Galotti, K. M., Baron, J., & Sabini, J. P. (1986). Individual differences in syllogistic reasoning: Deduction rules or mental models? *Journal of Experimental Psychology: General, 115*, 16–25.

Newton, E. J. (2001). *Individual differences in strategy development*. Unpublished doctoral dissertation, University of Essex.

Newton, E. J., & Roberts, M. J. (2000). An experimental study of strategy development. *Memory and Cognition, 28*, 565–573.

Reder, L. M., & Schunn, C. D. (1996). Metacognition does not imply awareness: Strategy choice is governed by implicit learning and memory. In L. M. Reder (Ed.), *Implicit memory and metacognition* (pp. 45–77). Mahwah, NJ: Lawrence Erlbaum Associates, Inc.

Roberts, M. J. (1993). Human reasoning: Deduction rules or mental models, or both? *Quarterly Journal of Experimental Psychology, 46A*, 569–589.

Roberts, M. J. (2000). Individual differences in reasoning strategies: A problem to solve or an opportunity to seize? In W. Schaeken, G. De Vooght, A. Vandierendonck, & G. d'Ydewalle (Eds.), *Deductive reasoning and strategies* (pp. 23–48). Mahwah, NJ: Lawrence Erlbaum Associates, Inc.

Roberts, M. J., Gilmore, D. J., & Wood, D. J. (1997). Individual differences and strategy selection in reasoning. *British Journal of Psychology, 88*, 473–492.

Roberts, M. J., & Roberson, D. (2001). Predicting strategy usage for the compass point directions task: Spatial ability versus verbal ability across the lifespan. *Cahiers de Psychologie Cognitive/ Current Psychology of Cognition, 20*, 3–18.

Saville & Holdsworth Ltd. (1979). *Advanced test battery; Manual and user's guide*. Thames Ditton: Saville & Holdsworth Ltd.

Siegler, R. S. (1996). *Emerging minds: The process of change in children's thinking*. New York: Oxford University Press.

Siegler, R. S., & Jenkins, E. A. (1989). *How children discover new strategies*. Hillsdale, NJ: Lawrence Erlbaum Associates, Inc.

Wood, D. J. (1978). Problem solving – the nature and development of strategies. In G. Underwood (Ed.), *Strategies in information processing* (pp. 329–356). London: Academic Press.

Afterword

What do we know, and what do we need to know about reasoning strategies?

Maxwell J. Roberts
Department of Psychology, University of Essex, UK

Elizabeth J. Newton
Department of Human Communication Science,
University College London, UK

The preceding chapters have identified many findings regarding individual differences in the use of reasoning strategies, and have discussed their implications both for theories of reasoning and for theories of strategy usage in general. It seems appropriate to bring together in one place the most interesting findings and recurring themes.

The chapters in this volume have demonstrated that individual differences in reasoning strategies are detectable for a wide range of tasks, can have important consequences for performance, and are explicable in terms of current theories of strategy usage. Although task demands and task format may influence the strategies that people are likely to use (Morris & Schunn, chapter 2; Gilhooly, chapter 3; Dierckx & Vandierendonck, chapter 5), even within these constraints, individuals are likely to use different strategies. This may result from past experience with the success and failure of different alternatives, to the extent that adverse experience with particular strategies may bias people against using them, even in circumstances where this would be advantageous (Dierckx & Vandierendonck, chapter 5). Alternatively, not all strategies may be available to all people, with the best performers at the original strategies being the most likely to identify improvements which improve their performance still further (Roberts & Newton, chapter 6). Overall then, simple deduction tasks have proved to be an ideal test-bed for the investigation of general theories of strategy usage.

Not all patterns of strategy usage identified are understood: Despite finding clear preferences, along with cross-task consistency, Bacon, Handley,

and Newstead (chapter 4) have not yet explained these patterns of performance. It might be tempting to claim that such usage reflects past experience,
especially as measures of spatial versus verbal working memory capacity did
not predict this (but see Gilhooly, chapter 3). However, positive evidence for
this would be required, especially as competing explanations based upon
levels of verbal or spatial ability, or even stylistic preferences, have also been
put forward to explain strategy choices. Explaining people's natural strategy
preferences, i.e., those in the absence of intervention from an experimenter, is
potentially a difficult task: Do people fail to use strategies because they are
not aware of them, or because others have been selected in preference?
Instructing subjects to use each of various strategies, then subsequently
requiring them to choose between them (e.g., Lemaire & Fabre, chapter 1;
Dierckx & Vandierendonck, chapter 5) undoubtedly provides a more
controlled environment, although possibly at the risk of underestimating
or overestimating the importance of particular determinants of strategy
selection.

Other findings and suggestions discussed in previous chapters have implications for general theories of strategy usage. One example is that people may
need to evaluate strategy validity, both for self-discovered and for taught
strategies. This possibility has been neglected up till now, and may well be an
important determinant of whether people are prepared to adopt a new strategy (Roberts & Newton, chapter 6). In this case there is a need to identify the
circumstances in which this procedure is important, and to understand the
processes that people apply when they achieve (or fail to achieve) this. In
addition, whether there proves to be a 'window of opportunity' versus a
simple 'progressive relationship' model of strategy discovery will be of
importance not just for theories of strategy discovery, but also in the class-
room (Newton & Roberts, chapter 7). A window of opportunity model
requires high levels of vigilance in this respect. Task difficulty must be set so
as not to be so difficult as to prevent learning, and not so easy as to discour-
age this. To date, strategy discovery has proved to be far easier to suppress
than to promote.

Finally, a number of findings suggest intriguing future avenues of research
to explore, in that patterns of performance, currently thought to be well
understood, may actually conceal far richer phenomena than suspected.

Elsewhere, many researchers have suggested that people are extremely flexible, that strategy usage varies on a trial-by-trial basis, and that this is a
characteristic of human behaviour. Of course, people can only vary in their
strategy usage if more than one useful strategy is known, and even then there
is a possibility that this variability itself varies as a function of the task: The
more that different strategies vary in their overall effectiveness, the less likely
that people will switch between them on a trial-by-trial basis (Dierckx &
Vandierendonck, chapter 5; Roberts & Newton, chapter 6). This suggestion

is relatively straightforward to test, and is important given the alternative, that trial-by-trial variability (or the lack of it) is an artefact of strategy identification procedures, either because a single retrospective report tends to result in a single reported strategy, or because the requirement to give a retrospective report after every single trial encourages more experimentation than would otherwise be the case.

Assuming that trial-by-trial variability is a genuine feature of certain tasks/task formats, and that variability results from a genuine attempt to optimise strategy selection (as opposed to arbitrary switching), a further important suggestion is that strategy selection on a trial-by-trial basis may not be a cost-free procedure (Dierckx & Vandierendonck, chapter 5). In which case, not only may individuals vary in how successfully they apply this process, but also the potential benefits of investing resources into this process may vary from task to task and situation to situation. Again, this implies that trial-by-trial variability need not be an inherent feature of all reasoning. In particular, variability will be low when the benefits of applying the best strategy are likely to be outweighed by the costs of identifying it. Speculatively, individual differences may occur at this meta-level, so that some people persist in engaging costly strategy selection procedures even when the benefits are likely to be low, whereas others fail to engage in relatively undemanding procedures even when the benefits are potentially high.

Overall, although strategy selection seems to be well understood in terms of the simple principle that good strategies in the past are more likely to be used in the future, once we acknowledge that strategy selection procedures are not necessarily cost free, it follows that people will differ in how likely they are to engage them, and also in how successfully they apply them once engaged. Inevitably, we realise that strategy selection procedures are not as well understood as we first thought, and that trial-by-trial variability, far from being a universal feature of human cognition, may only be a consequence of combining certain types of people with certain types of task.

Another important avenue to explore concerns how people are able to detect their own success. For example, the non-application of a trial-by-trial strategy selection procedure may reflect some sort of metacognitive deficiency, or alternatively may reflect satisfaction that one particular strategy will yield adequate success for the entire task in question. This will suppress the search for alternative strategies already known (Dierckx & Vandierendonck, chapter 5), and perhaps a search for new strategies not yet known (Newton & Roberts, chapter 7). Where feedback is available, knowledge of accuracy is straightforward, but people appear to be aware of this even without feedback. In fact, this is not so mysterious: There are numerous cues to accuracy, such as strategy failures (Dierckx & Vandierendonck, chapter 5) and representation consistency (Roberts & Newton, chapter 6). Again, there may be individual differences in people's ability to evaluate their success, as well as their levels of error tolerance, which may well mediate whether searches take place to identify alternatives amongst known strategies, or for entirely new strategies. In addition, given that estimates of accuracy and actual accuracy are never perfectly correlated, we need a clearer understanding of people's uses of potential cues to this, and whether changed patterns of strategy usage can result in circumstances in which these cues may be misleading.

A recurring issue in this book is that strategy identification must be performed extremely carefully by the researcher. This is inevitably more difficult than to implement a study that neglects individual differences. For the latter, it is straightforward to aggregate over subjects and dismiss misfits as unimportant, or artefactual, or representing experimental error. Instead, larger numbers of subjects are required and it is also necessary to analyse at the level of the individual. It undoubtedly helps if researchers have clear ideas in advance as to the potential strategies that may be applied, as well as their likely effectiveness (Lemaire & Fabre, chapter 1; Morris & Schunn, chapter 2). However, evaluating the likely effectiveness of various strategies cannot be achieved simply by observation of spontaneous selections, as differences in past experience and psychometric profiles may influence both strategy selection and strategy execution. There really is no substitute for instructing subjects to use all potential strategies over all possible item types, provided that suitable precautions are taken in order to ensure that subjects are following instructions (e.g., Lemaire & Fabre, chapter 1; Dierckx & Vandierendonck, chapter 5; Roberts & Newton, chapter 6). In fact, accurate identification of strategy usage at the level of the individual remains the biggest difficulty to overcome when embarking upon such research, as the range of methods outlined in the preceding chapters is testament to. As a general rule of thumb, a single source of evidence should never be relied upon. Hence, we have trial-by-trial reporting in conjunction with performance data (Morris & Schunn, chapter 2), overt behaviour in conjunction with performance data (Dierckx & Vandierendonck, chapter 5), retrospective reporting in conjunction with performance data (Roberts & Newton, chapter 6; Newton & Roberts, chapter 7 – occasionally with overt behaviour too), selective interference of different strategies by placing loads on different working memory subsystems (Gilhooly, chapter 3), or even a combination of all of these (Bacon, Handley, & Newstead, chapter 4). Clearly, appropriate methods of identification are non-trivial, and it is at this point in the research that a die-hard strategies sceptic can dismiss the entire corpus of findings to date. We hope that the findings presented in the preceding chapters would at least give such a sceptic pause for thought before such a reaction. Without understanding reasoning strategies, we cannot understand human reasoning.

Author Index

Subject Index

DATE DUE
